ANDRÉ GIDE

ANDRÉ GIDE

His Life and His Work

LÉON PIERRE-QUINT

Translated from the French for the first time by
Dorothy M. Richardson

ALFRED·A·KNOPF
New York
1934

Originally published as
André Gide.   Sa Vie, Son Œuvre.
Copyright 1932, by Librairie Stock,
Delamain et Boutelleau, Paris.

PREFACE

EVERY idea, and every philosophical system, is the expression of a personality. Between the work and the life of André Gide there is a closer connection than between the work and life of any other writer. His ethic is continuously illuminated by his life, his evolution, the discussions going forward within his consciousness, and the characteristic shades of his personality. The biographical portion of this book has been facilitated, moreover, by the fact that Gide again and again confessed himself, and these confessions are the centre of his life's drama.

The second part of the book is devoted to a study of the most characteristic features of Gide's art. Before deducing thence any ethical ideas, and particularly any individualist ethic, the author analyses the nature of the examination of conscience; inquires how the interior of a personality can be reached, self-deception can be avoided, and sincerity arrived at.

Gide has never established a system. But the diverse thoughts one discovers in his books, often in apparent contradiction with one another, form together a living whole: his ethic. This it is that I have tried in some measure to reconstitute in the centre of this essay.

Finally, I have laid considerable stress upon the social consequences of this ethic — consequences that are to-day amongst the author's most lively preoccupations and perhaps give to his work its real significance.[1]

[1] My thanks are due to MM. Jacques-Émile Blanche, Jean-Richard Bloch, Jacques Copeau, Henri Ghéon, Edmond Jaloux, Pierre de Lanux, Paul-Albert Laurens, Roger Martin du Gard, Eugène Montfort, Henri de Régnier, Jean Schlumberger, and Paul Valéry, who have kindly helped me with their recollections in the first part of this book.

I may add that all the conversational portions introduced in the course of this biography, in the person of any speaker, come direct from a *journal* or a *confession* or a *correspondence* — but that in order to avoid overloading my book with foot-notes I have not invariably indicated the sources which have been the most frequently used.

Finally I desire to express my gratitude to the foreign collaborators whose valuable help has enabled me to draw up the bibliography appearing at the end of the volume.

CONTENTS

PART ONE

HIS LIFE

PART TWO

HIS PSYCHOLOGY AND HIS ART

PART THREE

HIS ETHIC

PART FOUR

HIS SOCIAL CRITICISM

PART I

HIS LIFE

CHILDHOOD

ON his father's side André Gide is descended from Huguenot peasants of the harsh Cévennes, on that of his mother from judicial functionaries inhabiting lush, green Normandy. According to Gide, the geographical opposition of his origins is one of the causes of the contradictions to be found in his character.

When, however, a pastor united Paul Gide, professor of jurisprudence, and Juliette Rondeaux, a wealthy heiress, the marriage was primarily a union of religious traditions and bourgeois traditions. In this austere grouping André Gide was born, in Paris, on November 22, 1869.

*　　　*

The author himself tells us [1] that at the age of six he was still a cunning youngster, chattering indiscreetly to the servants and stamping on his playfellows' mud pies. He is to be seen, in a photograph, with a pale, unchildlike face, dressed absurdly by his mother in a heavy plaid garment.

At the École Alsacienne he was an idler and was very

[1] *Si le Grain ne meurt.*

soon expelled on account of bad habits; a precocious sexual instinct had awakened in him like a rebellious force. Within this shadow lying upon his early years, it is not surprising that his demons should have come to birth,

When, however, during his eleventh year, his father died, he emerged from his state of semi-somnolence. But from this moment his mother's love closed in on him, enveloping him with a solicitude that made its weight and its importance felt at every moment.

From this time forward he grew up in an atmosphere of sadness, surrounded by three women who were dominated by the fear of thinking or acting otherwise than with perfect rectitude. There were Anna Shackleton, an old maid to whom his family gave a home, and his Aunt Claire, obsessed by the fear of losing caste: — We owe it to ourselves — she would insist — to travel only first-class; and at the theatre to go only in the dress-circle. . . . *We owe it to ourselves.* . . .[1] This bourgeois motto was the source of endless discussions. Finally, his mother, close at hand, a symbolic figure of Duty, dressed always in black. She was an unpretentious creature, full of *goodwill*, timid, austere, and strict,

Between her and her son misunderstanding was already beginning to dawn. One day, having told her that one of his companions had declared himself an atheist, young André

[1] In general, various kinds of quotations in this volume are distinguished thus: (1) quotations from texts: "........"; (2) quotations from conversations in texts: — .... "; (3) oral quotations: — (at the beginning, only, of the phrase).

inquired: " What does that mean — atheist? " " It means a wicked fool." His mother's replies were always definite, final, and admitted of no possible rejoinder. When the child's questions became more pressing, she would say: " You will understand later on. . . ."

Little by little, young André was reduced to a family type. His home seemed to him to be the centre of the world. He imagined nothing beyond its enclosure, unless it were a universe wherein wealthy, bourgeois, puritan families, similar to his own, were indefinitely repeated. His standard of beauty was the flat inhabited by himself and his relatives in the rue Commaille, with its many-branched crystal chandeliers and its heavily gilded salon, whose furniture was enveloped in loose covers. Later on, encountering poverty in the form of a needy comrade, he was to experience uneasiness and failure to understand the wretchedness he saw.

Meanwhile, when his mother wished to send him back to school, he suddenly became subject to nervous crises. He would fall down, apparently in pain, trembling and throwing himself into contortions. One day when his uncle Charles Gide [1] passed him without noticing his movements, the child rose without difficulty, ashamed and furious. Simulated crises? Even so, simulation is in itself the beginning of a neurosis.

Thus it was that he escaped the compelling discipline of school-life. An " irregular . . . frameless . . . scattered existence " went on from that time forward within the gen-

---

[1] The great economist; died in March 1932.

eral severity of his upbringing. Madame Gide took him to Lamalou and then to Gérardmer, for the benefit of his health. This brought him the joy of running about over cliffs and rocks and amongst waterfalls. And he became, for his age, a considerable botanist: collecting butterflies, insects, larvæ. He observed the antics of rabbits, the flight of swallows, or just the little circles made by raindrops falling into a hollow.

Across this vagabond existence professors and teachers of the piano pass in succession, grotesque marionettes, ignorant and narrow. One tells him of his unhappy married life; another takes him to look for rooms. In the circumstances it is a miracle that he learned anything at all.

He spent the winter with his father's family at Uzès. When he visited one of his cousins, a pastor, he was never allowed to go without a homily, a blessing, without being prayed for and prayed with. In each house there was a Bible. Young André found nothing more touching than these pictures of family-life where the grandfather, surrounded by kneeling children, full of sublime confidence in God, gives thanks to Him " without petitions."

*   *   *

André Gide is sixteen years old. His rather withdrawn, enigmatic expression brings to mind an adolescent John the Baptist. His elusive eyes are inwardly adream. Thick, sensual lips, shadowed by a light down, accentuate the fervour of his sombre visage. He wears a knotted tie whose floating ends subside upon a waistcoat buttoned very high. Sudden, excessive movements of friendliness, followed by mistrust-

ful withdrawals, betray the drama of pride and timidity
going on within. Already he practises self-examination and
has begun to keep a " *journal intime.*"

At the age of puberty he goes, through a world ravaged
by original sin, protected by a cuirass of innocence. The
demands of the flesh are a horror to him. ". . . It will be
best," his cousin Albert tells his mother, in his presence,
" for this big boy to go home with you in the evening when
you come to dinner with us. . . ."

On discovering that one of his comrades in order to
reach home goes through that sink of iniquity the *passage
du Havre*, he flings himself on his knees, shaken with sobs.
" Oh, I implore you. . . . Don't go there! . . ." Nevertheless one spring evening he is himself accosted by one of
those women " who have the voices of ghouls or of sirens."
" You needn't be so scared, you handsome lad! " Immediately he blushes, his temples throb, and he takes flight almost in tears, under the impression that he has had a narrow escape. " Oh, shocking! " he writes in his " journal."
" If that is the life one must live, I prefer my dream . . .
my dream . . . chimeras rather than realities." Even his
reading is supervised. He reads aloud, to his mother, the
books in his father's library. Théophile Gautier's *Albertus*
makes them both blush. Stanzas are skipped. From this occasion onwards, however, supervision is relaxed.

And then there comes a craving for books. Poets, all the
poets, good or bad. Victor Hugo, Baudelaire, Sully-Prud-
homme, and Heine intoxicate him. The most important
events of his life, between fifteen and twenty, are the read-

ing of two widely different books: the Bible and the *Arabian Nights,* each arousing equal enthusiasm.

More often than not he shares the joys of his discoveries with his cousin Emmanuèle R—. Since his twelfth year he had been attached to her with the whole of his passionate tenderness. She was a gentle, quiet young girl of well-nigh supernatural virtue, who regarded her mother's elopement as an almost ineffaceable dishonour, and the young André had then sworn always to protect her " against fear, against evil, against life." [1] In their childish love there is already an intermingling of religious fervour. One Sunday in church, listening to the pastor's sermon, he sees himself, in a vision, holding his cousin by the hand: " both in the white raiment " mentioned in the Apocalypse, treading the steep ascent to the " narrow gateway " and looking towards the dazzling, pure sky. . . . Thus they grew up together, meeting each year, during the holidays, on their parents' estates in Normandy.

At the age of sixteen Gide is prepared for his First Communion. During his preparation the pastor's teaching seems to him so dry and grim that he is suddenly moved to ask himself whether he has the Protestant vocation, whether, without knowing it, he is a Catholic. As a matter of fact, no dogma gives him any satisfaction. But, once free from studying the Catechism, with what joy does he turn spon-

[1] Cf. *Les Cahiers d'André Walter, La Porte étroite* (English translation, *Strait is the Gate*), and *Si le Grain ne meurt.*

taneously to God! It is the following summer. His course is finished. He lives the life of an ascetic, sleeps on a plank, plunges at dawn into icy water, rises in the night to pray. With these pious transports he combines profane labours, once more taking up Greek grammar and algebra. He " makes a copy of the fourth book " of the *Ethics*, " leaving out the annotations in order the better to grasp the whole . . . the continuity of the propositions." [1] This seraphic state of affairs persists for months. . . .

*   *   *

Here he is at life's gateway, free from all monetary anxiety, disposing of his time as he chooses. Oh, happy pre-war days, when idleness was countenanced, was honourable! Although his mother still kept guard over him, she was unlike most parents in not discouraging his vocation as a man of letters. She was content with noting down, under " Expenses of André's career," the costs of printing her son's early works,

He is now possessed by a project for a book in which he shall put down everything: the *Cahiers d'André Walter*. The work seems to him " so noble, so pathetic, so decisive," that he has no doubt that its publication will win for him the hand of Emmanuèle. Life, indeed, is " less than nothing without her," and he always pictures her as " accompanying him everywhere." . . . Thus he confidently goes his way towards a future which he sees arranged just as he wishes: " I would not change with anyone," he cries. But life had not yet revealed its most terrible aspects, and

[1] Cf. *Les Cahiers d'André Walter.*

they were suddenly to undermine his proud inward equilibrium.

In order to write his book he rents a little chalet near Annecy and shuts himself up there, with a piano. Writes, from dawn to dark. He has stopped his clock and his watch. But when, for a little relaxation, he goes to the window — the chestnuts are in bloom — there is an end to his serenity. The unsatisfied desires of the flesh, neglected and repressed, surge up in him with an irresistible drive from within, adopting all manner of by-ways to remind him of their existence. If he takes a walk in the village, his eyes are drawn to the faces of children. Look at that young jackanapes plunging into the river. How good it would be to bathe with him! To become a brute without thoughts. Presently he decides to go out only at night. But by night the fear of sin becomes more horrible. Odds and ends of melody haunt him to the point of nervous derangement. A frightful woman, with the face of a doll, rises before him and lifts her dress. Disappearing, she opens a mouth that is like a black pit. " Oh God," he cries, " preserve me from madness! " [1] But he cries to the Eternal in vain. His faith wavers. Ah, those fair, childish dreams wherein he saw himself, " in white raiment," ascending with Emmanuèle into felicity! To-day he knows what is at work within the sheltered heart and the chaste life of the ascetic. In vain he tries " to do violence unto himself." [2] The Devil has entered his retreat.

[1] *Les Cahiers d'André Walter*. Undoubtedly Gide represented André Walter as being more severely tried than he was himself.
[2] *The Imitation of Christ*.

Nothing in his education had prepared him to anticipate this conflict. At the outset he sees it as unjustifiable. Wonders whether his interpretation of duty is at fault, or whether his moral training has been of the best. It cannot be the will of God that a man should agonize in this fashion. Would it not be better to give rein to his desires? " How? . . . I know nothing, I am ridiculously ignorant in these matters. Besides, where? One of those strolling women? . . ." Oh, for a counsellor, a master, a guide! He reflects that he cannot be the only one on earth who suffers in this way. He would like to reveal his sufferings for the benefit of others who doubtless are having similar experiences. Thenceforward he dreams of dropping his mask, publicly revealing the trouble within.

But at the age of twenty, though horrified to discover his moral principles slackening, he is still held in check by his religious fervour and his ingrained habits. He resists both his doubts and his senses. This is the beginning of the terrible conflict with his puritan upbringing.

The hero's contest with the flesh is the subject of the *Cahiers d'André Walter*, but it is treated in conformity to the Symbolist tendencies of the day, in a musical, ethereal manner. The book is finished. It is a manuscript made up of very small sheets of poor, thin note-paper, ruled in squares, covered with a cramped, almost infantile script, entirely free from erasures. It was with this book that Gide proposed to answer the anxious questionings of a whole generation.

He was consumed with impatience. Letters from the capital were like gulps of fevered air. Away there he sees his friends getting going, full of excitement; ambition in full flare. " I shall be too late! " he cries; " I shall be out of everything! " Going back to Paris and without even attempting to find the undiscoverable benevolent publisher, he has an ordinary edition printed at his own expense " to satisfy the appetite of the public," which he imagines " should be quite considerable."

There were no sales. In grief and anger, he had the whole edition destroyed in favour of an *édition de luxe* of 190 copies.[1] (Had there been many more, they would to-day be too few.) A few of these, provided with dedications that were all fervour and emphasis, he sent to authors of whose work he had not read a single line. Some of the answers were enchanting.

This " pathetic and wonderful Virgin's Breviary," wrote Maeterlinck to him, is ". . . now and again eternal, like the *Imitation*. . . ." " This is a product," wrote Huysmans, " of . . . abominable vulgarities. . . ." Henri de Régnier invited him to go with him to visit Monsieur de Heredia. Mallarmé called him " *le Rare Intellectual* " and asked him to come to the rue de Rome " on Tuesday evening towards eight o'clock, before anyone arrives, so that we may be able to talk." And thus it was that Gide, trembling, curious, and enchanted, entered the " hot-houses " of Symbolism.

*   *   *

[1] Two editions had been prepared by Gide. The *de luxe* edition should have appeared first, but was kept back by delays on the part of the printer. (See Bibliography.)

1890! A thrilling moment of time for a young man seeking his path in the world of letters. One could feel that something was happening. Literature was in a state of division. The opposition between the "*boulevard*" and the "*avant-garde*" was livelier than ever. The Symbolists fought disdainfully, wishing to remain obscure, rare, isolated. The naturalists accused them of neurosis or of mystification and set up in opposition the massive editions of their own novels.

The work of the Symbolists appeared only in small periodicals, as rare as they were evanescent. Each coterie, in order to make itself felt, ran its own. Gide interested himself in several of them, together with his first great friend: Pierre Louÿs.

The two young men had met at the École Alsacienne. — You're fond of poetry? Louÿs had said one day on finding Gide reading Heine. Soon after that they became friends.

Supple and delicate, having overgrown his strength as a boy, but full of the irresistible ferment of abounding youth, Louÿs, while waiting for " women and genius," [1] flung himself into life and tried in vain to drag poor Gide along with him. The latter, bogged in scruples and reticences, was nevertheless, inwardly, as passionate as himself.

Together with Franc-Nohain, Michel Arnauld,[2] and Maurice Guillot, the two school-friends derisively founded the *Potache-Revue*. Then came *La Conque*, a modest little

[1] Louÿs's *Journal*.
[2] Michel Arnauld was the pseudonym beneath which Marcel Drouin, afterwards Gide's brother-in-law, soon made himself known.

production, of eight pages, price ten francs. Old Parnassus
patronizing Symbolism, Leconte de Lisle and Heredia side
by side with Bérenger, the future " controller of oils " during the war, and Léon Blum. But *Le Centaure*, which succeeded *La Conque*, was a splendid compilation with original engravings in colour, signed: Jacques-Émile Blanche,
Puvis de Chavannes, Odilon Redon. . . .

But Louÿs was nominally the sole editor. Gide, feeling
that Symbolism was not *his* movement, kept in the background.

Nevertheless for four or five years he was within these
circles, of which he very soon became " one of the most
luminous Levites." [1] Surrounded by Quillard, Hérold,
Viélé-Griffin, Henri de Régnier, Mockel, and Bernard La-
zare, he allowed himself to be carried along by the movements of the coteries.

There were interminable discussions: Wagner, Hegel,
the Lake Poets, and the Pre-Raphaelites. *Vers libre* had
just made its appearance. Manifesto succeeded manifesto.
All writers were poets. . . .

In the midst of this abundant blossoming of groups Gide
had already discerned a few rare writers who later on were
to make themselves known. Mallarmé became his venerated
master. Invited to his " Tuesdays," he listened religiously,
sometimes moved to tears, to this humble little bourgeois
pursuing in the presence of his disciples his intangible
chimera: the Pure Idea arisen from the Word.

It was at this time that he discovered, through Louÿs,

[1] Rémy de Gourmont.

Paul Valéry. Amongst the little Symbolist clans these three stood out as more inspired and more idealistic than the rest. Valéry was quite a young man, with remarkably expressive eyes, a brilliant talker, and absorbed, like the others, by the problem of the pure idea, " the purest that can possibly be conceived." [1] Gide predicted that he would be the most important man of his generation.

The three friends devoted their time to all kinds of exercises in prosody: acrostics and so forth.[2] An assiduous, passionate correspondence, mostly consisting in interminable byzantine discussions, was carried on between Gide and Louÿs. One might have taken them for two theologians treating of the divine essence. Louÿs's letters, in Gothic script, sometimes in " uncial," as he said himself, were written in violet ink with a golden-brown gloss; sometimes upon splendid vellum, like mediæval illuminated missals. Although he wrote with surprising swiftness, Louÿs, who was already obsessed by his mania for palæography, spent whole nights in producing these letters.

Absorbing as he found the pursuit of art, Gide nevertheless lived during these years in a state of gloomy, superficial agitation. He was a tall, thin young man, chaste, sober,

---

[1] Introduction to *La Méthode de Léonard de Vinci.*

[2] Occasionally they improvised sonnets, each doing a line in turn. Or Valéry would write on a visiting-card:
> *Les Trompettes des chars sonores du soleil* . . .
> *Vingt fois ont sonné l'ombre et clamé le sommeil*
> *Mais Louÿs ne repond plus depuis le seize avril.*
(The trumpets of the sonorous chariots of the sun . . .
Have sounded darkness twenty times, and proclaimed sleep,
But Louÿs gives no answer since the sixteenth of April.)

affected, with rather colourless eyes, the abundant curly hair of a poet, and an absurd, almost black beard. He spoke but little, through closed teeth, in words of rare distinction. Beneath a vast black felt hat, he was already romantically draped in a mysterious brown cloak, as he always has been ever since. Sometimes he had in his hand, or secreted in his pocket, the Bible that had been with him since childhood, which he would constantly produce, " in the presence of exactly those people whose . . . scorn was most redoubtable."

In the literary salons, whither he allowed himself to be drawn, ill with nervousness, he made only " a few scared appearances. . . ." But in " *le monde où l'on s'ennuie* " a new face is always welcome. At the house of the Beignères he talks with gentle young Marcel Proust, who appeared as a protégé of Anatole France. Gide represents the *avant-garde*. Someone asks: — Is it really true that you understand Mallarmé? And he is shown the sonnet beginning: " *M'introduire dans ton histoire* . . ." the cause of more than a little hilarity on the part of the ladies. . . . — Explain it to us. . . . Suddenly become the centre of attention and, enlivened by the general irony, he recovers his courage. But on another occasion, having sat down to the piano, he stopped suddenly with his feet on the pedals, his hands inert on the keys, panic-stricken, unable to go on. . . . It was about this time that he met Wilde, elegant, flattered by all, and with the eyes of a conqueror. " I don't like your mouth," said Wilde confidentially; " you have the

straight lips of one who has never told a lie." Then he broke
into laughter, leaving Gide thoroughly out of countenance.

Human relationships had become nothing less than torture. Even amongst friends he was unable to be *natural*.
He cultivated artificial poses and, being uneasy as to his
gestures, practised them, like an actor, at home in front of
the glass. His presence froze everyone up: no one dared to
risk anything verging on the improper, and his awareness
of this fact did but increase the discomfort of this puritan-
in-spite-of-himself. Henri de Régnier composed a laconic
epitaph: "*Ci-Gide*." [1] On the anniversary of St. Bartholo-
mew, Louÿs sent him a telegram: "*Ils t'ont oublié. . . .*" [2]

Pierre Louÿs, occasionally given to rather broad jesting,
had sworn to "thaw" his friend. He experienced a sort of
sadistic pleasure in shocking his modesty. In spite of his
persistent efforts he had not so far succeeded in getting
Gide to visit his bachelor quarters in the rue Rembrandt.
On one occasion he even sent him a telegram, through Mauclair, announcing his suicide, but Gide, suspecting a strata-
gem, took Hérold with him to his friend's rooms and made
him precede him. Louÿs, in pyjamas, opened the door and
shouted: — Can't I even be allowed to make love in peace!
But when Louÿs went so far as to send the inmates of a
disreputable house at two o'clock in the morning to knock
at the door of the flat where Gide was living with his mother,
the jest led to serious disagreement.

[1] A parody on the "*Ci-gît*" ("Here lies") of French tombstones.
[2] "They have forgotten you."

Thus did his useless youth and his fruitless chastity prolong themselves. " Commandments of God," he cries, " how far do your boundaries extend? " [1]

All at once his bonds lose their constraining power, and everything gives way in him. He has rebelled. Everything about him seems unendurably ugly — his past, his family, even his flat in the rue de Commaille. He must get away, away, away!

His friend Paul-Albert Laurens has decided to set out for Tunis. They will make the trip together. As timid and chaste as himself (though devoid of religious scruples), Laurens is equally resolved to be adventurous. Doughty as a mediæval knight, Gide sets forth to conquer his personality, to dispel both his ignorance and his fear of humanity and the unknown. At the same time he separates himself from his Bible: this book upon which he had so continually sustained himself is left behind when, in October 1893, he begins his journey to the oases of the Sahara.

On the boat, with the sea all round him and actually carrying him, at last, for the first time away from his childhood, he feels that henceforward he will pursue his desires to their end, not drawing back however difficult, ruinous, and dangerous these may be. . . . " All must be made manifest, even those things that are the most baneful. ' *Woe unto him by whom the offence cometh,*' but, ' *it needs be that offences come.*' "

[1] *Les Nourritures terrestres.*

2

THE REVELATION OF THE DESERT

IT was in Algeria that Gide was seized by an overwhelming desire for life, a feverish desire to be, to enjoy, and to love. Sunlight, nature, the ardour of plant-life, young creatures, and *the simplicity of love* freed him at last from the embraces of puritanism. " Nathanaël, I no longer believe in sin! " No, earth is not accursed! Glory be to the human body! Here no remorse tarnishes the beauty of the children of the desert. In this harsh, burning region, far from civilization, pleasure, of whatever kind, is natural: it is taken and given and the sun purifies all. To Gide are revealed both himself and the true nature of his desires.

For two almost uninterrupted years he remained in this world of the *Arabian Nights*. It was his most lyrical period. And yet he had never been so ill as during these two years. He believed himself tuberculous and thought he would die as his father had done. He soon gave up an intended and, for him, very exhausting expedition to southern Algeria and was obliged to winter at Biskra.

Here began his slow, wonderful convalescence. The oasis

19

of Biskra, with its white terraces, its " séghias," those precious little waterways, and its " lagmi," or palm wine, a
natural sap that needs merely to be drawn! Refusing the
doctor's verdict, he challenged his fate. The recovery of
health became his main concern. " I want to live! " he cries,
" to live! " [1] He surrounded himself with native children
and the spectacle of their health and their joyous movements helped him to conquer his illness, whose origin was
largely nervous. When his mother hurried from Paris to
nurse him, she was soon compelled to return. He wished to
heal himself alone, without help.

He gave up his sombre garments and shaved his beard.
When it was gone, he was a little afraid lest his unmasked
face should fully betray the audacity of his new way of
thinking.

In the course of his second visit to Algeria he met Oscar
Wilde and was drawn by him into fresh irregularities.
Wilde, then awaiting his lawsuit, febrile, overwrought,
half-crazy, and surrounded by a remarkable band of
hangers-on, allowed himself to be led by a kind of fatalism.

And, like Wilde, Gide abandoned himself to every kind
of pleasure. One morning, after having held all night in
his arms " a perfect little savage body, ardent, lascivious,
and full of darkness," he ran about alone in the open like
a madman, feeling light, floating, released, giving rein to
his overwhelming joy. Why should not all his nights, from
now on, be equally glorious? He imagined a transformed

[1] *L'Immoraliste* (English translation, *The Immoralist*).

world, free of rules and restraints, a new era in human life. . . .

It was in this exalted mood that he wrote *Les Nourritures terrestres:* Let us burn our useless books, break the links with the past, and the soul, gradually drained clear, will enter into communion with the whole of nature in a carnal, mystical pantheism.

Gide tried as far as possible to prolong his stay in Algeria. He even bought land, with the idea of settling for good in this chosen country. A young Arab boy was his servant: Athman, fourteeen years old and very black, dressed, to please his new master, in a single garment of red silk. Gide initiated him into the mysteries of French prosody. They went about together and played like children. Athman became so attached to him that Gide would gladly have taken him to Paris, had not his mother met the suggestion with extremely animated protests. Madame Gide had been frightened by the excessive enthusiasm betrayed in the letters of her son. For in writing to his mother, to Emmanuèle, and to Pierre Louÿs he had been unable to hold back the news of his metamorphosis. He would have liked to confide to the whole world the secret now dwelling within him. . . .

When he returned to Paris, his disillusionment was so cruel that for a moment he meditated suicide. It did not seem possible that nothing should have changed! The same cafés, the same Symbolist writers hidden in the same fortresses! All about him " everyone was busy," as if he had not come back, as if he had not a tremendous message to deliver. Presently he escapes from his dejection, taking refuge in his sense of humour: " Ah well, it's nothing to me. Am I not writing *Paludes*? "

But suddenly he is called to La Roque, where his mother is dying. Kneeling near the motionless body, beside which only himself and an old servant keep vigil, he rediscovers the gestures and the prayers of his pious childhood. Re-opening the Holy Scriptures, he weeps with all his heart.

It was almost immediately after his bereavement that he married his cousin Emmanuèle R—. The young girl believed in his mission, foresaw for him a life that should be a veritable splendour of exemplary austerity, and feared that she might prove a hindrance therein. Faithful to his childhood's vow, he wished to make her happy, devote himself to her, protect her, and lead her towards a happiness which, he believed, with a certain temerity, could be hers as well as his own. He did not reflect that happiness cannot be given, but only exchanged. One cannot make another happy unless, reciprocally, the other can give happiness.

But at this time Gide hoped to be able to reconcile the contradictions in himself: pagan joy and mystic love, the God of the *Arabian Nights* and the God of the Bible, Jesus, Apollo, and Bacchus. With the intrepidity of youth, believing all things possible, he believed also in the possibility of a grand, sublime adventure which should bear them both through and beyond happiness to something more . . . to " sanctity." [1] His marriage stands therefore

----

[1] *La Porte étroite.*

at the centre of his life, explaining and dominating everything. In order to understand it, one must call to mind the
dénouement of *La Porte étroite* and modify it: imagine
Alissa, at the end of this book, marrying Jérôme instead of
running away.

The quiet, simple ceremony was celebrated on October
8, 1895 in the little church at Étretat.

*   *   *

But it has hardly taken place before Gide realizes that
he is confined within an alien system of obligations. His
whole tenderness goes out towards this woman, but his
whole spirit is turned in another direction. He discovers
that she has a life of her own, and is faced with a fresh
responsibility. The thought of the irrevocable fills him with
fear. All is confusion within him. . . .

During this very year he finished his *Nourritures terrestres*, wherein every kind of satisfaction finds a place. But in
the following year he writes the story of *Saül*, whom he sees
as conquered and enslaved by his desires. Then he pub-
lishes *L'Immoraliste*, belauding his former audacities.
Nevertheless, although he feels himself stifling when he is
with pious people, he has ceased to believe in systematic
rebellion and regards untrammelled liberty as impious. He
is once more a prey to the doubt that had held him during
his adolescence. And once again, but this time more vividly
and more urgently than ever, the dramatic problem of his
whole life rises before him: " You want to be of some use.
It is essential to discover by what means."

For twenty painful and anxious years he is to turn and

turn the moral problem this way and that. During this distressing period he adopts in turn every possible ethical position, works it out to its conclusion in a book, and rejects it. The disconcerted critic is unable to keep pace. Francis Jammes is held up in the course of writing an article upon him by the impossibility of encircling his personality. Gide himself admits: " I am never anything *but* that which I believe myself to be, and this *varies* incessantly." So he wanders . . . until at last, by dint of a prolonged, laborious, and voluntary effort, he attains serenity.

It is in this painful ascent that we are now about to follow André Gide: in the persevering struggle of a man who sets out to attain self-knowledge and self-possession.

3

"LET EACH FOLLOW HIS BENT . . .
BUT IN AN UPWARD DIRECTION"

THE DAY after his marriage Gide returned with his wife
to the Algeria for which he had an inconsolable nostalgia.
But disillusionment awaited him. Winter and the absence
of warmth makes the country unrecognizable. The charming children of Biskra and Blidah, whose mere presence
had healed him four or five years ago, are now grown men,
vulgar, deformed by their daily work, trapped by the desire
for gain. Gide supposes it is his own youth that has died.
" I have," he writes, " most certainly passed the age at
which travelling is a joyous enrichment." [1]

One by one, like fragments of dead skin, the hopes of his
past life drop away from him. The trio composed of himself, Valéry, and Louÿs is dispersed. Valéry, finding in
Rimbaud and Mallarmé absolute perfection, the furthest
limits of poetry in two different ways, had retired to a silent
retreat from which he was not to emerge until the war. With
Louÿs, Gide had quarrelled. " Be unique," he had already
written to him from Algeria, " come, come! " But as soon

[1] Letter to Édouard Ducoté.

as Louÿs had joined him, his fantastic, invading, tyrannical personality seemed more unendurable than ever. One
wanted sunlight, the other shadow; one conversation, the
other silence. They were not to meet again.[1] Whilst Louÿs
went on to captivate the general public with his *Aphrodite*,
Gide retired into obscurity.

His friends in the old group had left him. Even with the
best of them, Henri de Régnier, he had fallen out.[2] It was
admitted in Symbolist circles that he had aroused hopes
with his rather esoteric little brochures (*La Tentative
amoureuse*, *Le Voyage d'Urien*), but by this time he was
regarded as lost.

— Gide will never do anything, said Heredia a little
while before his death.

When *L'Immoraliste* appeared, the *avant-garde* was completely taken aback. The book was a " novel "! But if Gide's
writings were now more explicit, the larger public was not
aware of the fact. Surprising as it seems to-day, he had the
reputation of being difficult to understand. Official criticism
made fun of his small editions. But when one has no more
than one or two hundred readers, one prints accordingly.
It took years to exhaust the first five hundred copies of *Les
Nourritures terrestres*. Although it was something quite

---

[1] At the time of his mother's death Gide wrote a farewell letter full of
deep feeling: ". . . It is useless and vexatious publicly to display our in-
consistencies. . . . Let us leave it at that. . . . I think respect for the
past . . . will preserve us from slander. . . . Next to your brother it is I
who have perhaps loved you best. . . . Farewell. . . ."

[2] Henri de Régnier had published an exquisite, frivolous novel in the
eighteenth-century manner: *La Double Maîtresse*. Urged by the indignation
of his friend Viélé-Griffin, another terrible puritan, Gide let himself go in
an unnecessarily severe criticism in the *Revue blanche*.

new, it was ignored by the press.[1] *Saül* was left on its author's hands. Antoine himself, after having at first been interested in the play, refused it on the ground that the first acts were Shaksperian, but the last . . . Maeterlinckian.

After having been something of a " great man " in the Symbolist movement, Gide felt that nothing could be more painful than this injustice. His horizon closed in on him and he felt as if he were speaking in a void.

He has now reached the lowest point in the curve of his life; he feels that something within him is at an end and that there is, so far, nothing to take its place. There is a sort of break in the continuity of his existence, a prolonged emptiness such as is to be found in the lives of the greatest writers. No event of any importance marks this period, during which desire tempts him and true satisfaction remains absent.

" I am doing nothing," he admitted; " I neither read nor write. All this spring I was waiting for the summer and throughout the summer I have waited for the autumn." [2] Between 1902 and 1908 — that is to say, between *L'Immoraliste* and *La Porte étroite* — Gide produced nothing but brief critical articles. He could not fix his thoughts. He strained at the leash. " I am aware all the time that I am already over thirty, and *in order to be what I am,* I have

---

[1] Save for Ghéon in the *Mercure de France*, Madame Lucie Delarue-Mardrus in the *Revue blanche*, and Edmond Jaloux in the *Renaissance latine*. These few articles, appearing in the smaller reviews, sufficed to save the book from passing entirely unnoticed.

[2] Unpublished correspondence.

not a moment to lose." [1] But he was held up by a nervous disorders recalling those of his childhood. Obstinate insomnia left him gasping with fatigue. Every kind of treatment was tried. Now the lungs, now the liver, were said to be out of order: doctors prefer to treat bodies rather than minds.

He returned to Champel and there passed a veritable " season in hell." Or he would suddenly go off alone and hide himself in a small village lost in the depths of the country. " If you knew," he wrote to Ducoté, " in what a state I have passed three sleepless nights, you would approve of my going off and leaving everything, duties, engagements, serious occupations, and pleasures." [1] La Roque was his mooring-place. At the first contact family life always had a soothing influence. But the respite was brief. In Paris he stayed only for short periods. Towards 1904, with the idea of entertaining friends and relatives, he built a " villa " at Auteuil, altogether too vast, and arranged with an almost too cunning emphasis on the necessity of securing for everyone the possibility of tranquil work. He never took the trouble of finishing the interior fittings and was off and away whilst the architect was still busy. . . .

He travelled through Germany and Austria and, by preference, along the Mediterranean basin: Spain, Italy, North Africa, whither he returned five or six times in the course of ten years; later on he went as far as Greece, Turkey, and Asia Minor. All his life Gide has been a wanderer, rarely remaining more than a few weeks in the same place. But during this period of his youth he produces the impression

[1] Unpublished correspondence.

of a traveller who is " surrounded." At the end of *L'Im-moraliste* he himself describes this tragic state of restlessness: the traveller reaches an unknown town in the evening, worn out, at the end of his tether; the next day, too impatient to look round and as if pursued by some sort of demon, he leaves everything to go . . . somewhere else, always farther on.

Uneasiness had entered his life, following him step by step, never leaving him. At every turn, with every thought, he felt the necessity for self-justification, for putting himself right with his conscience. His inner life was an interminable dialogue.

This uneasiness became an obsession. When visited by a stranger, his first question would be: — Tell me, are you uneasy? In pronouncing these words, leaning towards his interlocutor and slightly dropping his voice, he seemed to evoke the whole of human anguish, because, for Gide, the question could have only one meaning: — Do you fear God?

Now and again, at the end of his endurance, he would feel the necessity of confiding in someone. One day he asked Félix Bertaux point-blank, his face expressing his concentration on the question: — What does the communion of saints mean for you? As Bertaux remained silent, he told him later on: — I cannot tell you what it has meant for me. . . .

When, after much inward debating, he published his " confessions," the pleasantries of certain journalists, and the irony of one section of the public, roused his contempt.

To a friend who chanced to meet him at this moment, he exclaimed tragically and tormentedly: — And to think that there are people who find all that simply amusing!

There are few (with the possible exception of Nietzsche) whose passion for truth has equalled Gide's. With the whole of his being he desired nothing so much as absolute sincerity. And yet this man was obliged to lie to God as he did to society. The particular nature of his desires had set him in opposition to his education, his surroundings, and his religion. Herein lies the whole drama of his life. Moreover, he was troubled over the problem of God only in so far as this problem was inscribed in his flesh. He could not resign himself to guilt:

— Is it my fault — he reflected — that I experience certain desires? Would it not be treachery, since God has given me the gifts of thought and of speech, not to express that which is within me?

But the moment he followed his inclinations, he recoiled, aghast, since for dogma there is no such thing as physiological fatality and *each is responsible for his soul* and can guide it in a chosen direction, giving way to his desires or resisting them.

" What can a man do? " asked Gide. Where is truth? Where is unattainable truth?

Then, supreme succour, he turned once more with joyous relief to the Gospels. Little by little the book became luminous. No, there are no prohibitions in the words of Christ: " Happy is he who . . ." Jesus repeats, " happy. . . ." It is the devotees who have reduced the image of Christ, and religion that has ended by crucifying Him a second time. But suddenly, like a diabolical sneer, came the question: Can one call oneself a Christian so long as one is tempted by pleasure? Can one combine divine and creaturely love? Can one reconcile heaven and hell?

— Oh, *I am afraid* of blasphemy! . . . he admitted.

Later on, one day when Gide explained to me that Christ had never announced anything but joy and happiness:

— On earth? I inquired.

— Yes. The Kingdom of God is eternal joy in the instant, in the present, down here.   Read *Num Quid et tu.*

— But why, in your book, do you allow a belief in another life, an after-life?

— *I was* afraid. . . . And like a traveller returned from afar, he seemed still to tremble at the memory of the risks his soul had run.

" Afraid." This word was frequently on his lips. He meant: — I am afraid . . . to follow my thoughts to their conclusion, yet I cannot exist in a state of compromise.

It is, in any case, difficult to picture the oppression exercised by sexual prejudices in pre-war days. On certain individuals the state of public opinion pressed very heavily. There was reason to be afraid! In this already far-off time adultery seemed to be the sole licence tolerated by society. Every other irregularity was banned by the psychologists. Jean Lorrain and Pierre Loti, in order to get their books accepted, were obliged to transpose the sex of their characters. Juries and law-courts maintained a threatening attitude.[1] Twenty years after his drama with Verlaine, Rimbaud was still banned by the press.[2] Wilde was pilloried by a stampeding England. Leaving prison, the one-time conqueror became a wretched derelict and abandoned himself to the vilest debauches. In Paris he was avoided whenever he appeared on the boulevards. When Gide met him, he sat down with him on the terrace of the Napolitain — an action calling for a considerable amount of courage — but with his remarkable frankness he admits that he himself sat with his back to the passers-by.

Even in France those who defended Wilde were very rare at this time. Nevertheless, his *Salomé* was performed at the Œuvre by way of protest against the revolting condemnation, and a few did not hesitate to treat the play as a symbolic success. Gide and Édouard Ducoté arranged a dinner for Wilde and a few of their friends. In *L'Immoraliste* Michel, in the midst of a salon, ostentatiously embraces Ménalque, who also stood under condemnation.

Wilde's tragedy had stimulated Gide's desire for freedom. He admired the aureole of the great pariah and aspired to the same fate, but as martyr rather than as victim. He felt, obscurely at that time, but still with certainty, that a day would come when, in his confessions, he would reveal the secret of his whole life, the whole drama of his thought, everything. He knew that he could escape the im-

---

[1] In the Rémy case the accused was condemned, on insufficient proof, solely on account of his sexual life.

[2] Rimbaud offered *Le Temps*, from Aden, an account of the Italo-Abyssinian war, which was refused solely on account of his past.

passe only by the force of an entirely puritan logic, whatever might be the consequences.

— All that ought to break forth, and will break forth. . . .

This moment, the aim of his existence, was to be that of his liberation and would make an end of his anguish. But the truth he was to bring to mankind still seemed to him so unstable, so horrifying, and so scandalous that he headed off its approach; he needed to grow accustomed to it. Was it possible he could be right in face of all the world?

He was afraid, too, not only of his thoughts, " but of the fear they inspire in certain friends." Even the most daring writer fears those nearest to him more than the public.

— I must confess — he is to say later on — that love, too, can turn one very much away from oneself. . . . But that is a question on which I have no right to speak. . . .

Thus did scruples and ruinous solicitudes incline him to compromises which were hateful to himself. His way of disappearing, his flights, and his exaggerations were entirely the result of an exceptional honesty, desirous of breaking through the contradictions of life.

— Where is truth? he asked from the depths of his anguish.

Meanwhile he felt the immensity of life, palpitating on the earth within reach of his hand, and the fear of failing to enjoy it supplied a fresh source of disturbance. — I *fear*, he said, that every desire, every potentiality I shall not have satisfied during my life will survive and torment me.

He was driven by an insatiable curiosity as strong as was his disquietude. One day, in a small Algerian town, meeting the strange cortège of an Arab wedding, he followed it step by step as far as the courtyard of the nuptial dwelling, where Muslim fanatics immediately began to threaten him. It was not until a friend drew him aside that he came to himself, awaking as from a dream. Absorbed in the spectacle, he had lost all sense of expediency. His curiosity was a sort of " avidity of the spirit and of the senses," a perpetual love of taking risks.

In seaports it rose to a kind of paroxysm. When on his way to Algeria he passed through Marseilles, the tumultuous town, with its enormous commercial activities, the foreigners passing through it, and the prostitution haunting its old streets, whipped up the ardour and the thirst that were in him to turn to account every source of gratification. Having made a considerable impression upon Lieutenant Dupouey and gained his friendship, in order to remain on the pinnacle where he believed the latter to have placed him, he said with a smile:

— If I do not become the hero of an adventure, or take my life within six months, what will Dupouey think of me? —

Under the influence of *Les Nourritures terrestres*, there had sprung up between himself and his friends a kind of emulation in regard to the taste for " experiences ": a visit to a bar, a conversation with a sailor, a stroll round the docks — what Nietzsche calls " evil frequentations " — such things seemed to them points of departure for all sorts of extraordinary enterprises.

But in the midst of his audacities Gide hesitated, tacking about. He had become almost as tremulous as a butterfly and seemed to be the victim of a diseased inability to be still. His mobility had become a legend. He was always outdoors. To stay with him in Paris was to see less of him than ever. Sometimes he would be awaited for a whole evening. One day Edmond Jaloux asked for him at the Hotel de Noailles in Marseilles, where he was staying, and as he was not there, the porter explained:

— Oh, Monsieur Gide still does nothing but come in and go out.

Unable to abandon himself to pleasure without remorse, Gide exaggerated its value. He would speak of desire with the same awe as he would speak of sacred things, in murmurs, with delectation, with concupiscence. For him, voluptuousness was something immense, moving, and terrible. Nevertheless, in the face of the spectacles which were presented to him, he would display ingenuous astonishment as if he were seeing them for the first time, would look mysterious, smile knowingly, make sudden avowals followed by abrupt reticences.

By this time he had made the acquaintance of Henri Ghéon, who remained, until the War, his most intimate confidant, accompanying him on all his excursions. Yet Ghéon carried on a medical practice at Bray-sur-Seine and supported his mother. Detained all day by his profession, he would drive into Paris at night in a little car, an originality in those days, and sometimes would not return until the morning, bringing friends with him.

Together the two led a free and tumultuous existence.

They amused themselves by being at once mysterious and provocative. . . .

— One must live dangerously. . . .

With Ghéon, Gide indulged in all manner of extravagances. They had got Gide's youthful guide, Athman, over from Algeria and for some time went about in Paris accompanied by this young Arab. Athman was present at the literary meetings of the group. He even passed from the rank of servant to that of poet, and publications were hoped for in the near future.

This was towards 1900. The Exposition Universelle ruled Paris. Gide and Athman would stroll up and down in front of the Tunisian *souks*, set up amidst the booths, roundabouts, and other attractions. One of these small Arab cafés was used as a decorative background by Jacques-Émile Blanche when he painted his friends' portraits. In one picture [1] is to be seen a slender young man with a drooping, Vercingetorix moustache and garments that are not quite those of an artist and not quite those of a tourist. This person looks at once grave, chilly, and dejected. His uncertain glance seems to seek something upon which it may rest. It is Gide. At his side, seated on an Oriental carpet, is Ghéon. With a head like that of a bearded satyr, and a frankly Rabelaisian smile, he looks full of good nature, mordant vivacity, and jollity. In the background are Eugène Rouard and Chanvin. In the centre, in sumptuous native dress and looking a little bewildered: Athman ben Sala.

[1] Now in the gallery at Rouen.

By the end of a few weeks the young Arab was full of literary pretensions and, realizing that he had become something of a burden, took refuge, successively, with various friends of Gide. On returning to his country he became a great marabout, took hashish, and wrote increasingly extravagant lyrics. In his fashion he had reconciled heaven and hell.

Meanwhile the years were passing. To anticipate a little: by 1907 Gide is again more continuously at work. He has published *Le Retour de l'Enfant Prodigue*. Several projected books are growing clear in his mind and he is shaping *La Porte étroite*.

He has advanced step by step, determined not to make an imprudent move, unless at a moment he shall consider opportune. He has expressed this progression of his thought in *La Porte étroite*, but still envelops it in an almost impenetrable mystery. The evocation of his ascetic youth is indeed so fervent that the reader may well be mistaken as to the meaning of the book, apparent only in the concluding lines. Alissa, having renounced Jérôme from religious motives, suddenly finds herself, at the moment of death, confronting an empty heaven. It is " the abrupt, disenchanting illumination " of her whole life. Will she give way to blasphemy when she realizes that she has sacrificed the substance for the shadow, the fullness of love for a nonexistent morality, and that she is about to die alone, without either God or Jérôme?

At this moment of his life, still struggling against himself,

Gide all at once asks why he should be condemned, like
Sisyphus, to the perpetual rolling of his stone? Would it
not be more *natural* to leave it at the bottom of the valley
and sit on it? For in the end one grows weary of useless
effort and can see no meaning in this obscure and painful
labour everlastingly renewed. Why make vain sacrifices?
Why this rigidity of soul? Why?

He had just got through the first stage. The period of
emptiness was nearing its end. Meanwhile the painful conflict with the devotees who will soon begin to exercise pressure is still to continue. But now he sees his way ahead:
" Let each one follow his bent . . . but in an upward
direction."

$$*\qquad\qquad *\qquad\qquad *$$

Whilst Gide was thus struggling, alone and restless, the
moral and literary influences of his little books were slowly
and gradually extending. He still benefited by the notoriety
of the Symbolist groups: to have been known to ten of the
avant-garde writers meant, even for one who was unknown
to the great public, the admiration of the young.

Now and again a brochure by Gide, despised of the critics
and difficult to obtain, would find its way by devious paths
to some adolescent lost in the country and would overwhelm
him. Isolated in various parts of France, new readers made
contact with the author, and a literary group was about to
come into being through the drawing together of the best
of these scattered, distant friends.

Almost always Gide's contact with them was the result of
an effort to discover the author of a critical article on his
work. Ghéon, commissioned to write an article on *Les Nour-*

ritures terrestres for the *Mercure de France,* had written to Gide and visited him. With infinite caution and many reservations Gide showed him the proofs of an unpublished work. This book was an immense revelation to Ghéon and filled him with the unbounded enthusiasm which was the origin of their friendship.

In the same sort of way Gide unearthed Jacques Copeau, who had just read *L'Immoraliste* with transports of admiration. In his *journal intime* he questioned the author, called him by name, waited for him. He wrote a brief notice of this book for a little dramatic review and then went off to Denmark to be married. In Copenhagen he received a note in beautifully written round-hand, no more than a few words, a little mysterious, as Gide knew how to make such communications, and inciting him to the response for which, wordlessly, it called. . . . And with what delirious joy did Copeau respond! When he returned to France, Gide doubtless expected some pathetic adolescent; but it was a young man of thirty who came in, robust and assured, with a large black beard. This did not prevent their becoming excellent friends.

Sometimes it amused Gide to take people by surprise. He had discovered at Marseilles a small volume of Symbolist verse, *Une Ame d'Automne,* dedicated to himself and signed Edmond Jaloux, who was then a youth of eighteen. One day on returning to his rooms Jaloux finds there his friend Miomandre and a stranger, a tall young man who rises and introduces himself: — I am André Gide. Enormous sensation!

His direct, personal influence on his friends was even

more astonishing than that of his books. He had passion
for teaching: — I shall read you pen in hand, he would
say when a manuscript was brought to him, and he would
return it with marginal annotations, suppressing, above all,
useless words. If his ascendancy and his exactions as a
writer now and again reduced the already feeble to powerlessness, how much, on the other hand, did creative minds
profit by his discipline!

— At the age of twenty — Ghéon relates — I was writing
just anyhow, ceaselessly pouring out poems, plays, and
criticisms. . . . I met Gide; and I then understood the
meaning of effort, difficulty, art. For years afterwards I
scarcely wrote anything at all. Now my pen goes straight
ahead: my instrument is fashioned.

— When — Jean Schlumberger explains to-day — I
gave Gide my first book, a bad novel by a very young man,
I knew nothing of literature. I had read Loti, d'Annunzio,
and, haphazard, a few fashionable novelists. It was Gide
who set me on the right path and gave me new literary
horizons.

Gide played this role of enlightener to the next generation
also:

— I had just published *La Danse de Sophocle* — declares Jean Cocteau — when I got to know Gide. Together
with Ghéon, he had amused himself by writing, for the
N. R. F., a very severe criticism, which nevertheless expressed on the whole a certain sympathy. To reply would
be to show that I understood. So I wrote, thanking him.
Dorchain and Rostand had emitted dithyrambic eulogies.

Meaning nothing at all. Gide and Ghéon came to see me in the rue d'Anjou. I was completely ignorant. It is Gide who has shown me art and the modern world, who enabled me to discover Rimbaud, and style. What do I not owe to Gide! . . .

How many of " *les jeunes* " were experiencing at this time the same feelings of gratitude! Jacques Rivière, who had saved up in order to buy Gide's brochures one after another, suddenly devoured by an inward fire, by the need for heroic sacrifice, wrote to his friend Alain Fournier: " Become a disciple of André Gide. . . ." Edmond Jaloux, after reading Ménalque's narratives in *L'Ermitage*, discovered in himself the taste for adventure and for freedom from ties: — What did I not learn in the course of our many walks in Marseilles! he declares to-day.[1]

*   *   *

There are writers a meeting with whom may be the turning-point of a life. Gide was one of these. He made his impression at the first contact. He would receive his visitor with a mixture of brusqueness, hauteur, and controlled fervour. A tête-à-tête with him was an unforgettable experience.

Usually one went to see him at Auteuil, in his *villa des Sycomores*, a baroque building, style 1900, with circular windows in a row all along the façade.

---

[1] It is from the time of these conversations that Jaloux dates the deep appreciation of the great English, Russian, and Scandinavian novelists to which he owes his standing amongst our critics as the one who is most deeply initiated into the spirit of foreign literature.

The door was opened by an old, rather infirm servant, kept on by Gide's goodness of heart. One waited in a bare stone hall, whence rose a wooden staircase with a red balustrade. In the shadow a vast composition by Maurice Denis: *Hommage à Cézanne*, recently presented by Gide to the Luxembourg.

The rattle of the descending lid brought to an end the sound of the piano. Doors were shut. One heard Gide's piercing voice in the distance. He appeared, in a knitted jersey with very long sleeves, and wearing mittens.

— I was expecting you, he said. . . .

Immediately one felt that he was pleased to see one, and that his time was at one's service. Talk began, in a charming familiar fashion.

The " villa " was so vast that in order to keep warm one had to sit close to a large open fireplace. The rest of the room was gloomy, sad, almost dark. A little office-lamp on a small table supplied all the light there was. One took refuge with Gide in this warmed and illuminated corner which he was to fill with such an intensity of life. Seated sideways, almost turning his back on his interlocutor, he leaned forward, arms on knees, or balanced himself, his hands clasped round one knee. From time to time he stirred the fire with the tongs and put on a fresh log.

— Talk, I beg of you. I am giving you my full attention.

The visitor felt that he was understoood. Gide possessed the art of questioning, and presently the great questions were reached.

A long, heavy silence full of feeling. Then:

— I must indeed talk about myself, though I do not find it easy. . . .

He fixed his mind's eye upon a distant point, as if to summon thought thence and to make it concrete, so that it might be grasped by his friend, to whom he went on talking without turning his eyes in his direction.

The conversation lasted for hours. . . . Confidences were exchanged. . . . His awkward, ungainly body might play him false, but he well knew how to set forth his ideas, how to make them really present. In a most remarkable way he made the best of his defects as well as of his qualities. In reading aloud he revealed what almost amounted to a genius for acting.

Now he has gone to fetch a book from the first floor. He comes back by a little spiral staircase from which he emerges as if coming through a trapdoor. Seated at a table before the open book, he comes to life. His voice, whose register is extensive, fills out as it rises, passes from modulation to modulation, and sinks, finishing the extract in a tone of the deepest possible gravity. Then he plays with his spectacles, removing them, putting them on the table, taking them up again; all with a masterly deliberation. Everything contributes to the impression he makes: his surroundings, the atmosphere, his gestures, the sincerity of his emotion. In intervals of silence he follows the effect of his spoken words upon the face of his interlocutor. Gide likes to captivate, little by little to prevail over the mind of another, to take possession of it and become active therein. One is aware in his friendship of his need for absolute intellectual possession.

Roused and overwhelmed, the new-comer goes home with the feeling of carrying away treasures. Already he looks forward to further meetings with the master, to an intimacy that will be nothing less than an endless exploration of the deeply stirring regions of the inward life.

But he has counted on the future too readily. It was always when one thought one had secured him that Gide escaped. On the occasion of his first meeting with Copeau, Gide suggested, although they had already spent a long evening together, that they should take a turn in the open. It was midnight. The happy Copeau, enchanted by this proof of sympathy between them, failed immediately to grasp the fact that it is easier to " leave anyone under a street-lamp than to get him as far as the stairs."

— I think — said Gide when he left him — that there is nothing to be gained by going any farther to-day.

The moment he was interested in anyone, Gide could be passionately interested, sparing no pains to prevail with him. But suddenly he would flag and his curiosity would subside. He would seem like another man — indifferent, remote. Nothing could hold him. . . .

The fear of its vanishing does but make a presence the more precious. Gide liked to transform his abrupt disappearances by introducing into them the element of surprise. When one thought him in Biskra, he would turn up in Paris. Due to return from a journey on a given day, he would arrive the day before and, whilst his friends were waiting on the platform for his train to come in, would unexpectedly appear in their midst. . . . Then he would enjoy their astonishment with a smile full of malice and benevolent indulgence.

He loved putting people on the wrong scent. To the disciple who talked to him at great length and enthusiastically he gave an approving nod and then, with a single word, put him out of countenance:

— Allow me to refrain from exclamations! ” [1]

This was yet another of his ways of disturbing and awakening:

— I have no dislike of taking people in, he admitted.

Asked for a favour, for one of his books or an inscription, he would immediately be annoyed and evasive. But by the time the solicited service seemed to be forgotten, he would spontaneously turn to the applicant and present him with a splendid copy of one of his works, a rare copy, such as not even his intimates possessed, or perhaps, as an apparently unique mark of confidence, he would read to some new-comer extracts from his own “ journal.” He liked to give to each one unequalled pleasure and to exercise over every mind a special influence. But his gesture must be made at a moment chosen by himself, at the propitious moment wherein it corresponded to a need or to an expansive movement of his own consciousness. More important than anything for this uneasy soul was the safeguarding of his spiritual independence.

[1] Letters of Jacques Rivière to Alain Fournier.

On one occasion, believing that one of his German admirers had come to Paris in order to " tap " him, he had his response ready in advance: " If I were to help you, you would cease to interest me." [1] But when Gide openly refused, he often gave assistance secretly. His delicacy of feeling prompted him to help anonymously or through the medium of a third person. In spite of their manifold deviations, the fidelity of his sentiments was beyond question.

Following such tests, an invitation to visit Gide at one or other of the Normandy properties he had inherited was the consecration of a friendship. One would discover a totally different man, familiar and charming: Gide without his pathetic mask. In contact with the earth, he tended to become his natural self.

He would bicycle to the station to meet the arriving guest. Getting out either at Lisieux or at Criquetot, according to where the visit was to be paid, one would immediately be taken off to explore the neighbourhood. In the spring the countryside was deliciously leafy and moist. Between that of La Roque and that of Cuverville one was aware of the difference separating the two Normandys: Calvados and the Seine-Inférieure, one smiling, the other wind-swept; one all pasture, the other almost entirely cultivated, with farms mysteriously hidden behind screens of beech-trees.

Gide's two properties were just as little alike. La Roque-Baignard, which came to him from his mother, was a Louis

---

[1] *Conversation avec un Allemand.*

XIII château with a moat full of water, a postern gate, a dovecote, an inset tower, where Francis Jammes declared that one morning he had found an owl in his shoe. Cuverville, inherited by his wife, was a house with a severe rectangular façade, pierced by windows at regular intervals. If Gide has described La Roque in *L'Immoraliste*, it was Cuverville that gave him his background for *La Porte étroite*. His friends recognize there the wall with Alissa's secret door. Every part of the garden bears a name: there is the *Allée Noire* and the *Allée aux Fleurs*; in the immediate neighbourhood the *Valleé de la Misère*. . . . Not far from La Roque is another château, overgrown: the château of Isabelle.[1]

In the summer, married friends brought their wives to Cuverville. Each couple had a suite of rooms. Madame Gide showed herself wonderfully kind and considerate. Visitors were so numerous that it was not easy to arrange dates. " Brother, brother-in-law, sister, aunt, cousin, and nephew keep us here . . ." wrote Gide to Ducoté, and, in another letter: " We hope . . . to keep [the Drouins] until we go back to town. The Jean Schlumbergers have been here for a

[1] This is the Château de Formentin. The characters in this work, like those of almost all Gide's novels, are borrowed, in their main outlines, from reality. Monsieur Floche is named Floquet. The famous Bible, annotated by Bossuet, was sold for a ridiculously small sum to an antiquary when the authentic " Isabelle," at the end of her resources and prevented by creditors from cutting down the trees in the park, tried to raise money as best she could. Jean Schlumberger remembers having seen her, in his childhood, waiting like a beggar at the gateway of his father's estate. They gave her twenty francs, in order to be rid of her. Gide invented neither her adventures, nor her invalid son, nor her flight with a coachman.

(The English translation of *Isabelle* is contained in the volume: *Two Symphonies*.)

fortnight. We expect Copeau this evening and Ghéon in four days time. . . ."

Amongst his own people Gide was a simple, lively head of the family. Here it was that one learned to know him. Relatives would come from their own part of the country to seek his advice in the matter of a divorce, or the education of a difficult child, or some religious question. People confessed to him. This uneasy spirit was looked upon as the grand leader, the grand pastor. It grieved him deeply to be unable to help. In these Protestant families, however, every infringement of the rules of conduct became a dramatic problem. But Gide could usually reconcile the apparently irreconcilable. At other times he showed himself a stickler for the strictest honesty and could not bear to see his nephews or his nieces cheat at games.

Yet the children adored him. There were always crowds of them about him at Cuverville, and he delighted in them. He made them play, and played with them at hide-and-seek and blindman's-buff. The young men and girls of the party would often join them. He would go off with the whole troop to fish amongst the rocks and in the ponds and admired those who knew how to catch cuttle-fish and squid, pierce their ink-sacs, and handle them. One would cut off one of their long arms and attach it to a line to catch the rapacious prawns. There was much laughter. Gide would tell stories of fish and plant-life. . . .

Amongst his brother writers he showed the same zestfulness. — You cannot imagine, wrote Jacques Rivière to his mother, " in what a paradise we are living, just now. . . .

Gide [is] enchanting. . . . We are up to larks the whole
day long. Yesterday [he] impersonated a little old gentleman; he played Perè Ubu: . . . ' *Sir . . . we are going
to "slllay you "!* . . .' There are no great minds without
a sense of humour. . . ."

The days were passed in excursions and games. In the
evening, after dinner, Gide would translate *aloud* the poems
of Keats or Whitman, Goethe's *Torquato Tasso*, or the works
of Novalis. When the conversation became general, he liked
to lead it round to some question of morals or of literature.
And while thus spending himself he still found time for
plenty of work and for encouraging his friends in their
own.

In this way, little by little, a group was formed round
about him. It was not a school of æsthetics. There were no
" manifestoes." A certain number of men were drawn together by a shared zeal for art and for truth. Gide gave himself without reserve, sharing the joy of his discoveries.
Common enthusiasms gradually formed the real soul of the
group.

Certain names constantly recurred in the conversations:
Wilde, whose work was at that time severely criticized by
Gide, Whitman, Nietzsche. Between 1895 and 1905 Henri
Albert's translations of Nietzsche, in the *Mercure de France*,
were, each one of them, revelations for the small circle.
Ghéon, refractory at first, then fanatically enthusiastic, was
a gay and cheery Nietzschean. As for Gide, all his puritanism found satisfaction in the magnificent formula for freedom: " to surpass oneself. . . ."

But the great man of the period was, incontestably, Dostoievski. His human and his demonic side were found equally captivating.

It was under the influence of this great novelist that Gide became interested in the analytical novel. For the time being, the French novel was non-existent. The work of Zola and of Huysmans was finished. There remained Boylesve, pleasant, but insignificant. Gide introduced to all his friends the great Russian novelists, also those of England, notably Thomas Hardy and Conrad, and gave them a taste for psychological chiaroscuro; an influence strangely forgotten to-day, and yet the more considerable in that it was opposed to the purely musical lyricism of Symbolism.

*   *   *

If it is to remain vital, a group not only must have common admirations and exclusions, but must also gravitate round a review. The review is born, dies. By means of this experience the group is strengthened. Thus it was that from *L'Ermitage* came forth the *Nouvelle Revue Française*.

In 1896 *L'Ermitage*, a valiant little Symbolist organ, about to die, was bought by a mild, timid, self-effacing young poet: Édouard Ducoté. The moment he was its editor, he wrote to André Gide and thus achieved the review's salvation.

Gide undertook to be a regular contributor [1] and brought along his friends: Jammes, Ghéon, Copeau, Emmanuel Sig-

---

[1] He remained only a short time with the *Revue blanche*, where he had succeeded Léon Blum as literary critic (and whose " commentaries " were, later on, edited by Ghéon).

noret,[1] Claudel, " great and solitary," and, once or twice,
Paul Valéry himself. Very soon Gide became the ruling
spirit of the paper. He would always rather " incite to
activity than himself be active."

Ducoté sent him the manuscripts and he commented on
each one of them: " I'm delighted that you are getting contributions from Léautaud . . ." or: " De Fargue's poems
are rather too reminiscent of Rimbaud. . . . Never mind,
they are sappy. . . ." When he wished to refuse certain
worthless verses, he wrote to Ducoté: " If, as I admit I hope
you will, you have the good taste to find them bad, send them
back. . . ."

Thus it was that under his influence *L'Ermitage* became,
and remained for twelve years, the best poetic review of the
period. But the mark of its origin was still apparent. Ducoté
was too weak and too kindly entirely to get rid of the original contributors. (Hugues Rebell, Adolphe Retté, Stuart
Merrill, etc.). One day it was decided to reduce the number
of the contributors to twelve. But discipline was not maintained. And, besides, some of the twelve proved faithless.
Soon there were but four, then two, and the experiment
broke down.

The aim of these second-rank Symbolists was to keep the
review far above contemporary polemics, to steer clear of
reality and remain within an ivory tower.[2] *L'Ermitage* had

---

1 A young poet, regarded by the group as a sort of prophet, who died
prematurely.

2 The Dreyfus affair went its way and miraculously failed to stir the
feelings of any of the contributors. *L'Ermitage* was almost the only review
to let it pass unnoticed. Gide, on the other hand, took sides in the matter and
signed the Dreyfusard manifestoes.

therefore never more than two hundred subscribers. In 1905 Ducoté, disappointed, wished to give it up. But it survived for another three years.

Its format was now that of the larger reviews. Rémy de Gourmont, from the *Mercure*, joined Gide on the " editorial committee." Regular features were established.[1] But Gide, held by no fixed rubric, followed his fancy, engaging in polemics with Barrès, Maurras, and Montfort, holding dialogues with himself in his *Billets à Angèle* and in *L'Interviewer*, endeavouring, above all, to preserve, through all " *pretexts*," " *an unprejudiced mind*."

In 1908 *L'Ermitage* died once for all. . . . " What was wanting," explained Gide to Ducoté, " was a little more pride, decision, abnegation, and solidarity." These " conditions of a work of art " he was now about to find amongst his friends. The group was in existence and was looking only for an organ wherewith to express itself.

But everyone was afraid of being insufficiently experienced in dealing with printers and booksellers. Having learned that Eugène Montfort, who, so far courageously and alone, had managed and edited *Les Marges*, was wishing to enlarge his paper, Gide's group felt that the two schemes might be combined. *Les Marges*, moreover, had a home, subscribers, and a living.

Montfort agreed, was made editor of the *Nouvelle Revue Française*, and was given a free hand.[2]

[1] Michel Arnauld undertook *literature*, Jacques-Émile Blanche *music* (which he treated with admirable understanding), and Maurice Denis *art* (already defending Cézanne and the new school of Matisse).

[2] Montfort was the one-time editor of the *Revue naturiste*, which in

When the first number appeared, on November 15, 1908, Gide recognized disaster. The leading article, signed by Marcel Boulanger, was entitled "*En regardant chevaucher d'Annunzio* (Watching d'Annunzio Caracoling)." The press review, by Léon Bocquet, was headed "*Contre Mallarmé* (Against Mallarmé)." The revered Master had been given over to a smart, fashionable critic.

Gide's one desire was to break with *Les Marges*. Laborious negotiations were set going: — The whole difference between us — Montfort explained to Schlumberger — is that while *you* take Gide seriously, *we* regard him as a nobody. One side wanted a " tribunal," the other to go straight ahead until the public came to the review. Then Montfort started *Les Marges* once more and kept it going with the help of collaborators until recent years. Gide bravely began all over again. In February 1909 he issued a second first number of the *Nouvelle Revue Française*.

This time only three names appeared on the managing committee: Jacques Copeau, Jean Schlumberger, and André Ruyters. But to these must be added, in order to complete the list of those who formed the real nucleus of the venture: Ghéon and Michel Arnauld. Gide, of course, evaded any official title.

The review was installed in Schlumberger's flat (which he still occupies), in the rue d'Assas, near the Luxembourg. It had no financial backing beyond the funds supplied by Gide and Schlumberger. The latter gummed envelopes and

---

1895 attempted a reaction against the Symbolist movement by a return to life and spontaneity.

made parcels, giving up all his time. It was the heroic time of beginnings.

Meetings were often held in the quarters of the painter van Rysselberghe, known as Théo. Gide would always sit a little apart in a corner of the room. But it was he who was the real leader, the animating spirit, giving an example of unparalleled literary fervour. The collaborators read their contributions to each other. And with what extreme carefulness and severity did they correct each other! In these circumstances everyone was modest almost to the point of humility. When the epithets in a text were too numerous, they were suppressed. There were long discussions over a single word, over its critical bearing. Art took precedence of friendship. There were no concessions.[1] At the request of his friends, Schlumberger agreed to rewrite an entire article. When Pierre de Lanux took the post of secretary at the rue d'Assas, he felt proud to belong to a review that could thus blackball the contributions of an editor. Such possibilities certainly existed nowhere else. Gide, fearing above all things a mutual burning of incense, the standing danger of group-life, had even forbidden notices of his own works and those of his friends. This discipline was maintained right up to the War.

Thus did the *Nouvelle Revue Française* endeavour to be a genuine movement of reform amidst the commercialized, deliquescent literature of the day. The main idea was to

[1] When, in 1911, Ducoté expressed his surprise in finding his name omitted from the prospectus, Gide replied: "Well, no. . . . The omission was not involuntary. . . . I make neither excuse nor protest, but it pains me to think that you could doubt the faithfulness of my affection. . . ."

oppose sophistication in literary affairs, to fight against
" the decadence of administration in this century," [1] and to
fight for the recognition of *artistic morality*.[2] There was to
be no new dogma, but a return to a true classicism, to the
desire for an inward perfection, but for one that should
permit every kind of audacity. These traditionalists therefore defended " barbarians " such as Claudel, Péguy, or
Suarès. They set out, in fact, to make a critical revision of
values.

After the appearance of the special number devoted, upon
his death, to Charles-Louis Philippe, the review began to
make itself felt amongst the élite. About this time Octave
Mirbeau, in the course of an interview, suddenly began sing-
ing the praises of *L'Immoraliste*. *La Porte étroite* was arousing notice, and its publisher, Valette, was greatly astonished
to find a book by Gide actually selling. Why, henceforth,
should not the review publish the works of its contributors?
In 1911 it attached itself to a publishing house. Gaston
Gallimard put money into it and managed it in the spirit of
the group, whose value he fully understood.

After the publication of the first books (notably Gide's
Isabelle, Claudel's *L'Otage*, and Larbaud's *Barnabooth*)
manuscripts began pouring in. One day Gide called on
Pierre de Lanux, the secretary. He wished to see the rejected
manuscripts; felt curious about them.

---

[1] Montesquieu.
[2] On the death of Catulle Mendès, Gide wrote a celebrated article
against the platitudinous praises of the great press, of the Brissons and the
Clareties who declared Mendès to be the greatest poet of the day. To-day
Mendès has fallen into the " mortal silence " predicted by Gide.

He was attracted by one signed Jean-Richard Bloch.

Carrying off the manuscript, he read it sitting on the outside of goodness knows what horse-tram, got off after reading a few pages, telegraphed his congratulations to Bloch, ending with the word: " Come! " Jean-Richard Bloch came to Paris. He was a young professor, an admirer of Romain Rolland and of humanistic naturalism. Never mind. Already one was aware of the ebullience of ideas and images which were to enrich his work. His first book (*Lévy*), refused by the *Mercure*, appeared in the *N. R. F.* editions.

Soon afterwards Gallimard sent to Cuverville *Jean Barois* by Roger Martin du Gard.

— Perhaps not an artist, but certainly a tremendous fellow, was Gide's response.

This tremendous fellow, an atheist, a hearty materialist, and the future author of that powerful novel *Les Thibault*, soon became one of Gide's best friends.

In this way, always on the look-out, he collected successively: Jules Romains and the " Unanimists," Alain Fournier, the author of *Le Grand Meaulne*, Jean Giraudoux, and Henri Frank, the author of the poem *La Danse devant l'Arche*. . . . The newcomer to the group was introduced to the older members, who at first were perhaps a little inclined to condemn him without a trial. But soon he was found worthy and was, so to speak, " anointed with holy oil." He then shared with Thibaudet, Jaloux, Bertaux, and all those who were in at the beginning the editing of the critical notes — a supreme honour.[1]

[1] The early works of the literary Cubists (Appollinaire and Salmon), not elsewhere taken seriously, were welcomed with sympathy by the critics of the review.

The prestige of the group had become extraordinary. One knows with what repeated and tenacious efforts Proust tried to reach this apparently inaccessible summit. How fascinating for the beginner was the sober white dress of the *N. R. F.* publications, with its red lines! For him, the authors, not yet very numerous, who figured in the little catalogue at the end of the books were privileged beings of a superior and purer race than that to which belonged the representatives of official literature.

In 1913 Jacques Copeau tried to bring the theatre into the same movement of reform. He wanted to fight the dangerous realism of Antoine, the versified dramas of Richepin, the " sophisticated productions " of Kistemaeckers, and the " reckless industrialization " of the stage.

The Vieux-Colombier was, indeed, an honest playhouse.[1] In scarcely a year and a half (1913–14) Copeau, too, had had time to make several discoveries. At the Théâtre des Arts he noticed Dullin, then apparently condemned to play nothing but villains for the rest of his life. On another occasion he engaged a tall, lank, timid young man, the son of a chemist, who had called on him to ask for a part. It was Jouvet. One may say, in fact, that the vital theatre of to-day originated more or less directly in the *N. R. F.* group.

In 1914 this party seemed to be winning along all fronts. The review had three thousand regular subscribers. Under the direction of Rivière, Copeau's successor, it expanded more fully and became better known to the general public.

---

[1] Copeau, who tried to make the actor something less of a " barnstormer " by creating a school of actors in training from their early years, was the first, in France, to simplify backgrounds and ended his 1914 season with the triumph of *La Nuit des Rois.*

Gide's interest became less direct. Always when a goal was attained, his first aim was to remove himself, for success can dull the mind.

Thus did he take another step forward. The artist in him had found his pathway. . . .

*　　　　*　　　　*

But while his group, enlarged by the arrival of fresh collaborators, was gradually making itself felt, certain of his oldest friends left it to become Catholics. A strange phenomenon: while Gide himself was evolving in the direction of becoming more and more anti-religious, they were returning to tradition and to God.

Gide, it is true, had tried to awaken consciences rather than to impose his own opinions: — When you have read my book — he said to each one, " throw it away " and " forget me." Moreover, it is the lot of every true master to be denied, but to live again in his disciples. Gide's friends, however, were scarcely themselves converted before they began to try to draw him along with them, to circumvent and to convince him in his turn.

This new conflict round about Gide had begun, in 1905, with the conversion of Francis Jammes. On July 5 of that year Jammes, feeling " youth and its follies on the decline," [1] entered the bosom of the Church. His poetry at once became pious and he tried to induce his friends to make the same renunciation. In writing to Gide on the subject, as he continued repeatedly to do, he says:

— Drop your miserable Nietzscheanism. . . . France

[1] *Mémoires*, by Francis Jammes.

has need of you . . . you must be converted. Look at my last poem; my poetic talent has not grown less; on the contrary. . . .[1]

But Jammes's arguments were not, so far, very alarming. There was, however, a man who had over the whole group an influence opposed to that of Gide. This was Claudel. Big, heavy, short, and square and all of a piece, with a brow that made one think of a bull, Claudel, who was a fanatical Catholic, spoke in simple affirmations and negations that were like the blows of a fist.

" This great ass of a Goethe," he would say . . . this " miserable Gourmont." . . .

His prestige as a writer attracted a number of those who felt themselves moving in the direction of religion. With a brutal shove he flung them into the abyss of God. In the course of his life he had converted numbers of writers. It was he who had carried off Jammes and who now wanted to get Rivière out of Gide's hands. Like the God and Satan of popular imagery, Claudel and Gide seemed to be fighting for a soul: for the soul of the timorous little professor Rivière was at this time. He comes, first of all, under the influence of the great poet, to whom he writes, towards 1907:

— I have doubts, I have doubts. Reassure me.

— Go " to Mass *every day*," answered Claudel. — You

---

[1] Proof, Jammes's poem, addressed to Claudel:
Je recommande à tes prières ces amis,
Gide qui toujours flotte et revient d'Italie;
Fontaine dont le cœur dit: oui, la tête: non;
Le fier Suarès, qui cherche Dieu; Edmond Pilon . . . etc. . . .

must pass through the furnace of the confessional. The rest will follow. The mind will grow stupid and accustomed to obedience.[1]

Rivière raised objections. But Claudel was content to insist with a superhuman tranquillity: " There is only one God. . . ." And the vastness of this certainty overwhelmed his correspondent: Claudel knew how to intimidate and how to appeal to the feelings of this anxious spirit. " My child," he writes, addressing him like a father. But Rivière felt: " I am nothing to you," [2] though he did not dare to express this sentiment in writing to Claudel.

But in 1910, in face of the adjurations of Claudel, the " poor fellow " gave up his professorship and joined the *Nouvelle Revue Française* as secretary. Under the influence of Gide he came to regard faith as a repose for the lazy-minded. " I cannot find God other than everywhere," [3] he reflected. Nothing brought him more exaltation than the words of *L'Immoraliste*: " The pleasure I take in each action is a sign that I ought to do it." But he added: " It takes more courage to conquer oneself . . . than to allow oneself to be conquered by a discipline. . . ."

Meanwhile Claudel was ageing. When Rivière's wife was pregnant, he wrote: " In my family, women in this condition ask for a consecrated ribbon in an old convent up in the mountains . . . and none of them has ever had a mishap." The ribbon, however, did not prove very efficacious, for, although the obedient Rivière obtained it, his wife fell

[1] *Correspondance Rivière — Claudel*, p. 52.
[2] *Correspondance Rivière — Alain Fournier.*
[3] *Les Nourritures terrestres.*

" very ill " and her little daughter nearly " died." [1] Whereupon Claudel, seeking for his spiritual son other indications
of Providence, points out to him the divine grace successively converting, between 1911 and 1914, Jacques Maritain, a former Protestant, Péguy, an anti-clerical, and
Psichari, grandson of the " ignoble Renan." Rivière, struck
by the fertility of these miracles, began, a little before the
war, to say his prayers and put himself in the way of finding
God (" *A la trace de Dieu . . .*").

A little later Claudel even wrested from Gide and re-
placed in Catholicism certain of the great writers of the past
whom the group admired. Rimbaud was posthumously converted in the following manner. Assisted by the brother and
the sister of the poet (Isabelle and Paterne Berrichon), as
well as by Rivière, he contrived a sort of pious conspiracy
against Rimbaud's memory. Mutilated letters were published, and biographies ending with a supposed death-bed
repentance. Yet the whole life of this rebellious poet protests.[2] But with Rimbaud a Catholic, did not the whole of
modern poetry immediately become religious and edifying
for young people?

Here again Gide entered the arena to fight against systematic misrepresentation. When Claudel wanted to spirit
away a letter from Rimbaud to Verlaine, containing blas-
phemies, all his sense of honour rebelled. " Arthur Rimbaud

---

[1] Nevertheless Rivière remained " infinitely grateful to God " for it. In
religion, whichever way things go, they are a confirmation of the divine
presence and even of the divine goodness.

[2] Did not Rimbaud write: " *Je ne me crois pas embarqué pour une noce,
avec Jésus-Christ pour beau-père*"?

is *my friend*," he declared, and if I love him otherwise than you do, I love him " in the way he prefers to be loved [by me]." [1]

At last, in 1914, Gide himself is taken to task by Claudel. *Les Caves du Vatican* (English translation, *Lafcadio's Adventures*, formerly called *The Vatican Swindle*) has just appeared. In this joyous *sotie* [2] Gide confronts the social and religious hypocrisy of contemporary bourgeois society with the easy garments and the equally easy conscience of the wonderful adolescent Lafcadio. When this book was reviewed (in the *N. R. F.*), Claudel was greatly perturbed and asked Gide, or, rather, implored him, to suppress the superscription of the third part: " *But of which king do you speak, and of which pope? For there are two, and no one knows which is the right one.*" This passage, quoted from *L'Annonce faite à Marie*, was not reproduced in the volume. But that was not all. Claudel incriminated another " abominable " passage, on page 222 (English translation, *Lafcadio's Adventures*, page 208), where Lafcadio imagines the Curé of Cavigliajo capable of " corrupting " the lad who is under his care.

— Unhappy Gide! cried Claudel.

On the strength of this scandalous text, he thought the favourable moment had arrived for taking up an offensive, for castigating the soul of his friend after the manner of a furious prophet and thus bringing him back to God.

[1] Unpublished correspondence with Paterne Berrichon.

[2] *Sotie:* a variety of satiric drama, usually political, in vogue in France during the fourteenth and fifteenth centuries. (Translator's note.)

After the appearance of *L'Immoraliste* Gide had no more sins to commit. Already certain suspicious rumours were afloat: " Gide, in the name of our friendship, for the sake of your own personal interests, and in the name of those who surround you, I beg you to tell me who is . . . if you are he whom . . . this wretched creature who . . ." Claudel called upon Gide to reply and, if it were not too late, to save himself!

Claudel's great blow had struck home. It reopened exactly those scars of Gide's uneasiness which were incompletely healed. The nobility of the letter, the reprimanding voice rising, expanding, as if coming from the beyond, moved him profoundly.

" Yes," he replied, " it is true." But will Claudel understand this avowal? Will he not be so beside himself with anger as to break with me for good? Of this there could be no doubt. But had not Gide promised to unveil, bit by bit, and to this very Claudel, the depths of his conscience?

Claudel, duly indignant, became authoritative and threatening: " There is one thing infinitely more odious than hypocrisy, and that is cynicism." If Gide had not confessed, he would have been a hardened sinner, but since he did confess, he is a cynic. Presupposed guilty, he must be in the wrong.

But Claudel also knew how to melt, and spoke with emotion of the " two beautiful and noble letters " he had just received from Gide, and added:

" At least promise me that this passage " (from the

Caves) " shall not appear in the book . . . *little by little, one will forget.*"

Then: — For my part, I will keep your secret. I return your letters herewith. I have spoken of them only to Jammes. I have also written to Father F——, under the seal of the confessional, telling him about you. Here is his address. You can go and see him.

And now confess yourself and remember that a sin followed by repentance, and consciousness of its sinfulness, is greatly diminished in gravity. Gide, if you tell everything to Père F——, you can be completely forgiven, and *it will all be as if it had never existed.*

But this time Gide rebelled:

" I can change nothing in what I have written. It would be an act of cowardice on my part. And I do not understand how you can say: *Little by little, one will forget.*"

He found such hypocrisy revolting. What seemed to him really abominable was the lie not only tolerated by the Church, but sometimes even favoured, in the interest of maintaining her prestige. He therefore never went to the confessor.

At the very moment when Claudel might have believed that he had been right in holding out, Gide has escaped! No doubt he had exhausted all the attractiveness of the subject. What had chiefly interested him was the union, in Claudel, of the man of faith and the great artist. For amongst the Protestants, given over to abstract examinations of conscience, there are no such combinations. Can it be that Catholicism favours the development of the playwright and the novelist? If Gide corresponded with Claudel for so long, was it not principally on account of his artistic curiosity?

But the collisions between himself and his friends are now to increase. July 1914! The divine punishment of war has fallen on mankind. The hand of God wreaks vengeance on the unbelievers. For the believers it is the moment to take action. And they will not let it pass by.

From the very outset the contributors to the *N. R. F.* were dispersed. Ghéon and Schlumberger joined up. " As for me," wrote Gide to a friend while waiting for his summons (which never came), " I am giving my whole heart and all my time to the refugees." His country being threatened, he would have been " ashamed " not to give his services. Gide's sense of fitness was very highly developed.

For about eighteen months he worked regularly at a Franco-Belgian centre, devoting himself to the wretched derelicts cast up there. In the atmosphere of unanimous sacrifice his virtue was redoubled.

There came upon him at this time a kind of mystical crisis. In *Num Quid et tu* he engages in a dialogue with Jesus. It was the last great return of religious fervour. But even now his interpretation of the sacred texts was that of an " anarchist " and he hated dogmatic devotees, whether Protestant or Catholic, more than ever.

Meanwhile, as a result of the shock of war, conversions were multiplying all about him. Jacques Rivière, alone in a German prison-camp, made the act of faith. And then, rather suddenly, the earliest and most faithful of the group, the headlong, joyous Ghéon, in his turn entered the Church.

His conversion took place at the front, and, ironically enough, through the medium of another of Gide's friends: Lieutenant Dupouey. This young officer, whom he had met only once or twice, had just been killed. Ghéon, curiously overwhelmed, learned from the almoner that he had died, on Easter Day, in a state of extraordinary religious exaltation, having communicated that same morning; and he had therefore, according to the almoner, celebrated the day of resurrection in heaven. Dupouey's wife, a fervent Catholic, to whom Ghéon had written, told him substantially: — You will find it difficult to believe me, you will not believe me; but since my husband's death I am transported: I know that he is with God, that he sees God. And Ghéon, feeling his life in danger every day, began to believe these words. . . .

Meanwhile he kept Gide informed as to the progress of his religious faith, and Gide encouraged him. When he was definitely converted, Gide wrote: " I embrace you, *you* who have gone ahead of me."

But he soon realized, once again, that between him and the orthodox there was an abyss. Having been fervently sceptical, Ghéon was now religious with equal fervour. At the time of Gide's correspondence with Claudel, an indignant Ghéon rapped out at him: — Look here! Surely you are not going to be converted! And each time Gide returned to the subject he replied: — All that doesn't in the least interest me!

But now he was driven by a terrible proselytism. At all

costs he wanted to drag down *L'Immoraliste*.

In his letters to Gide he recalled their period of shameful dissipation and implored his friend to renounce his unworthy past. Like Claudel, he tried to touch him upon the most sensitive spot: his secret, hidden conscience. The priest always wants to interfere with a man's life. Is it not Tiresias, Gide reflected, who reveals to Œdipus and to those about him that his happiness is rooted in a lie, in incest, in crime? [1] Gide felt that an attempt was being made upon his private dwelling. He felt that he was being attacked, not because he believed himself guilty, but because he wore a mask. Undoubtedly this was the most poignant drama of his life, a sort of final test.

And now there came upon him, imperious and ineluctable, the necessity for open explanation.

Already, before the war, he had written *Corydon*, a study in sexuality, but of this work there had been only a limited edition, twelve copies privately printed for a few intimate friends. He now felt more than ever certain that this book was destined for publication. Already he imagined the attacks and the sarcastic comments it would call forth from society. Legal measures he anticipated without dismay. For he knew that this careful work was based on observation and common sense.

But *Corydon* was merely an impersonal study. It is his personal memoirs that now, in solitary retirement at home, he begins to put together. He comes forward in person and

[1] No doubt it is this moment in his life that was to supply him, later on, with the idea of his play, *Œdipe*.

speaks. It is the story of his own life that he tells in *Si le Grain ne meurt.* — You can put down everything — Proust had told him — but never say " I." No matter! He will courageously " follow his bent." In his struggle against the priest, against everyone, truth seemed to him to be his best weapon, and the story of his life the most brilliant justification of his conduct.

Thenceforward he is at the top of the hill. Immeasurable joy flows through him. Although these two books are not to be given to the public until much later on (there was no question of publishing them during the War), they bring him, nevertheless, a sort of liberation; he has definitely emerged from the enclosure of religion and its traditional morality. — Leave thy house and thy dogmas, thy goods and thy ties, says *l'Enfant Prodigue* to the younger brother. " Go . . . be strong. . . . Forget us; may you return no more. . . ." Gide will not return.

*　　　　*　　　　*

When the new German offensive broke out in 1918, Gide decided to rejoin his wife, who was determined in no circumstances to leave Cuverville. In spite of the danger of invasion he had no hesitation in going and even said a moving and pathetic farewell to some of his friends. For a time there was no news of him. His friends were anxious. Then one day they learned he was at Cambridge, bathing in the river and perfecting his knowledge of English.

The war was over. And a kind of second youth was about to begin for him.

4

SERENITY

AT the age of fifty Gide has returned to the very depths of his own being. He has recovered the audacities he had suppressed during his youth. " The indwelling monster is vanquished! " he cries.

When visited by a new-comer, he always asks:

— Are you uneasy? And immediately adds:

— Because, personally, I am no longer so. I have left off fighting my demon. I no longer resist my desires.

Is desire an evil? He does not know. But he is no longer troubled. Pleasure or asceticism, heaven or hell; these contests no longer exist for him:

— I let these contradictions live within me — he says.

— . . . I have left off analysing. . . . This is my way, a good way, a true way. . . .

*   *   *

His brow has cleared. For some long time he has ceased to wear his long moustache, and his uncovered face seems no longer to have anything to hide. If now and again he allows the ravages of the past to appear, a momentary mask, as soon as his features are in repose he regains his tranquil assurance. His shoulders have broadened. His voice is full of gaiety, sweetness, and seduction.

The truth is that this man who was once so timid has learned how to outwit his timidity. True, he still greets one with a constricted smile and sometimes takes leave abruptly, without venturing to give his hand, just raising it to the level of his head in a sort of salute. But if he freezes, he can also burn. One feels that the puritan ancestors still abiding within him and compelling him, in spite of himself, to these awkward gestures have fundamentally nothing in common with the man as he is to-day. A new being has come to birth in him, simple, joyous, and free and, as if emerged from a dangerous crisis, daily fuller of life.

His heart is now so light that he begins to sing fresh *Nourritures terrestres:* " Whither my desire reaches, there shall I go! " Never has his taste for adventure been so lively. He regrets nothing but lost time: " Ah, I have lived too prudently up till now! " he says.

An insatiable curiosity drives him onwards. People and things, an unexpected meeting, everything, attracts and enchants him. It is the post-war period. Jazz is beginning in towns. He goes to the circus, the music-hall, the cinema; sees the first Chaplin films; makes the acquaintance of the young painters, the actors, the new writers of this hopeful period; is called the " uncle " of the " Dadaists," who recognize themselves in his Lafcadio.

*   *   *

For some time he goes about amongst these extraordinarily violent young people, whom he finds prodigiously interesting. No doubt the relationship was not always serene,[1] and Gide retained, from earlier days, a sort of fear of the world he was entering and of his new friends. Nevertheless, curiosity won the day.

He was asked to contribute to *Littérature*, which was not yet the " littératuricide " review of the group. " We can't produce the review without you," declared these unexpected disciples. He accepted, joyously seeing " gratuitous action " increase in his work and please these " modern " poets.

— Which of my books do you like best? he asked them.

— *Les Caves du Vatican.*

— I am delighted! That is the one I like best myself!

When the Dada manifestoes began to appear, he watched them all assiduously, with a rather conspiratorial smile: the " judgment of Barrès," the launching of the " Twenty-three Manifestoes " (" No more painters, no more writers . . . no more anything, anything . . ."), and was amused, above all, by the first stupefaction of the public. At the Salle des Indépendants, where these young anarchists of art, intimidated by the boards, recited magnificent excesses with their arms glued to their sides, he cried: — Use gestures! and the saying became proverbial.

A little later, however, in 1919, when he published *La Symphonie pastorale*,[2] a short narrative wherein he worked

1 For the group gave itself up to curious exaggerations. Tzara, their leading publicity chief, organized the Dada advertising campaign; Aragon, in a cap and red belt, flung invectives at the powers that be; Breton, with exquisite politeness, announced the end of the immense farce known as " art."

2 The English translation, *The Pastoral Symphony*, is contained in the volume: *Two Symphonies.*

off his old religious preoccupations, the disappointed Dadaists protested. Soon after that he broke with the group.[1] He had decided to make no concessions to these young people, much as he liked them. — My problem, he told Jacques Rivière, has always been to try to last rather than to try to please.

In this expansion of his spirit the desires of his youth were realized one by one along unforeseen paths. When he was twenty-five, he already dreamed of a favourite disciple. Was it not to him that he dedicated the first *Nourritures terrestres*? To " you, my Nathanaël, whom I have not yet met, I give this name, not knowing your own which is to come."

Henceforward he will not need to seek imaginary names. . . .

A few years later he left for the Congo with Marc Allégret, a young companion who drew him thither. Was it not an early dream come true? " Caravans," he had cried thirty years before in Algeria, " why may I not go off with you, caravans! " And now he was going to find them, in the south of the desert, which was their stopping-place.

Before leaving France, and as if to get rid of a burden, he sold part of his library, notably the books of old friends

[1] Undoubtedly Gide, as usual, began by establishing affectation. " You do not like the first part of *La Symphonie pastorale*," he wrote to Aragon. " Are you likely to care for the second? Indeed, I hope not." The breach came about as a result of a conversation between Gide and André Breton, reproduced by the latter, *word for word*, first in *Littérature* and then in his book: *Les Pas perdus*.

who had betrayed their proper destiny. " Let us burn useless books. . . ."

Claudel wished to see him again: in thinking of the dangers of the expedition he had felt, he said, a sad presenti-
ment — that Gide would die. Though perhaps impressed,
Gide does not allow this prophecy to hold him back, but the
farewell between the friends was none the less pathetic.
Claudel regarded it as a final parting. It was therefore the
more embarrassing for both to find themselves together
again, the next day, in Madame Mühlfeld's salon.

In the course of a single year Gide, with an equipage of
a hundred bearers, whom Marc superintended, explored the
forest of French Equatorial Africa from one end to the
other. What a joyous undertaking it was, and what a triumph! In spite of his age, his health was proof against the
severest tests. He cheerfully walked twenty-five miles a day.
All about him was the formlessness of the wild, the fighting
of monkeys, and, from time to time, fever and tornadoes.
In his travel diary [1] are to be found notes on the local flora
and fauna, on the different varieties of cicindela (tiger-
beetles) and the habits of the mason-fly and the termite.
Like Goethe, towards the end of his life, he had become a
servitor of reason; little by little the poet within him is
joined by the man of science.

It was in the course of this same journey that he came
upon the horrible exploitations practised by the white colo-

[1] *Voyage au Congo* and *Le Retour du Tchad* (English translation of
both in *Travels in the Congo*).

nists, and caused an inquiry to be held on this subject.[1]
— Ah — he thought — amongst miserable humanity how
difficult it is to be a man!

Meanwhile, during his absence, he had published *Les
Faux-Monnayeurs* (English translation, *The Counterfeiters*), for, unlike most authors, he had no desire to supervise
its launching in person. Yet it was his most important work,
a narrative of five hundred pages and with thirty-five characters. At last, under the influence of Dostoievski, he had
produced his " first novel," as he called it himself; and it is
his masterpiece.

It had given him untold labour. The successive points of
view that he had held during the course of his life and that
hitherto he had worked out to their conclusions singly, each
in a separate book, he here brings together in a single work.
He had given the whole of himself in this novel, which is,
as it were, the blossoming of his maturity,[2] and he is now in
sight of equilibrium.

Yet when this book appeared, it was received with a
freezing indifference, if not with hostility, while his earlier
works were attacked on all sides.

*   *   *

Before attaining serenity, Gide was to fight yet one more
terrible literary battle. Implacable enemies had resolved to
destroy him. But it was exactly in the course of this last

---

[1] See Part IV, Chapter iv, on " Work and Colonization."

[2] Gide had declared that he meant " to put everything into this novel."
He had made the same declaration when he was twenty years old, in regard
to *Les Cahiers d'André Walter*, but the " everything " had greatly changed.

struggle that he succeeded in gaining acceptance for his work.

Though still unknown to the crowd, he had nevertheless a high moral standing amongst the élite. The *N. R. F.* particularly had become a power in the world of letters and excited the envy of very many writers who were not connected with it.

It had reappeared in 1919 and was immediately a prodigious success. Valéry, whose glory Gide had predicted, made a triumphant entry into literature. Marcel Proust, whom he had at first misunderstood and then sought out, won the Prix Goncourt in 1920, and immediately his name, so far totally unknown, became famous. Jean Giraudoux, with the startling images of his *Nuit à Châteauroux,* enchanted a whole group of " the elect," while Paul Morand, first with *Tendres Stocks* and then with his brilliant *Ouvert la Nuit,* made fashionable a new modern style. Gide and his friends had indeed made a sort of " trust " of the best writers of the time.

It was at this time that a group of those who were excluded began to feel that they were being directly interfered with. Amongst them was Henri Béraud. He could not understand why the works either of Gide or Proust or Valéry, all of which bored him to death, should sell so readily, particularly abroad. He believed therefore that Jean Giraudoux, director of propaganda at the Ministry of Foreign Affairs and a friend of the *N. R. F.,* must be favouring this house at the expense of others.

Taking his stand upon this commercial territory, he be-

gan in 1923, in *L'Éclair*, a veritable crusade against the
" long faces " [1] of the Gidean Huguenots, setting up against
their " tedious " literature work such as his own — that is
to say, " the roaring fun of the tipplers of Beaujolais " and
the " droll stories " of " the enliveners of estaminets."
Whereupon the press, suddenly liberated, let itself go.
" Go it, big 'un! Keep it up! Keep it up! " shouted a provin-
cial journalist.[2] " *Hoch Literatur!* " cried M. Camille
Mauclair, in speaking of the *N. R. F.*[3]

Giraudoux, meanwhile, did not find it very difficult to
exculpate himself. This he did quite simply in the *Nouvelles
Littéraires*. But Gide remained silent, and Béraud grew
furious. The longer the one remained silent, the more fran-
tic did the other become.[4] Finally, having noticed that these
polemics had given him an unexpected importance, Gide
sent his adversary, ironically, and as if by way of thanks, a
box of chocolates, with these few words: " No, I am not un-
grateful, my ' familiars ' have misrepresented me." His
Souvenirs de la Cour d'Assises being due to reappear at
this time, he had even dedicated this new edition to Béraud,
but at the last moment the dedication was withdrawn.[5]

For matters had taken a fresh turn. Béraud, beside him-

[1] Cf. " *La Croisade des longues Figures,*" by Henri Béraud.

[2] M. Édouard Dulac, editor of the *Pau-Pyrénées*.

[3] We may mention the protests against this " absurd malevolence " made
by Paul Souday, Léon Daudet, and Fernand Vandérem.

[4] Moreover, Gide had some fun out of it. For example, the editor of a
small review (*L'Œuf dur*) having sent him the proof of an article by
Béraud, entitled: " Nature has a horror of Gide," he returned it simply
marked: " Ready for press."

[5] In the first edition of the book one can see that the fly-leaf, which held
this dedication, has been cut away.

self, was using bad language. There was even some talk of
a duel. But what really mattered was that in the long run
his attacks, together with those of the press, had really affected the group: — Throw enough mud, and some of it
will stick. Copeau thought he detected disaffection in the
audiences at the Vieux-Colombier. Valéry noticed that bib-
liophiles no longer fought for his *éditions de luxe*. Was the
N. R. F. to rank in the eyes of the great public as an
" incense-burner " or a " mutual admiration society "?
Béraud, in fact, credited his enemies with his own motives.
For him the world was divided into two hemispheres: on
one side, friendly critics who give praise; on the other, adversaries — that is to say, those who withhold their admiration.

At this moment, when the *N. R. F.* seemed to be stricken,
another offensive was launched from an entirely different
quarter, this time nationalist and Catholic. It was led by
Henri Massis, a young neo-Thomist who, in the *Revue universelle* and in his *Jugements*, made furious personal attacks upon the enemies of his doctrine. These attacks
lacked, perhaps, the prophetic accents of a Claudel, but
they were supported by trenchant reasoning and numerous
dangerous quotations.

In 1921, and again in 1924, did Massis fling himself
upon Gide. Claiming to unmask him, he maintained that his
methods of seduction, his success, and his value were all
due to the subtleties, the escapes, the trickery and lies of
impotence. Moreover, this deceitful being, by means of a

fallacious method of criticism, turned sacred dogma and
the holy principle of responsibility and the intangible unity
of man to the service of his own appetites. But, above all,
Massis incriminated Gide's redoubtable influence, his per-
fidious and corrupting effect on the young.

Rouveyre and Béraud, moreover, had also cunningly insinuated corruption of " those who fell into his clutches."
And now there appeared a pamphlet entitled: *Un Mal-
faiteur* (*An Evil-doer*), wherein a self-styled father of a
family accused him of causing the death of his child, who
had taken his life after reading *Les Nourritures terrestres*.
This leaflet, with a preface " from beyond the tomb " by
Archbishop Christophe de Beaumont, can scarcely be taken
seriously. Has not the moral reformer in every age been
suspected of imaginary crimes?

Nevertheless Gide was moved to indignation in seeing
himself thus disfigured and his honesty called in question.
Would it not be the best method of giving a true picture of
himself and answering all his enemies if he were to set forth
at last the facts of his life? It seemed to him that the moment had arrived for the publication of the memoirs he had
written during the war. Yes, the printing of thousands of
copies of *Si le Grain ne meurt* had now become a matter of
urgency.[1]

Hitherto he had drawn back because he knew that this

---

[1] Like *Corydon*, this work had appeared almost secretly, not more than
ten or twenty copies being printed. These clandestine publications had made
Paul Souday inquire impatiently: — Is M. Gide going to publish or is
he not?

book was going to shock the most tenacious prejudices of
public opinion: its sexual prejudices. And indeed it contained, *set down in the first person*, confessions and statements that were only too sincere and seemed the more
unavowable because no one had ever dared to make ac-
knowledgments of such a kind.

But although in general Gide is wary of actively committing himself, he was perfectly aware in this case of the
consequences of what he proposed. He was ready to risk
losing honours, privileges and the advantages of social life;
he preferred to be " dishonoured " rather than to be hon-
oured for being that which he was not. He hesitated, moreover, all the less in doing his duty in that truth is contagious
and would liberate others besides himself.

In vain did his friends bring pressure to bear on him,
imploring him to postpone publication at least until after
his death. But Gide, knowing how relatives " arrange "
posthumous publications, stood firm.

In the basements of the *N. R. F.*, packed in cases, the
copies of *Si le Grain ne meurt* lie waiting for him to give
the order for their distribution. Time passes. . . . Will he
draw back at the last moment? Far from it. He has made
up his mind to publish, in addition to this book, a large
edition of *Corydon*, his study of the sexual instinct, and
almost one after the other, in 1924 and 1926, these two
books appeared publicly.

Collective reactions are even more unpredictable than individual reactions. *Corydon* and *Si le Grain ne meurt*

caused, properly speaking, no stir at all. Press notices were few, the more so because copies of this book had been sent to no one. For Gide this result was more serious than a scandal. He felt himself excluded from society.

His best defenders, in intellectual circles, deserted him. Certain friendly critics believed him to be the victim of obsessions; others silently disapproved of him. " The measure is full! " cried Paul Souday in the *Temps*. For Rouveyre it meant " an infection in the world of letters." Charles du Bos denounced Gide's " generalized inversion," and Gabriel Marcel " the frightful spectacle " he offered.

Amongst the Catholics it was felt that he had burned his bridges and need no longer be considered. All means must be employed to overthrow his ideas, prevent them from doing harm, and keep the damage within bounds.

For Massis he had become a real " demoniac." The supreme scandal was that in the midst of the degradation to which he had fallen as a result of the avowal of his horrible secret, and in spite of his refusal to believe in a future life, he should pretend to know happiness! A *happy infidel* — what a diabolical imposture!

Meanwhile, other members of his group had deserted him.

Ever since the war, in fact, conversions had gone on occurring all about him. Following Jammes and Ghéon and Dupouey, Copeau, disheartened by his difficulties at the Vieux-Colombier, had suddenly closed his theatre, thrown up everything, and taken refuge in God. Paul-Albert Laurens, the companion of his first tour in Algeria, had followed in his turn, then his friend Charles du Bos, and then a young Jew, Réné Schwob. The wave of religion carried off contributors to the *N. R. F.*: Jean Cocteau, to whom Maritain opened his arms, the poets Reverdy and Max Jacob, and Gabriel Marcel, the metaphysician. And finally Jacques Rivière, who on his return from Germany had at first gone under to a new profane influence, that of Proust, died in 1925, "miraculously saved," according to Madame Rivière.

By this new phalanx of proselytes Gide was assailed more vigorously than ever. Each one of them took him in hand.

"Whether I believe or do not believe, what is that to you?" he answered.

There was now no hesitation in his resistance of this unique battle-front of devotees. He "stood his ground within his own conscience." [1] But they came for him again and again.

— Leave me alone, he cried, for he felt it impossible, without growing angry, to speak any further of the gross "falsehoods" of the religions, and the "hideous egoism" of families.

* * *

But though in this way he surmounted all attacks, it seemed to those nearest to him that he was beaten. In the end they had come really to fear his influence. They believed his advice to be bad and suspected his intentions.

[1] Luther.

They no longer asked him to intervene as heretofore, and this for him was the most painful of all.

— The approbation of a single *honest man,* they told him, is all . . . that matters, and your book will not obtain it.

— Alas, answered Gide, anyone who approves my book ceases to seem honest in your eyes.

— No, no; it is not my doctrine that is at fault. . . . You incriminate my ethic; I blame my inconsequence. Where I was wrong was in believing that perhaps you might be right. . . .

— Henceforward, he resumed, that which is not is that which could not be. He was obliged to " consent to take his chances alone."

And yet he added sadly: — A man abandons himself when he has nothing but himself to consider; I exert myself only through love; that is to say, on behalf of others.

*　　　　*　　　　*

Much more quickly than he could have hoped, there was a change of opinion in regard to him.

From time to time he would receive from some outstanding personality the kind of appreciation that showed him he was understood. When Sir Edmund Gosse wrote to him from London, this letter seemed more precious than a hundred laudatory press criticisms.

Edmund Gosse did still more: shortly after the publication of *Si le Grain ne meurt,* he invited the London Royal Society of Literature, which was about to nominate a French candidate for membership in place of Anatole

France, to choose André Gide, who was unanimously elected.

The younger generation was grateful to him for having braved unpopularity. Under the influence of Freud, the work of Proust, and his own work, people were perhaps beginning to regard certain sexual prejudices with less embarrassment than hitherto, and that which at one time had seemed inadmissible gradually began to appear almost natural.

His other books began to fall into their right places. Each one of them had been ten or twenty years in advance of the period; now they had all made up for lost time. In literary criticism, names Gide had loved and helped to make known, Rimbaud, Lautréamont, William Blake, Dostoievski, Conrad, Rilke, either held their own or were increasing in value. The *N. R. F.* was at the height of its fame. With a sudden drive, as it were, the work of Gide had got home.

And now his most irreconcilable enemies seemed to bow before the accomplished fact: Paul Souday placed him on a level with the great contemporary writers, and Henri Béraud, taking advantage of the appearance of *L'École des Femmes* (English translation, *The School for Wives*), " congratulated " him on having written this " vital and moving book."

Abroad he was admired with a still greater deference. His sixtieth birthday was acclaimed by the whole of the German press and in academic and theatrical circles as an event for intellectual Europe. In the United States the translation of *Les Faux-Monnayeurs* became a huge publishing success.

Thus did glory come to him: glory that is the outcome not of honours and decorations but of the esteem created by a life and its work.

Gide has long since renounced all such vanities. Indeed, he never felt himself at a greater distance from them. Salons, though no longer intimidating him, seem vacuous. He prefers to surround himself with professors, savants, foreign critics, and young people. " Youth," he says, " attracts me more than beauty. There is a certain freshness, an innocence one would like to recapture." [1]

This man, described by his enemies as a sombre Machiavelli, is found, when one sees him at close quarters, to be living, with remarkable light-heartedness, in an astonishing state of detachment. Gide knows that nothing is more dangerous than glory. Therefore he aims only at detaching himself therefrom: he does not wish to be held by anything.

It seems to him that it is he who now possesses true evangelistic feeling. Did not Christ teach that one should sell one's goods, lay aside everything? Is not that his essential teaching? Now, nothing is more alien to Gide than the sense of property. He really needs to feel detached. He has got rid of the estates that belonged to him, selling La Roque and his Auteuil villa. (If he keeps Cuverville, it is because his wife is attached to the place.) He camps wherever he goes. Avoids being " waited on." When alone, he does not

[1] Unpublished Journal.

care to arrange comforts for himself or spend on his own
account.

His adversaries, by way of travesty, have declared him
avaricious. But are these not the Pharisees, clutching at
their luxury and their wealth? On the other hand, a single
characteristic rules Gide's serenity: this taste for getting
rid of encumbrances and for the gratuitous activity whereby
the sense of the infinite is restored. The question he has
been asking himself all his life: — What can a man do?
How shall he " serve "? — he now answers through the
mouth of Œdipe: " By renouncing his goods, his glory, and
himself."

Yet Gide is well aware, however natural he may find detachment from the things of this world, that the Devil will
always get his own back in some other way.

. . . Arrived at this point on his journey, he looks
round for the companions with whom he started out. What
has become of them?

Many of them have disappeared: Pierre Louÿs into
wretchedness and debauchery, Proust into glory, Ducoté
into obscurity. Others, having, like Ghéon, deserted mid-
way, have attempted a resuscitation: the Catholic theatre.
Francis Jammes has withdrawn from everything, to Orthez.
On receiving a letter from Gide, he sent in reply nothing
but a fragment of coarse brown linen in an envelope (very
good quality linen, too, Gide notes). Meanwhile, even Valéry and Claudel, in spite of their genuine greatness, are
content to lean upon the powers that be: the Academy and

the State. Sole survivors of the original small group, Roger Martin du Gard, Jean Schlumberger, and Gide have steered a straight course to the end.

Gide's influence, moreover, lasted and expanded for nearly half a century. His books are active and lead to action.[1] They help the individual to wrestle with himself as did Jacob with the angel. They infuse a strange strength and often enable the weak who are hesitating on the brink, the water's edge, suddenly to risk the plunge. Then Gide receives enthusiastic letters burning with gratitude. Sick people write to him who have, with his help, recovered a taste for life, even in hospital, and adolescents, troubled as to their place in the world. Young girls come to him with their confessions. Strangers take up his time in asking for advice. There is even an old madwoman who for years has daily sent him lengthy outpourings of delirious love, the homage of a mind that is beyond the bounds of reason, as if ironically to remind the author of *Paludes* of the dangers of literary vanity.

*　　　*　　　*

Meanwhile Gide's thought ceaselessly progresses. He feels that he has not yet sufficiently penetrated the vital core of his consciousness: a fresh task.

— For too long — he admits — I have spoken through something or someone. . . .

[1] Gide has also exercised a direct personal influence. In this connexion should be mentioned the annual gatherings at Pontigny, organized by M. Desjardin. It is here that Gide has come in contact with some of the best foreign writers and notably, immediately after the war, with German writers. Very many are those who cherish deep-seated memories of those " *décades* " during which intellectual problems were discussed (the subject being fixed in advance) and of which Gide was often the animating spirit

At the present time he has given up fiction. He wishes to reach the reality of social life. Since his journey to the Congo he has been haunted by the colonial abuses. Is it possible that almost the whole of humanity may be thus groaning in chains? Wrapped in serenity, Gide cannot rest satisfied, and, like all wise men, he keeps watch " on the left."

— As to my last book — he says — I must first of all live it. . . .

But will he have time? He has begun reading Karl Marx's mighty tome. He watches the drama being played out away there in Russia, in the future. Henceforward it is in that forward march of humanity, perpetually getting ahead of itself, that Gide places his real hope of a beyond.

— Tell me where you want to go."

— Straight ahead," says the old, blind Œdipe, in amongst people."

Although the idea of death no longer causes Gide any uneasiness, it nevertheless forces upon him a term for the payment of a debt: he would like to be able to finish his work, to give it a clearer, more forcible consequence, and thus to die satisfied, giving back to earth, as he has always promised himself to do, a " grateful and enchanted spirit."

PART II

HIS PSYCHOLOGY AND HIS ART

GIDE'S work as a whole may be regarded as a prolonged debate on the subject of morality. Throughout it one hears, as if from some mysterious corridor, the incessant voice of conscience.

Beginning with his earliest books, he gives us *interpretations* of Greek or biblical legends, and often, setting out with a realistic or dramatic or poetic legend (as in *Philoctète, Bethsabé,* or *Narcisse*), he composes a small treatise on morality. His essays, even when they touch upon æsthetics, are primarily concerned with ethics. In the same way, almost all his characters are arranged in relation to an idea of good or evil. As the sculptor works upon his marble, so Gide upon his moral material.

Thus, in the most important of his novels, *Les Faux-Monnayeurs,* although we meet there almost every variety of human being, a certain grouping is discernible: on the one hand, more or less rebellious and perverse children and young people — such as the troubled Bernard, Armand, who has wandered from the path, Vincent, hovering between various lines of conduct — and on the other, pastors, pro-

91

fessors, and parents, in bondage to traditional precepts.
There is only one exception, Lady Griffith, a wealthy, elegant, beautiful woman who cares for neither God nor the
Devil and is therefore " the despair of the novelist." She is
" soulless," " two-dimensional," and thus fails to interest
him. For the same reason the characters of Marcel Proust,
who do not suffer from moral disquietude, make upon Gide,
in spite of the wonderful way in which they are handled,
the impression of being merely puppets. For Gide, the
moral conflict alone gives people their reality, their consciousness; and this consciousness ought to accompany
them, like a borne shadow, at every step of the way. Gide
should believe the legend of the man who sold his shadow
and thus lost the reality of his life.

One might apply to Gide's own work what he has said of
Dostoievski's: if French authors are usually preoccupied
with the " passional . . . intellectual " and family relationships of their characters, Gide, like Dostoievski, is
mainly interested in " the individual's relationship with
himself or with God. . . ."

Nevertheless, and apparently paradoxically, Gide's aim
throughout life has been nothing less than to escape morality. " Away with morality " is already the conclusion of
André Walter, or, more exactly, away with *traditional*
morality. The truth is that Gide tried to get past morality
into a state of " gratuitousness " where at last the individual can live light-heartedly, at his own disposal, detached from perpetual preoccupation with duty. This state

of supreme " gratuitousness " represents for Gide the summit of a new individualistic ethic.

But before reaching it he was obliged to analyse, in the inner life, the various motives of human activity. Driven to criticize traditional morality, he has been led to psychology, which in its turn has led him to a higher morality. Moreover, it is from observation of the psychic life that he has drawn the great laws of his art.

Thus morality, psychology, and art appear in the work of Gide as three aspects of a single spiritual effort, and it is only for the sake of convenience that we shall consider each in turn.

The most impressive meeting-place of these three aspects of his thought is the examination of conscience: on one hand the reflective centre, and on the other that of action or of inspiration.

Nearly all Gide's characters are given to constant self-examination; hence the moral colouring we have remarked in them. The youthful Vincent would like to seduce a woman who is taking a cure in a sanatorium where he too is being treated. He hesitates, tries to justify himself. Tells himself they are both ill and must die. What holds him back? Why should he refrain? Thus, while he courts her, a conflict goes on within him. His self is divided. There is one who acts and one who watches and judges.

These two selves deliberate the matter together, and this dialogue, going forward in the depths of the conscience, seems to Gide to be the source of all true inward progress. " To suppress the inward dialogue is to arrest life itself."

Gide considers the examination of conscience not only from the moral, but also from the intellectual point of view and finds therein the same advantages as are to be found in a dialogue between two different persons. In philosophy is it not the aim of the Platonic dialogues to reveal an idea under all its aspects and to make it live in its progression? If Socrates called the art of his dialogues " maieutic," it is exactly because it allowed him to *bring to birth* the precious contents of the minds with which he deals. The examination of conscience ought to have the same result, with the sole difference that the interlocutors are the two aspects of a single self.

In order the better to elucidate these interior conversations, the holder of them can set them down in writing. And we find nearly all Gide's leading characters keeping a " secret diary." Sometimes this diary constitutes the whole novel (as in *Les Cahiers d'André Walter, Les Nourritures terrestres, La Symphonie pastorale*). Sometimes the narrative alternates with the diary of the chief character, as in *Les Faux-Monnayeurs*, where Édouard appears as seen from within by himself and from without by the author: at once reflecting and acting. The motives of his actions are analysed from one point of view by the hero himself and from another by the author, and the reader, seeing everything from these two angles, has the impression of dealing with real persons.

This consideration under two aspects, which Gide sees as a vital factor in the examination of conscience, he also regards, in the realm of creative art, as the best method of achieving reality. And it is in order the further to penetrate reality that he has introduced into his best work a kind of duplicating process. In *Les Faux-Monnayeurs* the chief character, Édouard, who is a novelist, writes a novel which is the same as that of Gide, in so far as it has the same characters, under other names, and the same plan of showing them from two angles. The whole book is, so to speak, projected inwards. Each character, each event, placed as it were between two parallel mirrors, is reflected by both of them and creates the illusion of inexhaustible depths. This is what Gide means when he writes: "Nothing . . . has actuality for me unless I can see [it] reflected."

He has made extraordinarily good use of this method, which, in certain scenes, leads to the most disquieting misunderstandings. In order to intimidate little Georges, a boy of thirteen, already a thief and an accomplice of counterfeiters, Édouard reads him a scene from his novel which represents a man like himself in the act of administering a reprimand to a boy like Georges. Édouard's novel goes ahead of Gide's. The future mingles with the present, and the whole work is the greater for the fact of its apparent evolution along lines moving at different rates.

Nor is this all. Even the title of the novel has both a concrete meaning (the story of the counterfeiters) and a symbolic meaning (false coins, false value, suggesting to Gide the idea of insincerity; both the mutual flatteries and the dissensions of his characters). The two novels, proceeding throughout the book, are related to the twofold character of the title: one is a *realist* novel, presenting the facts as such, the other an *idealist* novel, presenting their figurative meaning. Gide has compactly criticized these two genres. Realism he accuses of being no more than flat, meticulous, and uninteresting photography of reality (the usual formula of the commercial novel). Idealism he judges as follows: " Under the guise of a novel of ideas, we have so far been treated to nothing but execrable tendency novels (*romans à thèse*). . . ." One may deduce thence that the duty of the writer is to make, within the work itself, the synthesis of these two genres.

This twofold fiction presents also the " conflict between the facts set before the author and the ideal facts " — that is to say, the conflict between that which the author aims to do with reality and what reality compels him to do, the conflict between the work as originally conceived and the realized book. In *Les Faux-Monnayeurs* Gide introduces this fresh point of view by explaining, in Édouard's journal, what he had wished to attempt, and by showing, in the narrative, what has materialized. And it is this point of view that led him to publish separately, in his *Journal des Faux-Monnayeurs*, reflections on the book which he was not able to introduce, directly, in the work itself. " Think," he remarks in this connexion, " how interesting we should find a similar record kept by Dickens or Balzac, or a journal of *L'Éducation sentimentale* . . . the history of the work, of its gestation. . . ." This journal, compared with the book, re-creates, for Gide, the drama of life itself.

And this complex reflection of people and things, this multiple decomposition of reality (sometimes reminding one of Pirandello) is to be found throughout the whole of his work. For he has found duality in the most diverse aspects of life: in art, of fiction and reality; in the conscience, of thought and action; in society, of the individual and the group; in love, of sensuality and tenderness. Is not man himself body and soul, and the world matter and spirit? Like a good Christian, Gide sees it under the sway of a perpetual duality. Between God and the Devil the conflict never ceases.

Gide's work has therefore the semblance of a battlefield where combat never ceases; life becomes a stake, risked terribly at each moment, obliging the individual to keep his energies continually at a stretch.

Does this mean that this kind of generalized manichæism is the ideal destiny of man?

Gide is obliged to admit that this duality, whenever one of these two aspects of a personality dominates the other, may lead to an acute and painful disturbance of poise. The I who judges assumes a monstrous, immeasurable importance, while the I who acts effaces itself and disappears. Thus nothing is more dangerous than abuse of self-examination as practised notably by the Protestants, who submit even the least important of their actions to the judgment of conscience. This exhausting confrontation results in a feeling of inferiority and an anxiety which makes them incapable of acting without remorse. The resultant nervous disturbance is sometimes so great as to lead to madness or to suicide.[1]

" When one is in such a divided state," says Armand, a victim of Huguenot education, " how shall one be altogether sincere? " And he explains: " Part of me holds back and watches the other commit itself, observes . . . and condemns or applauds. . . ." In order to correct his painful inward dualism he involuntarily exaggerates it, and on his face, which he dares not show uncovered, he wears a ceaselessly grimacing mask.[2]

It can even happen that these separated elements of consciousness fail to be reunited. What then arises is a recognized pathological condition known as dual personality. This condition has often been described, both by writers and by psychiatrists.[3] Gide himself, who has never quite been able to escape from his puritanism, has suffered in this way. " I . . . do not quite grasp," he writes, " when I watch myself act, that the one I watch *is the same* as he who looks on. . . ." Yet the very fact of his stating the case in-

[1] Statistics have revealed that there are twice as many suicides in the Protestant Swiss cantons as in the Catholic.

[2] Nietzsche, another child of Protestantism, has made considerable use of the image of the mask, which to him seems indispensable for everyday life.

[3] There is, for example, the famous play *Le Procureur Hallers,* and Giraudoux's *Aventures de Jérôme Bardini.* Here we encounter a person, in the one case a magistrate and in the other a sober employee, who, at certain times of day or night, becomes someone else. He escapes, furtively, and disguises this unknown aspect of himself. In psychiatry one of the best investigators of such phenomena, which he calls cases of secondary personality, is Dr. Janet.

dicates that he remains within the limits of normality. His
resistant sanity has saved him even in his most troubled
moments.

He has, nevertheless, experienced, to the point of obsession, both in his psychic and in his creative life, the tor-
ments of duality. The author of the journal, the " contem-
plator," has often absorbed the artist to such a degree that
he has gone so far as to ask himself whether all he was
feeling was not the work of the one who, at home within
himself, analyses and judges. ". . . Man experiences what
he imagines himself to be experiencing. Thence he proceeds
to thinking that he imagines himself to be experiencing
what he experiences. . . . Between my loving Laura,"
says Édouard, " and imagining that I love her . . . what
God could see the difference? " This being so, is not everything in our consciousness merely illusion and nothingness?
By observing himself while he writes (and projecting into
his books the twofold results of this observation), does not
the novelist allow exactly that reality to escape which he
believed himself to be penetrating the most deeply?

This raises the whole question of introspection. Auguste
Comte, we know, denied the possibility of its existence by
affirming that a man cannot stand at the window and watch
himself passing in the street. With this statement he excluded almost the whole of psychology or at any rate
limited it to the observation of others than oneself — that
is to say, to a kind of psycho-physiology. From that point
he reached as far as to banish personal analysis from the

domain of art and considerably to limit its application. . . .

Yet art rests on introspection. For it is the proper and mysterious attribute of art to fuse the two persons who hold converse within, the one who inspires and the one who is inspired, the muse and the poet. In the act of creation, as in all intense activity, the ego and the self end by coinciding, until we have the illusion that they are but one. And it is exactly at those moments of poetic or of " gratuitous " activity that a man recovers his sincerity, his freedom, and his availability.

Thus while the duality of our nature causes us to sway between two contrary and successive states, we progress only by the reconciliation of our inner antagonisms. All moral and psychic life should tend to recover, beyond our duality, the profound unity of our being. No doubt the world of consciousness and the external world present themselves in the form of a dualistic opposition, but the goal is nevertheless unification.

" Our whole universe is the prey of discord," declares one of Gide's most astonishing characters, the old music-teacher, La Pérouse. But he adds, suddenly transported by a sort of ecstatic adoration: ". . . Perfect harmony, continuous; yes, that is it; perfect harmony, continuous. . . ." This is the supreme expression of serenity, of eternity.

The contradiction, moreover, inherent in every human life, is that if, one day, absolute harmony were realized, life would stop and cease to be. " Ah, how we must wait before harmony is resolved! " cries La Pérouse.

2

"GOOD REASONS" OR MORAL ARTIFICE

THE HERO of *Paludes* keeps a secret diary. " There are," he says, " two parts in my agenda. On one page I write what I am going to do and on the opposite page I set down, each day, what I have done. Then I compare the two. . . . — This morning, opposite ' Try to get up at six,' I wrote: ' Got up at seven.' . . ." Thus he nourishes his sense of duty.

What is this Duty? What is this conscience, which seems to keep watch and to be for ever rebuking, as if it were someone independent of one's personality? Baudelaire calls it an ironic voice, inviting us, preferably at night, " To recall what use we have made of the day which is past. . . ." A terrible eye, says Victor Hugo, whose gaze nothing can arrest, will pursue Cain, be he never so surrounded, even to the depths of the most secret cavern.

To-day most people believe that " the voice of conscience " is with us from birth; that it is a kind of immediate moral sense, given by God, like our intelligence. Particularly since the eighteenth century and Rousseau, who believed the " natural man " to be fundamentally good and just, has conscience been considered as a sure guide, rescuing us each moment from the abyss, after the manner of an inner tribunal which we carry with us everywhere in order that it may decide our conduct. Protestantism, Kantianism with its " categorical imperative," and finally the ethics of the laity have popularized this notion in our own days.

Alas, Gide suspects, this voice that is said to be infallible is often merely fallacious, and the examination of conscience an incredibly clumsy moral exercise. The moment one observes its operations a little attentively, one hears nothing but the grating of the mechanism: hypocrisy has insinuated therein its corrosive and defacing acid.

" The moment I got up," says the hero of *Paludes*, " I read on my agenda: ' Try to get up at six.' It was eight o'clock. I took my pen, struck out the entry, and wrote: ' Get up at eleven.' And I went to bed without reading the rest." This single instance, ironically proffered by Gide, typifies the comedy perpetually played by those who examine their consciences, and of which they are vaguely ashamed: " And I went to bed without reading the rest . . ." adds the hero of *Paludes*. ". . . Blow out the lamp quickly," cries Baudelaire, " so that we may hide in the darkness! "

This art of self-deception appears in the *bad reasons* discovered for self-justification and transformed into *good reasons*. " It is not so much his actions that I despise," says Éveline in speaking of the unfortunate Robert, " but *the reasons he gives for them.*" In this domain, where only lies or inventions will serve, the resources of the human mind are prodigiously rich.

The classical method of escaping responsibility is to shift it on to one's neighbour. When the starving wolf decides to eat the sheep, he accuses it, in order to justify his crime, of all kinds of imaginary misdeeds, and when the poor sheep protests, he replies: — If it's not you, it's your brother." — I have no brother." — Then it's someone belonging to you. . . ." The " good reason " may be stated thus: Since I do not wish it to be myself, it shall be he. . . .

Éveline's father one day makes a confidante of his daughter and tells her of his disappointment in marriage. Ah, if only he had been better understood and seconded by his narrow-minded wife, what would he not have done! Whilst he is speaking, Éveline cannot " refrain from thinking that it had rested with him to get more from her than he did, and that since he had failed to make the most of his intelligence and of his gifts, he was not at all averse to laying the responsibility on [his wife]." Most of the failures and the incapables actually reason in much the same way: — It is not my fault that I have not succeeded in this, or that, says the child, it is the fault of my parents; of my colleague, says the business man; of the publishers, says the writer. . . . If every other excuse fails, circumstances are blamed, or ill luck, or destiny, neither of which is likely to protest. It requires courage and honesty to admit that one has only oneself to blame . . . with the possible result that at present, since everything still rests with myself, and my love of indolence, masked beneath " good reasons," stands revealed, I shall be forced to make an effort, a laborious and tiresome effort.

This transference of responsibility to others presents itself on behalf of the most diverse sentiments. Comic writers have often applied it to cowardice: literature is full of Tartarins who are always ready to swear that when they met the lion, it was the lion who was afraid and took flight.[1]

But Gide, carrying his analysis still further, declares here that the substitution taking place in the course of the examination of conscience is usually not a mere putting of one person in the place of another, but, rather, of a setting aside, within consciousness itself, of a real feeling of which the individual is both aware and ashamed, in favour of a kindred feeling not possessed by him, but commanding his moral approval.

The hero of *La Symphonie pastorale*, a married pastor, finds himself full of abounding love for a poor blind orphan girl, twenty years of age, whom he had brought to his home on the occasion of one of his parochial visits and whom, since, he has devotedly cherished. Actually what he is experiencing is a violent physical passion, but this is exactly what he does not know, because this guilty passion has concealed itself from his consciousness under the disguise of charitable duty. God, he tells himself, has put " a kind

[1] Political life, also, is a perpetual shelving of responsibility: not ourselves, but the Socialists caused the franc to fall; it is they who are without ideals, while we . . . On their side the Socialists reason in the same way.

of obligation in my path " and I cannot " escape it without a sort of baseness."

But the drama grows involved. The pastor's son, quite a young man, in his turn falls in love with Gertrude, the blind orphan, and very honourably asks his father's permission to marry her. Here, then, is the father, jealous of his son and seeking any means to separate him from the girl. But even this jealousy is unconsciously disguised as " bad reasons." Gertrude is too young, he tells his son, and then: — Your sentiments . . . seem to me to be guilty, because they are premature. It rests with us to exercise, on Gertrude's behalf, the prudence she has not yet learned." You shall go away for a while. — It is a matter of conscience."

The scene is admirable in its sublime hypocrisy. The more the pastor is devoured by jealousy, the more he talks of nobility, of duty, and of conscience. " An instinct as sure as that of conscience," says he, " warned me that I must at all costs prevent this marriage " (of his son with Gertrude).

How can he so incredibly deceive himself? Just because his guilty love seems to him to be as pure as the sense of duty and brings him the same joy and the same release. And just here is the supreme illusion: a man such as is the poor pastor imagines that a reprehensible desire, once yielded to, must necessarily create remorse. He forgets that the desire, stronger than ourselves, conceals itself in the depths of consciousness under a borrowed name and thus triumphs over our scruples.

Sometimes it is even more cunningly indirect, demanding for its accomplishment a stiffening of our whole being, which makes us believe, whilst we carry out our base action, that we are fulfilling a great and noble task. Thus Vincent, looking for " good reasons " for abandoning the woman he has seduced and her child, sets up for himself a kind of Nietzschean morality from which pity is excluded as shameful. Hence, in breaking with his mistress, he imagines himself to be accomplishing a task whose praiseworthiness is the greater because of his own tenderness of heart.

Strangest of all is the fact that a few months earlier when he met this woman, ill in a sanatorium, and alone in the world, like Gertrude, he thought, like the pastor, that his loving-kindness gave him a right over her. He then believed himself to be acting like a good Christian. In place of the transference of sentiments we have, in Vincent's case, the transference of moral laws.

Poor voice of conscience! Sophisticated voice, perpetually fooling us, playing conjuring tricks and concealing beneath the fine name of " duty " our most egoistic sentiments. Many of Gide's characters are thus victimized by its deceptions. The head of the *pension* Azaïs declares that he has given a home to the old La Pérouse, whom he overworks, solely from benevolent motives. Old La Pérouse himself gives the name of austerity to that which in his case is nothing but pride. In *André Walter* we see divine love, the mortification of the flesh, and the pure transports of the hero concealing a simple carnal desire, unsatisfied and rebellious. This latter transference, which is, moreover, the best-known type, explains why it is that mystical sects sometimes end scandalously and bigots tend to become mean and even fraudulent. . . .

It would thus seem that the entire inner life is nothing but a perpetual play of " bad reasons." The more moral a man is, the greater his need to deform and misinterpret this morality. It is in order to deaden the anguish born of his faults and his antisocial instincts that, without knowing it, he has recourse to the lie that gives him the illusion of purity. The more powerful is the sense of guilt, the more will the individual, in order to reassure himself and have an " easy conscience," use and abuse, on his own behalf, deceitful, insidious arguments.

Gide has indeed affirmed that devout people are more prone to hypocrisy than others. That is why all his clerical families live in complete blindness. It is stifling, killing, says Armand, speaking of his home. At the Vedels', each one gives way to his passions in secret, but, adds Armand, " Grandpapa . . . sees nothing but the fire, and Mother compels herself not to understand. As for Father, he forgets it all in God: it's easier. . . ." Thus, Vedal père prefers to give all his time to the poor, to his sermons and his meetings, rather than to see clearly all around him and, particularly, within.

Self-examination finally appears as torment and the conscience as a curse inflicted by God upon man since the day he ate the fruit of the tree of Knowledge of Good and Evil. If the eighteenth-century optimists were able to regard conscience as a saving guide, the romantic Byronic poets and the German natural philosophers held, with greater reason, that conscience, first and foremost, inflicts upon us the sense of our misery. Nor is it so much remorse that pains us as the vague impression of being played with when we try to judge our actions, and the fact of our inability of distinguishing good from evil, truth from falsehood, good arguments from bad; so much so that in the midst of so many windings we feel we must end by being lost altogether. God, says old La Pérouse, " sends us temptations He knows we can't resist, and if nevertheless we resist them, He revenges Himself on us still more," by throwing our minds into confusion. " Why has He ill will towards us? " Yes, why?

But indeed it is not God who has invented this moral duplicity whence come all our ills. It is man himself, in his ignorance. He does not know how to do without " authorization " for his actions. So long as he demands this from society, from religion, from others, and not from himself, duplicity will be general.[1] Gide has seen clearly that the hypocrisy of the inner life is born of the very form of traditional morality.

This it is, with its laws and its rites, which condemns the full blossoming of certain instincts and sometimes of even the most fruitful, and which obliges man to invent " bad reasons " in order, nevertheless, to give these instincts full rein. The human passions have a life of their own and will no more suffer brutal repression than our lungs will endure

[1] See Part III, Chapter i, " Individualist Morality."

stifling or our hearts arrest. When morality forbids them to show themselves, they take refuge in the unconscious as in a thick fog, and there, profiting by the darkness, they corrupt our minds, falsify our logic, and disarm us. It is in this way that the pastor's unacknowledged passion for the young blind girl reappears triumphant, pure, and innocent, transfigured into passionate charity.

This opposition between the deeper instincts and social institutions is also the starting-point of the Freudian conception of the life of the psyche. When our desires (and, for Freud, particularly our sexual desires) are repressed by the moral " censor," they soon surge up again, disguised, however, in the symbolic images of our dreams or in the pathological obsessions of neurosis. But these safety-valves for our instincts operate only at the cost of our nerves. In the case of " good reasons " the moral " censor " allows the travestied and unrecognizable desire to pass, but the price of this liberation is a sordid trick, debasing our intelligence and contaminating our whole personality.

One may say that if Freud in the realm of pathology has revealed the part played by our instincts, Gide has similarly revealed it in regard to normal life. For the one as for the other, all these transferences which safeguard the inner life of the individual take place in the unconscious. Our desires thrust down into the unconscious like roots seeking their nourishment in the earth. When these encounter stones and other obstacles to their development, they cleverly shape themselves according to the outlines of these obstacles, in order that the plant may live. Anyone ignorant of this subterranean labour and knowing the plant only by its visible part would be unable to care for it.

When we undertake personal examination, we are not unlike this uninstructed horticulturist. We are aware only of the small luminous point of our consciousness and know nothing of the immense surrounding darkness. If the inner voice seems to be unreliable, it is because we neglect the voice of the unconscious and listen only to that of consciousness.

"There are more things in heaven and earth than are dreamed of in our philosophy." Nor is our inner world less vast and mysterious. Gide has made it his business to explore its most unknown, its most obscure regions.

THE UNCONSCIOUS, THE DEVIL'S RETREAT

THE IDEA of the unconscious, which has revolutionized our conception of the inner life, is a relatively recent one. As is usual with admissions of ignorance, psychology has reached it rather belatedly. For a long time philosophers believed that the ego was fully accessible to reason. Man needs no small supply of modesty in order to admit that he can know but little of himself.

Bergson, with his wonderful descriptions of psychological life, is undoubtedly one of those who have most greatly contributed towards the spreading of the idea of the unconscious. Freud, his contemporary, proceeding from the study of neurosis, has demonstrated the primary importance of unconscious motives in human actions. And, also at the same period of time, writers and poets (Symbolists, Expressionists, and Surrealists) have sought inspiration in the most obscure regions of being.

It is remarkable that two of the greatest French contemporary writers should both have seen in the study of the unconscious the means of illuminating the depths of the human

soul. Thus regarded, each of them may seem to be Berg-
sonian, although Proust came to Bergson very late, and I
suspect Gide of having paid but scant attention to his work.
One may say, therefore, of each of them, that he did not
really come under Bergson's influence, but rather took possession of the ideas that were floating " in the air " of his
period and adapted them to the purposes of his own genius;
Proust searching in the unconscious for whatever reality
and lastingness there might be in love and in art, Gide compelling himself to seek there the point of departure for an
acceptable morality.

Here, then, is Gide bent over the unconscious, wherein
from the first he discovers the hiding-place of the worst
human instincts. Here it is, when oppressed by conventional
morality, that the individual represses and transforms his
underhand thoughts, his veiled covetousness, and his equivocal sentiments, all the desires that cannot become operative
without danger, and the Devil knows that they are legion!
Freud, whose profession obliged him to " roll," as he says,
" in all this mud," affirms, crouching in the depths of the
ego, such frightful desires as would make the " honest
man," if he knew of their existence, ill with shame and
horror: cupidity, hatred, murder, and incest.

The exploration of this dark cavern is anything but an
agreeable task. Entering it, says Gide, thought is something
like a dragon advancing " with invisible muzzle, snuffling at
everything it meets with a predatory curiosity." But the
thinker must not recoil. The unconscious is the chosen

hiding-place of the Devil within us, and just for this reason we must pursue and dislodge him.

This last image need not deceive us. Gide has never met the Devil, this personage capable of throwing, as Luther did in his, an ink-pot in the face of anyone who resists him. Gide refers rather to the demoniac spirit, the Devil crouched in the shadowy unconscious and amusing itself, while we indulge in self-communings, by suggesting all those miserable " good reasons," those lies and sophistries which presently we can no longer distinguish from the truth. He it is who, by transforming our best intentions, unchains without our knowledge our worst desires. He " plays with us like a cat with a mouse."

Gide, in his turn, seems to reap amusement from these manœuvres. Ambushed in company with the Devil, behind the characters of his novels, he observes the criminal tricks played upon them by their secret instincts. What rejoices him is not so much the sight of a man duped by the Devil, but the fact of tricking the Devil himself by surprising his secret. " You think he is your dupe," writes La Bruyère, " but if he is pretending to be, which is the greater dupe, you or he? " And Gide takes a passionate delight in letting his characters fall into the traps of the unconscious and afterwards revealing to the reader the illusions of which they are the victims. Thus he proves himself, on the whole, stronger than the Devil and puts a man on guard against his errors.

Gide opens the diary of the austere pastor, Vedel. What does he find there? Whole pages of " struggle, supplication, prayer, and effort " on the subject of his resolution not to smoke any more. " O God," writes Vedel, " give me strength to shake off the yoke of this shameful slavery." What can be the meaning of the word " smoke," for Gide knows that the minister has long since given up tobacco, and given it up, moreover, without difficulty? He understands. The word " smoke " stands for something else. . . .

One Sunday, at Neufchâtel, Gide meets the faithful coming home from church. "Their thoughts," he writes, " are washed and ironed by the sermon they have just heard, and piled neatly in their heads as in a clean linenpress." Then he adds: " I should like to rummage in the bottom drawer. I have the key." [1] Gide is never more delighted than in discovering in some serious person an irregular desire, ill-contained and revealing itself through the façade presented to the world. For him this spectacle is as amusing as that of the tail of a badly tucked-in shirt challenging the gravity of an eminent professor.

Turning, then, towards his public, Gide might say, as did Baudelaire: " Hypocritical reader, my peer, my brother . . ." why drape yourself in your dignity? Come, we are all tormented by evil. Don't protest! If you are sincere, you will recognize yourself in my heroes, in Vincent, in Michel, in myself. You tell me to hold my peace, and say that even if you are aware of the corrosions of some secret acid, there is no need to shout it from the house-tops. Dear reader, one should hide nothing. For my part, I shall tell everything. Enough of your foul lies! I shall tell every-

[1] Unpublished Journal.

thing. It will be strange and sad. In any case, it will be true. . . .

If in so many of his books Gide gives us the impression of fishing in troubled waters, it is because he is trying, above all things, to penetrate to the depths of human consciousness. Armed with his diabolical key, the key to the unconscious, he accompanies his characters, forces locks, opens hidden letters, and lifts lids. Now it is Bernard who steals a valise in order to read Édouard's diary; now Julius looking through Lafcadio's private note-book during his absence; and now Sarah looking through that of her father. But if the author intrudes upon these private bypaths, it is in order to discover the secrets of the human drama.

In the course of this continual pursuit we see him perpetually on the look-out for the smallest gestures, the most insignificant details. For he knows that instincts deeply repressed in the unconscious are betrayed only by slight nervous contractions, reflexes, imperceptible movements. And it is these signals, usually unperceived, that he must watch for if he is to dislodge these instincts. A competent observer watching a gambler seated, imperturbable, at the green table will discover the emotion that sways him, solely by the slight trembling of a finger. It is thanks to a curious little badge Georges wears in his buttonhole and to the fact that he blushes and does not answer when questioned on the subject that Édouard learns of the existence of a secret society made up of the boys who have been led astray by a gang of counterfeiters.

Inductively, then, led by these apparently insignificant

details, the author reaches down to their deep-seated origin. As a novelist, he proceeds as did Edgar Allan Poe or Conan Doyle in their detective stories. Individuals and families take all sorts of precautions to hide their secret passions, but they are no more successful than are criminals in covering all their traces. And it is these indications that Gide notes and interprets after the manner of a detective studying finger-prints or grains of dust. Thus, in *Isabelle*, it is by means of a series of such small indications that we penetrate step by step, side by side with the author, the shameful secret of the château. In this respect the story is admirable. The scenes are wonderfully graduated until the moment when we discover that Isabelle is a girl-mother cursed by her parents, who no longer dare to receive her save secretly, at night.

If, however, Gide is so intensely preoccupied with the smallest signs of vile and occult passions, it is not only an infernal curiosity that urges him on. After all, he asks, are these deep passions so frightful? Since they exist within us, must there not be some good reason for their existence? Does not society work against its own interests in condemning them, and are there not, among them, forces that may be fruitful for the individual?

It is a remarkable fact that many of the great figures in history owe their greatness to the very instincts it is customary to deprecate. Sunk in vice and debts, surrounded by rogues, astray, and repudiated by his own class, Julius Cæsar, calling upon the enormous and so-called evil energies within him, became the extraordinary social reformer and great military leader whom we know. And during the last war did we not see men who were supposed to be " done for " become " heroes "?

Gide remarked that the greater number of savants, writers, and thinkers have suffered from an inward lack of balance. And it is exactly their irregular passions that have permitted the release in them of intellectual creativeness. Almost all the great mystics have been neuropaths. Mahomet, Luther, and Dostoievski were epileptics. " Pascal's abyss moved with him as he went." [1] " Nietzsche and Rousseau had their madness." [2]

But we must beware. Gide does not pretend that genius has always been either mad or " abnormal," or that vitiated instinct is *in itself* creative; but only that the latter brings with it so unendurable a disorder of the consciousness as to move certain minds to create within themselves a new order, personal and original, that will give birth to a work of art. Thus " within the origin of every reform," he writes, " there is always . . . a small physiological mystery, an anomaly . . . a malaise, the malaise of the reformer." [3] In a state of well-being, on the other hand, a man's mind will be satisfied with things as they are and will go to sleep. [4]

[1] Baudelaire.

[2] Cf. Gide's study: *Dostoïevski* (English translation, *Dostoevsky*).

[3] Cf. Gide's study: *Dostoïevski:* " Dostoievski was not great because he was an epileptic, but because, being an epileptic, he was nevertheless able to do his work."

[4] Therefore it may sometimes be dangerous to attempt at all costs to cure a neurosis, particularly in an exceptionally gifted person. For it may be that this neurosis has become the very mainspring of his being. In *Les Faux-Monnayeurs* (page 262; English translation, *The Counterfeiters*, page

Thus it becomes easier to grasp what it is Gide finds so deeply attractive in troubled natures. He seeks them out because he feels they are more valuable than others, because their rebellious desires are capable of producing the most unexpected, the most moving, and perhaps the most fertile results. On the other hand one may be sure that nothing is to be expected of a man who can submit *without difficulty* to all the rules of politeness, of morality, and of religion. Such a man's personality is bound to be very empty and poor.

This is why Michel prefers to the " feeble, weakly, too well-behaved " children who interest his wife the young good-for-nothings of Biskra, who, by their mere presence, help to cure his neurasthenia.

And yet is there not now and again an equivocal sentiment within the author's liking for scandalous passions? Is he always looking for a revelation of the unconscious? And never for perversity in its own right? When he seems to admire debauchery, when, for example, he writes: " I have known . . . all the vices," when he chooses to name a book *L'Immoraliste*, does he not seem to be desiring evil for its own sake?

I must admit that nothing has ever seemed to me more

---

189) Édouard seems to reproach the Freudian lady doctor for displaying " the most intimate workings . . . [of a] mental organism " so openly that " there is not left even the smallest thicket or clump behind which to take shelter from peering eyes." Yet Freud saw that the antisocial instincts, when they are " sublimated," may become the source of the very greatest things. He attacks only " repressed " instincts.

naïve than pride in shocking the moral susceptibilities of
society. The apache who delights to see his photograph in
the newspapers and for whom an appearance in criminal court makes a red-letter day is out for much the same
thing. This desire to collide with public opinion is indeed
a great tribute thereto. Vanity for vanity, I think I prefer
those who flatter public opinion to those who seek notoriety
by defying it. Nevertheless, there is in literature a whole
tradition of satanism. Apart from burlesque comedy, there
are the romantic and macabre bravadoes of the " Young
France " group, the Boussingots of 1830. There is Dorian
Gray, or, still worse, Monsieur de Phocas, who amuse
themselves by shocking the bourgeoisie with paradoxes;
or Barbey d'Aurevilly, rejoicing in the idea of a married
priest and savouring black masses at his side.

But in order to take pleasure in the idea of the Host
dragged through the mud, one must first believe that it con-
tains a divine presence. In the same way, in order to flout
vice, one must first be certain that it exists.

Thus when Gide writes: " I have known all the passions
and all the vices," the reference is to vice as understood by
conventional morality, in which he does not believe. But
since he uses the word " vice " without either commentary
or clear indication, his phrase remains equivocal.

As a matter of fact, Gide is by no means averse to shocking the reader by producing an impression of sacrilege in
order to rouse his attention, but he hopes that he will soon
be undeceived by the context and the better able to grasp
the underlying thought, which is altogether different.

In this direction none of his books is more characteristic than *L'Immoraliste,* whose title itself is a play on words: Michel is actually a very moral creature putting into practice and individualist ethic which is not that of the crowd. Thus when he declares — in a celebrated episode — that young Moktir, the Arab boy, has been his " favourite " since the day he saw him steal a pair of scissors, it is not because *according to social laws* the theft is reprehensible that he delights in seeing what would be nothing more than an uninteresting sacrilege, but because he sees in the theft the expression of wild, free instinct which may be the early indication of a nature rich in possibilities.[1]

There can, moreover, be no possible doubt as to the author's real intention, if one is willing to attend as closely as he demands. When Bernard, having stolen his parents' letters by removing the cover of the marble-topped table, thinks over what he has done, he asks himself: " Was it wrong of me to read those letters? " And perhaps it is wrong according to objective social morality, which condemns the action in itself, but not according to *his own* conscience, which feels the need of getting clear on the subject of his family. And this examination of his conscience reassures him so much that, if one were to accuse him of being a " lock-picker," he would be sincerely scandalized. Like Lafcadio, like all Gide's characters, he is essentially moral.

[1] The damaging expression: *One must be prepared for anything in his case* . . . is the same as the expression of admiration: *This is a man from whom everything may be expected.* The man of genius, like the debauchee, will behave unexpectedly — that is to say, without regard to conventional rules, by giving free rein to the energies of his deepest being.

It is therefore astonishing that Gide himself should so often have been regarded as an " immoralist." Doubtless he likes it to be known that he flouts current morality, but he soon reveals the fact that he pays tribute to another. It is true he takes a wicked delight in first allowing it to be thought that he believes in the rules he defies. But just as, when he plumbs the unconscious, he delights in getting the better of the Devil, so, in his art, does he amuse himself by mystifying the reader.

If his enemies have taken him for a devil incarnate, they have fallen into his trap. When Massis is horrified because Gide writes of one of Barrès's characters: [1] " If Racadot had never left Lorraine, he would never have become a murderer; but then I should not have found him in the least interesting," he does not see that it is not the crime, regarded as reprehensible, which interests Gide, but the inner condition, the more or less unconscious instincts which drove Racadot to this criminal action. Gide, fencing with words, reaches his aim. He succeeds in " scaring " his public by revealing to them the relativity of morals. It is for the reader to take note of his own prejudices.

Thus sacrilege, with Gide, is above all things a psychological device. It is a way of surprising, disconcerting, and " disquieting " the reader in order to allow him to perceive the extraordinary complexity of the inner life of every human being.

And indeed the confused, darkly stirring feelings hidden

---

[1] In *Les Déracinés*.

in the unconscious are not to be expressed in the densities of language. The proper business of the artist is to *suggest*. In seeking to disquiet the reader, Gide is trying to communicate to him, by suggestion, the sense of the profound mysteries of humanity which words are powerless to convey. It is for this reason that his sentences often seem to have a content in some way surpassing that which they contain.

The writer gives us his thought enclosed. It is in ourselves that it must blossom and expand. By this mysterious act of germination the work of art enables us to recover that in the inner life which is intangible but, in the true sense of the word, vital.

4

BEING AND SEEMING—SINCERITY AND
TRUTH

IN a state of duality, duped, victim of his own disguised desires, can the man who undertakes the examination of his conscience never reach truth? But even before he can ask himself how he shall attain to sincerity, society puts a preliminary question: Ought one to be sincere? Ought one, in every case, without exception, publicly to unveil truth?

It is an old problem of morality, but one whose melodramatic aspect, the aspect so often presented in the theatre, seems alone to be recognized,

What is the problem stated by Ibsen in *The Wild Duck*? Should we denounce the illusions of our friends or our relations at the risk of destroying their happiness? The answer forces itself upon us: in the first place we have no right to invade the privacy of others and settle, on their behalf, the difficulties of their moral life. Since truth is very often incompatible with happiness, one may risk one's own, but not that of another. One may reveal only

123

the truth about one's *own* life.[1] Thus the horrible secret which Gide's Œdipe wishes to divulge in the hearing of the people is primarily related to his own existence. " I do not want a happiness that is made up of error and ignorance . . ." cried the hero. " *For my part,* I have no need of happiness." Gide is undoubtedly one of those who has carried furthest the need for unmasking oneself and yielding up one's *arrière-pensées;* yet he has always refrained from speaking of those dearest to him, feeling that he could not assail their peace of mind.[2]

Those who have believed in the necessity of intervening in the lives of others have generally been religious-minded persons, confessors and puritans. The results of their desire to convert and to save the souls of their contemporaries have sometimes been revolting. Mark Twain tells an admirable little story of two old Huguenots who compelled a little girl to confess to her dying mother a petty untruth, a terrible fault in the eyes of puritan morality. That this might kill the mother matters nothing so long as the child is not left with the lie on her conscience. Let her acknowledge it quickly, before her mother is gone, lest the sin should become irreparable and inexpugnable!

It is against this unhappy principle of invariable *truth-telling* that Gide reacts by assuming an individualist attitude: one must tell only *one's own* truth. The former rule

---

[1] One ought also to consider the way such a revelation may react upon others.

[2] " I practise discretion," he writes, " only on behalf of what is confided to me. In regard to what I learn for myself, I admit that my curiosity is boundless."

is nevertheless generally given to the child, who will find it quite natural to answer one day, when his grandfather asks why he does not kiss him: Because you are too ugly. The horrified mother will exclaim: Child, you must not say that! — Why not? Haven't you told me to say what I think? Politeness and good manners will thus appear to the child to be a vast system of lies organized by grown persons, while in reality these conventions are a vital necessity; life would be impossible if one day our skulls were to become transparent and reveal all our thoughts. A moral law which flies in the face of such obvious facts is not only absurd, but is itself a source of hypocrisy.

It can happen, however, that the individual who tells *his own* truth may wound the feelings of those for whom he has affection. It is so in the moving incident, related by Wilde in *De Profundis,* where one of the friends of his youth comes to visit him in prison and tells him that he believes none of the calumnies spread abroad about him during his trial, and he will always remain for him the old Wilde he so greatly esteemed. . . . Tragic moment for the imprisoned writer! Ought Wilde to undeceive this friend and risk losing him? He did not hesitate to do so. Neither, in similar circumstances, did Gide.

The conflict here presented arises from the fact that our relations and friends " construct an image of us that bears very little semblance to reality," so that when we reveal our actual selves, they are filled with consternation. But more often it is we ourselves who have contributed to the mistaken opinion they have of us. We have either been unable or unwilling to show ourselves as we are from the first. Constant sincerity on our part would have eliminated the conflict. And one may therefore be allowed to point out that the question as to whether we ought to reveal our lives to those who misjudge us resolves itself into another: How can we escape being misjudged? And thus we rediscover our first question, the only one that really matters: <u>How can one be sincere?</u>

" Oh, Laura," cries Bernard, one of Gide's most sympathetic characters, " how I wish that all my life, in response even to the lightest touch, I could ring true, clear, and authentic! . . ." For Gide, sincerity is the point of departure for all real morality, every great undertaking. Without hesitation he calls it the loveliest of the virtues, but also the most difficult.

For almost everyone rings false, is the prey of false sentiments which stand in the way of mutual understanding, knowledge, and love. Take Passavent, for instance, the diabolical incarnation of insincerity, the very type of the " humbug." Gide makes him a man of letters, a poet of the *avant-garde*, absolutely unscrupulous, ceaselessly plundering his associates, incapable of anything beyond reducing the whole of life to words or epigrams. But what of the ordinary man, Robert, the average middle-class man? He, too, is playing up the whole time. When he defends fireside virtues, the grandeur of religion, of patriotism — things which fill his whole existence — what is he doing but playing a part, putting up a façade? ". . . All these marvellous sentiments," retorts his wife, with hatred in her voice, " according to you it would be madness [on my part] to wonder whether you really experience them! " But children, are not they at least sincere? Gide reveals them as even more desirous of boasting, more defiant and inclined to show off. One of them becomes a thief in order to astonish his playfellows, and little Boris takes his own life partly in a spirit of bravado.

In everyone vanity opens an abyss between being and appearing, between the reality of the individual and his representation of himself. " By a reversal of the natural order," writes Schopenhauer, " man seems to consider public opinion as the reality of his existence, while that which goes on within his own consciousness is regarded as the ideal part." And Nietzsche, in his turn, exclaims: " Do at least be a little honest with yourselves. We are not in the theatre . . . where the neighbour rules, where one *becomes* a neighbour."

But how avoid telling lies when one does not even know that one is lying? The worst of insincerity is that it is almost always unconscious. Our minds are so full of ready-made ideas, customs, conventions, and foregone conclusions that we do not even notice how they deform everything of which they take cognizance. A psychologist [1] who has made a special study of the evidence given in courts of law has estimated that nine tenths of it is worth-

---

[1] The philosopher Claparède.

less, not because the witnesses are necessarily dishonest, but because they have neither seen nor heard with any exactitude that which they report. Éveline, although she is sincere, is so prejudiced against Robert that everything he says produces a single resonance in her mind. " Hearing him speak, she hears lies." Man calls these prejudices his convictions. The stronger they are, the greater is his feeling of sincerity — and his blindness. Nor is this all. The character, as it solidifies and stiffens, acquires all kinds of false twists which become irreparable. Sometimes humility, sometimes ostentatiousness, infatuation, or pride, so characteristic of believers and ascetics, for ever sets the individual apart from his real self.

Conventional morality incites us to adopt these deforming attitudes. For even to have a passionate attachment to a moral ideal that is at variance with our own nature takes us outside ourselves and makes us artificial and hypocritical. To try to become the ideal being one is not built to be is to condemn oneself to *appearance* instead of to *reality*. Traditional duty puts us under the obligation of conforming to a ready-made model of virtue, the same for everyone and to which many can attain only by going disguised for the whole of their lives. But traditional moralists would appear scarcely to condemn those who *affect* to be " honest folk." What they fear most is the man who acts according to his nature, the natural man.[1] " Everything amuses you," writes the horrified Fénelon to one of his pupils, " everything scatters you and plunges you back into the *natural*."

---

[1] We have already read Claudel's dictum: " There is one thing infinitely more odious than hypocrisy, and that is cynicism."

Yet to be natural, to be oneself, is the whole of sincerity.
Gide has observed, not without surprise, that this idea of
sincerity, if introduced into traditional morality, would
ruin it.[1]

We are now nearing one of the fundamental aspects of
our author's thought. If sincerity consists in being oneself,
how can that self attain to it? How can we grasp our own
authentic feelings, down to their roots in the darkness of the
unconscious?

Gide has perceived how especially difficult it is to be
sincere in love.[2] Is it, he asks, love or hatred that Dostoievski's hero Trousotzki feels for his wife's lover? For many
years the three have been a unified group. When the lover
falls ill, the husband tends him as if he were his own son.
Then suddenly, when he believes him to be sleeping, he
tries to attack him with a knife. Immediately afterwards he
is weeping and sobbing. Had Trousotzki been sincere in
the demonstrations of friendship lavished upon the lover
during the last twenty years, and yesterday in tending him
with such solicitude? Perfectly sincere, replies Dostoievski.
He loved and hated him at the same time. But *he did not
know* whither this love would lead him: to " the kiss *and*

[1] Gide has raised this question in *L'École des Femmes* and, more particularly, in *Robert*. On carefully re-reading these two small books I have
come to the conclusion that their real subject, the actual conflict between
Robert and his wife, Éveline, revolves round this question of sincerity in
relation to morality. Whilst Robert quotes Fénelon with approval, Éveline
believes it right to seek the good in remaining sincere, remaining herself —
that is to say, in forcing herself to develop and accentuate the best that is
in her.

[2] In his novels Gide has not carried his analysis so far as did Proust.
It is in his critical work, and particularly in his *Dostoïevski*, that his ideas
on this subject are to be found.

the knife-thrust, both at once." These were the authentic expression of his state of consciousness.

Thus love and hatred, pleasure and pain, all the shifting fugitive emotions of our deepest being ceaselessly interpenetrate and combine like the drops of water in a lake. One may attempt to express and define them in circumscribed, fragmentary, motionless words, but the task is almost impossible. Into what language, then, can we translate our inner emotions? What name can we give to the extraordinary mixture of feelings actuating a Trousotzki?

And what makes sincerity still more difficult to achieve is that the ego, drawn along through time and ceaselessly evolving, is daily, hourly, modified, is changing every moment. When Robert married Éveline, it was the girl of twenty he loved in her. But today the beloved face that used to melt his heart has lost something of its glow; it's expression is lacking in warmth, and at times Robert cannot believe that the woman he now sees is really Éveline. Religious morality, however, making marriage an indissoluble tie, assumes, or wishes to assume, that love never changes. Actually, the sentiment that yesterday held truth, may today be empty of it. At what instant can we secure it, since it is never for two successive moments of its duration identical with itself? — You say, says Robert to Éveline, that I am not what you thought I was. But, then, neither are you what I believed you to be. How can one ever know whether one is indeed what one believes oneself to be? " [1]

---

[1] "It is a long way," says Bernard, in *Les Faux-Monnayeurs*, "from what I thought I was to what perhaps I am in reality."

" This word ' sincerity,' " cries Gide, " is amongst those whose meaning troubles me the most." — This irritating problem — he adds — is everything to me. To know whether I feel what I believe myself to be feeling; whether I am my single self, or double, or triple, or nothing; whether I flow from my consciousness or am coincident therewith; if, beneath the continuous deterioration of body and soul, anything of me remains constant. Here is the whole problem of personality ceaselessly modified in time and space; of dark, immense, disquieting personality, extending away along mysterious avenues, while consciousness illuminates only a very small point.

The scope of sincerity must therefore always be limited. All that man can hope is gradually to extend it more and more. Perhaps he reaches complete sincerity, at rare moments in *free activity* or in the *act of creation*, when the ego and its expression are merged in a living unity as, in infinity, asymptote and curve meet again.

*   *   *

From Gide's criticism of absolute sincerity flows an almost parallel criticism of the idea of absolute truth. Just as moral consciousness is unable to attain to the one, so also is intelligence unable to reach the other.

Nevertheless man, who imagines himself to be made in the image of God, has believed that his reason can grasp the whole universe, explain the world in syllogisms, and reduce reality to dogmas. Who shall " deliver " us, cries Gide, " from the heavy chains of logic? *Therefore* is a word the poet should ignore," [1] and a word, I would add, whose use should be forbidden to most of us.

Nothing is more characteristic than Gide's well-justified defiance of abstract logic, of vain philosophical discussions. He knows that no one has ever been convinced by argument, that light has never flowed thence, and that each party continues obstinately along his own way. — Don't corner my reason — Gide will say to those who contradict him, above all to believers. — I yield you the last word. Why " quibble "? Reason is always in the right. In prolonging itself the conversation will but increase our sense of the inanity of all discourse, and the vanity of all systems.

This particular attitude of Gide's has been more frequently misunderstood than any other. He has been accused of shirking the great problems and of running away the moment there is any question of taking up a definite position. But is not the giving of an answer very frequently being content with a mere formula? The public likes, " on hearing the name of Pasteur . . . to be able immediately to think: oh yes, rabies; Nietzsche? the superman; Curie? radium. . . ." But nothing is easier or less honest than this sort of summarizing, wherein all the complexity of truth is first reduced to a phrase, a sham, empty word, and then repeated with " violence, persistence, and uniformity," in order to drive it into the minds of the crowd. If this kind of conjuring with reality is to be called *answering*, then, certainly, Gide does not answer.

Does this mean that he has never shown himself a little

[1] Unpublished Journal.

too much afraid of logic? It is possible the artist in him
has kept him a little remote from general ideas. This it is
which explains his fear of philosophy, and particularly of
metaphysics, which for him is nothing more than the sterile
play of ideas. Yet the philosophers, like the poets, are
creators. . . .

Whatever may be his reservations, Gide has never been
malicious in regard to reason. To criticize it and to set
limits to the operation of its results is to enlarge it. It is
because man has been able to perceive that every truth is
relative to himself that reason is his glory and his pride. In
this sense Gide is a convinced rationalist.

But exactly because this remarkable instrument of reason
is in our hands, we ought not to abuse it as do only too
many religious people and other dogmatists. We ought to
use it with prudence, patience, and modesty. Gide himself
has given us an admirable example. His way of dealing
with deliberate and even with unconscious trickery, his
detestation of the falsification of texts for polemical purposes, his obvious desire to present the propositions he is
attacking, in his novels, in the most favourable light, his
habit of occasionally presenting his own view in the words
of an opponent [1] and always setting down documentary
evidence in its original form, without either paraphrase or
modification, makes his criticism of psychology the finest
possible tribute to reason.

For in the last analysis the proper business of reason is
to clear the path of pitfalls and misunderstandings and to

[1] Cf. *Robert.*

diminish the margin of error. This achieved, the task of reason is at an end. Being no more than a path which takes us in a given direction, it cannot reach the absolute. There is always a moment when we must leave the straight path of reason and plunge into the thicket. There is always a moment when, like Gide's Philoctète or his pastor, we must say: " I see no further, I do not know. . . ." In this there is neither evasion nor scepticism, in the bad sense of the word, but rather reason rising superior to itself. If Gide's work is primarily interrogative, it is because most problems are badly stated and vanish as soon as reason disposes of the sophistry implied in the very way they are set forth.[1] On the other hand, once the terms of a problem are clearly and luminously stated, the answer will usually be immediately evident. At this moment reason can but retire; truth speaks for itself and prevails by virtue of its immediacy.

It is an intuition of our deepest being, rising from the same source as sincerity, rarely surging up save in these exceptional moments of clairvoyance, enthusiasm, or delirium, when man calls upon all the forces of his personality, save in *liberty* or in *creation*. . . .

---

[1] The philosopher Meyerson has explained that control, as applied to science, consists solely in eliminating the chances of error; what is called a controlled fact, an exact fact, is therefore *nothing more* than a fact disentangled, as far as is possible, from the illusions of the senses and of the mind.

5

FREE OR GRATUITOUS ACTION

WHEN Prométhée [1] left the Caucasus and came down the
boulevard de la Madeleine " between the fourth and fifth
hours of an autumn afternoon . . . different Parisian
celebrities passed continually before his eyes. — Where
are they going,' Prométhée asked himself, and settling himself in a café with a bock he asked: — Waiter, where are
they going? ' "

And the waiter replied: — If his lordship could see them
coming and going every day as I do, he might as well ask
me where they come from. It must be the same place, as
they pass every day. I say to myself: Since they always
return, it is because they have not found . . .' " They have
not found their personalities, and it is because they seek
and do not find them that they create this impression of
useless activity.

Each one of us, however, is accompanied by an individual conscience, as is Prométhée by his eagle. " An eagle,
as a matter of fact . . . shall I tell you? We all have
one of our own. . . . But we do not take it about with

[1] *Prométhée mal enchaîné* (English translation, *Prometheus Ill-Bound*).

us in Paris. . . . Eagles are embarrassing. . . ." When Prométhée, still seated at his table on the terrace, " calls his eagle to him, the bird, enormous from afar but, close at hand, not so very big after all, comes for the café like a whirlwind, bursts through the window and, with a blow of its wing, crushes the eye of a customer. ' Just look what he's done! ' ": in a capital a conscience is a great encumbrance. It is more comfortable to sell it or stifle it.

Yet it is in becoming conscious of himself that a man becomes free. In making the effort of discovering his personality he may attain gratuitous action and find it a marvellous recompense. " I have thought for a long time," says Prométhée, " that it is just this that distinguishes man from the animals. A gratuitous action. . . . Do you understand? . . . An action . . . *born of itself* . . . therefore without a master; a *free action,* an original action? " [1]

But for almost everyone the effort which leads to liberty is too arduous and painful; and lucidity too terrifying. If a few are inclined to self-examination, they are hampered by the conditions imposed by their material existence. Man " is operated " by the habits, the heredity, the surroundings which determine his activities as a whole. Waking in the morning, he thinks he must go to the place where he works. Does he really think this? His thought is an unconscious reflex which makes him get up. He dresses, goes out, goes to his factory or his office. Is there a single gesture in his day that is not mechanical? A single instant during

---

[1] A gratuitous action is, for Gide, most certainly a free action. The whole of this chapter is founded upon that concept.

which he breaks away from his daily preoccupations and asks himself before acting: Why . . . yes . . . why? Yet even one moment of such consciousness per day would be worth having. . . .

In *Paludes* Gide shows us the idlers, the men of letters themselves, doing the same thing every day and hardly anything else. " Who is Bernard? The one who goes to Octave's every Thursday. — Who is Octave? The one who receives Bernard every Thursday. . . ." " To be happy in one's blindness, to believe one sees clearly in order not to try to see " is, however, the worst form of slavery. Behind a humorous exterior *Paludes* hides the distress inspired by the sight of average, mediocre humanity resigned to its fate.

Yet Gide believes that man can save himself. There is a note of hope to be discerned in his work. He opposes to gregarious humanity, to all those who try to " be as ordinary as possible," a few wonderful adolescents, such as Bernard or Lafcadio, who desire only to be themselves.

At the age of twenty body and soul, not yet scored by habits, still respond to the calls made upon them. Whether Lafcadio is climbing into a burning house to save a child or is simply walking up a mountain side, his movements are equally free and natural, inspired by the same joyous certainty and ease. He has not been submitted either to traditional education at home or to the routine of school. He has been taught to express his own temperament, to follow his bent. . . .

But this is not enough for the attainment of freedom. Each one must " follow his bent . . . but in an upward direction," and know how to sacrifice certain desires and temptations to the deep law of his being. Their appeal, sometimes very powerful, *isolated and almost independent* of us, distracts and turns us away from ourselves. When Lafcadio has given way to anger or to involuntary pride, he takes a small knife, " and thrusts it through his trousers pocket straight into his thigh." [1] By means of these self-inflicted punishments he submits his pride, his timidity, his obstinate, averted, hidden feelings to the light of conscience, where they fuse in a unique whole. In freedom he has learned to discipline his deepest instincts, which he liberated from their cavern. He has taken possession of himself (in the exact sense of the words, he has himself in hand). Henceforth he is ready to act. . . .

If I were to try to define a free action, I should say it is that which proceeds from the *whole* personality, its *whole* contents, from the conscious and the unconscious, from past and present, from body and mind. I should say it is an action which puts an end to our duality and reconciles us to ourselves. All the frictions of our inner life have ceased. Action and actor seem at last to coincide. Free action represents us, as the work of art represents the artist.

Here is Lafcadio, travelling by rail, alone in a compartment with Amédée Fleurissoire, a stranger to him. Lafcadio

---

[1] Lafcadio even keeps a record of these knife-thrusts in a little account-book, where one may read: ". . . For having answered before Protos = 1 t.; for having had the last word = 1 t.; for having wept on hearing of Faby's death = 4 t. (The t's stand for the thrusts of the knife.)

feels perfectly at ease and thinks to himself: This dismal, pimply fellow, standing at the door and struggling to fasten his detachable collar, as hard as cardboard — why shouldn't I throw him out of the train *just for fun, without any real reason?* " If I can count slowly up to twelve without seeing a fire anywhere in the country," the noodle will be safe. He counts: one, two, three . . . ten! A fire! One good push sends Fleurissoire flying out of the train to his death. Such is Lafcadio's " gratuitous action."

But is it really gratuitous? Has Gide chosen a good example?

No doubt this action strikes us as absurd. But absurdity is often one of the characteristics of free action. " If . . ." writes Bergson, " some novelist, breaking through the cunningly woven fabric of our conventional self, should show us, beneath our apparent logicality, a fundamental *absurdity*," this writer would have made us suspect the extraordinary nature and the wealth of our deeper self. Gide certainly reveals the absurdity of the action, but does he also reveal to us, by means of this crime, the extraordinary wealth of the character in question? Certainly the logic of feeling is quite different from that of our reason. " The kiss *and* the knife-thrust, both at once," wrote Dostoievski, " were [for Trousotzki] the perfectly logical solution." [1] In everyday life clear ideas and simple feelings remain crystallized on the surface of consciousness. But the true

---

[1] Gide maintains that the French novelists have not dared to depict such contradictory states of mind. They give their characters unity and continuity and make types of them: the miser, the jealous husband, the paterfamilias. A sentiment, or an isolated passion, rather than a man with the whole of his personality, is what they try to bring to life.

psychologist will break through the solidified crust and discover, deep down within consciousness, a mixture of in-
coherent images. In order to express the vital depths of a
personality, Gide has been moved to create " an inconsequent being," inconsequent in the matter of *reason*. An
inconsequent being? That is Lafcadio, exactly defined.

The inconsequence of his action ought, however, to correspond with a more inward, more secret psychological
mechanism than that of intellectual logic.[1] But this one does
not discover because his action is without motive.

Without motive? That is, indeed, another characteristic
of gratuitous activity. In free activity, writes Bergson, we
sometimes try " to discover what reason has determined
our action, and find that we have no reason at all (and perhaps even that we have acted against our reason). But that,
precisely, in certain cases, is the *best of reasons*." And
Gide: Lafcadio's " reason for committing the crime was
exactly that there were no reasons for committing it."

Here, however, we must make what is apparently a delicate distinction, but is nevertheless a fundamental one.
If *free activity* appears to be motiveless, it is because the
individual has not acted under the influence of any particular emotion (cupidity, jealousy, anger, or fear). He has
freed himself from these isolated desires. The true motive
of his action is, therefore, the *whole* of his personality.
This is what we mean when we say that the action has no

[1] If I needed to give examples of free, inconsequent actions, I should
deal with the works of Gide in succession. These may appear contradictory
when compared with each other, but each one has been a free, authentic
expression of his personality.

cause — that is to say, *no particular cause.* When one writes a book with one's whole soul, the cause of this action is neither the desire for wealth, nor for honour, nor for the astonishment of one's contemporaries. One writes this book without motives, because it has no other motive than the expression of the personality of the author, the representation of a faithful image of himself.

Yet, even in regard to *the most determined action,* it may equally happen that the motive escapes us; but then another kind of motive is in question, a *particular* motive. We shall examine later on the case of a certain Redureau, who, in 1912, murdered seven people, *apparently without reason.* Actually the action had many causes, which were not discovered because the effect (the septuple murder) seemed too disproportionate to its motives.[1]

Speaking more generally, there are actions committed under the influence of violent emotion surging up from the unconscious, obsessions so sudden and so irresistible that we believe ourselves to be acting freely when in reality we are acting as if under the influence of hypnotic suggestion. This resemblance is very confusing and makes free activity extremely difficult to recognize. Thus the most determined actions are sometimes the most deceptive. They simulate the spontaneous nature of free action; like free action they are inconsequent and apparently causeless. Yet they are its exact opposite.

[1] The motives were perhaps fear or anger, then terror in face of the enormity of the first act, and finally a certain lack of mental balance (denied, however, by the medical consultants) which allowed the first causes to become determining.

Does not Lafcadio's crime belong to this last category? Was he not impelled to his act by an unconscious, isolated obsession of his ego? By the irritation the painful spectacle of an ugly and clumsy person may produce in a young creature full of the sense of well-being? [1]

Yet Gide tells us that Lafcadio's crime is " disinterested." But can an action be disinterested that is carried out under the pressure of an unconscious obsession? Is it possible to claim that gratuitous actions in general are disinterested? [2] Must we not recognize that the egoistic and altruistic tendencies existing side by side in any complete individual join forces to compose the vital unity of the ideal gratuitous action? If Lafcadio were acting freely — that is to say, with the *whole* of his consciousness — his natural altruism and human sympathy would surely prevent him from taking life. It is because this altruism and this sympathy seem to be temporarily asleep, because they take no part in his action, that he throws Fleurissoire through the window. " The greater number of crimes being committed in a state of somnambulism," writes Valéry, " it should be the business of morality to awaken the sleeper in time."

---

[1] When Fleurissoire, clumsily handling the electric light switch, turns the light on, then off, then on again. Lafcadio thinks *impatiently:* " Will he soon have done playing with that switch? What is he doing now? "

[2] " Disinterested " is an expression that lends itself to a sort of play on words. When Bernard, or Octave, *interests* himself in his family or his country, he is more *disinterested* than when he discusses a matter of business with a tradesman. The *interest* moving us to act reaches an increasingly high moral level in proportion as the action becomes more and more conscious — that is to say, more free. But *interest does not disappear, it changes its nature.* In the end, in freedom, interest and disinterestedness seem to be one.

Nevertheless Gide depicts Lafcadio as being completely master of himself. Is it possible that from this self-possession there should come forth an action having the characteristics of a sudden impulse? We seem here to be dealing with unlikelihood, a psychological contradiction arising, we repeat, not from the intrinsic absurdity of the action, but from the action itself.[1] Yet it is difficult to speak of a lack of verisimilitude in regard to books such as *Les Caves du Vatican* or *Prométhée mal enchaînée*, two wonderful extravaganzas presented from beginning to end in a form designedly paradoxical and often grotesque.

But Gide himself has most certainly realized all the difficulties of the question, and it is perhaps for this reason that he had sometimes seemed to repudiate the paternity of the expression: " gratuitous action," or at least to consider it as a novelist's device. At other times, and particularly in relation to the Surrealists, he has recognized its importance, an importance which seems to have been overlooked, to my great astonishment, by certain of his most attentive readers.

Though the example of gratuitous action given in *Les Caves du Vatican* is disputable, Gide has nevertheless admirably described, *before the action*, the method which leads to self-consciousness, and, *after the action*, the conditions of the state of gratuitousness.

A free man passes beyond *traditional morality*; places himself, so to speak, above it. This is one of the most im-

[1] The idea of gratuitous crime seems to have been " in the air " during the Symbolist period. I find an analogous idea in the very title of De Quincey's essay: *On Murder Considered as One of the Fine Arts.*

passioning and also one of the most mysterious characteristics of freedom. Intelligence is incapable of understanding
it. All reasoning on the subject of freedom seems to lead to
determinism. A philosopher like Bergson may prove that
this reasoning is *erroneous*, but none the less its hold upon
our minds is so habitual that we perpetually return to it.[1]

In reality a free action is not in itself intelligible and we
can do no more than be aware of it. It comes forth like the
plant from the seed or the fruit from the flower. Like
everything that has the property of life, it can only be lived.
The philosopher who has the most ardently defended the
idea of liberty has been able to demonstrate it only by
refuting deterministic theses and then, having cleared the

[1] This reasoning is multiform, but based, I believe, always upon the same
error. Freedom, instead of being regarded as the faculty which admits of
the expression of the *whole* personality, is seen as characterized by its
power of choosing. Every time we declare (as we very frequently do) that a
free action might have been *other* than it was, we think of the individual
as having made a choice between the accomplished action and some other
action. This way of speaking *unconsciously implies* a false analysis of the
deliberation preceding the action. If the individual had had to choose between two actions, we must suppose two conflicting motives within him,
and his choice of one of the two. But if these two motives were of equal
strength, he would never have been able to decide. And if one was stronger
than the other, there was nothing for him to choose; he was no longer free.

This way of analysing free action ends either in determinism or in insoluble contradictions. It bears, in fact, upon the deliberation preceding the
action (and not upon the action itself), and it will never serve to explain
how one can pass from the one to the other. It regards as *invariable* motives
which are modified at every moment, as is also the representation, in
advance, of two possible actions. When, therefore, we maintain that a free
action might have been *other* than it was, we abstract the time-element, and
the expression becomes meaningless. What is required is a quite different
analysis of deliberation, replacing consciousness within duration, and
thereby enabling us to realize that all we can say of free activity is that
it is the expression of the whole self at a given moment of time. But reason
always reverts to the idea of choice, seen statically and creating the illusion
of determinism. Reason always tends to eliminate time.

ground, asking us to retire into ourselves and recall the rare moments in our lives when we have made decisions in conformity with all our aspirations.

I alone, then, can tell myself whether or no I have acted freely, I alone can appreciate my responsibility. Of course, so long as I am subject to the chain of cause and effect, society has a hold over me (and it is at these moments that society will give me the benefit of extenuating circumstances [1]); but when I attain to freedom, society cannot *judge* my action, because, for society, the motives and the intentions of this action have become unintelligible and there remains nothing but unlikelihood and senselessness. " A gratuitous action! " cries le Miglionnaire. " There is nothing more demoralizing! " And Gide adds: " I will not speak of public morality because there is no such thing."

The contradiction between free action and traditional morality is still more striking when considered from the point of view of Miglionnaire, who, in *Prométhée*, is " le bon Dieu." Since God knows everything, He foresees the future and knows in advance what man will do. How, then, can man act freely and be responsible for his actions? Centuries of theologians and philosophers have come up against this insoluble problem. " What I have done," says Gide's Œdipe (referring to murder and incest), " I could not not have done." And Œdipe rebels against the priest Tiresias, who demands repentance for a crime that seems to have been deadly. " Most base treachery on God's part," he cries, " to

---

[1] To-day, in principle, there is *responsibility* only when the action is *free* and *conscious*, only when liberty begins.

me, intolerable. . . ." No, Œdipe will not serve a God who seems to drive humanity into the pathway of evil. . . . When men reason about liberty, they believe they cannot act otherwise than as God has decided. For the Greeks, Fate was superior to the gods. It was written, thinks the Muslim, or at any rate it is thus that the European interprets his thought. Nevertheless, despite the reasonings of deceptive logic, freedom prevails, at certain exceptional moments, by virtue of an immediate and irresistible intuition.

But this individual intuition escapes the reasonings of others. Neither the moralist nor the judge [1] nor the priest can postulate responsibility in the case of a free action. And it is in this sense that it sets the individual outside moral and social laws.

This is not merely a figure of speech; it is a psychological truth. By means of a free action the individual liberates himself from his social wrappings, his respectability, his uniform. . . .

When he throws poor Amédée Fleurissoire through the window, it seems as though the young, free Lafcadio were casting forth conventional morality, as though light-heartedness were triumphing over the spirit of gloom, and as though Gide himself had got rid of all his puritanism. By action Lafcadio has cleansed his conscience and is reborn younger, happier, emancipated. " Oh, dizzy adventure! Oh, perilous pleasure! "

[1] See Part IV, Chapter iii, " Justice," where is considered the question of the particular point of view of judicial tribunals.

" Whichever way the wind blows from now on," he cries, " it will be in a good quarter." He feels that henceforth he can do anything and everything. That does not mean that he will do just anything,[1] but that *he is now adapted to life's most unexpected circumstances.* Similarly, when he tosses up before making a decision, he is not introducing the element of chance, for as often as not he ignores the result of the toss in order to act according to the deep-laid law of his conscience, having used the toss to help him not to turn away from making a decision.

Between thought and action, imagination and realization, most people deliberate, discuss, become involved in irrelevancies, and thus lose the best of themselves. A man who is not prepared for unpremeditated activity would doubtless be unwise to act spontaneously. But in a state of freedom the individual is always ready to act; that is why we say he is ready for anything, ready to take any risk. Moreover, he is afraid of nothing: he knows that the consequences of action are almost infinite, that action engages us in an immense, terrible, and unpredictable adventure . . . and that one has " no more right to revoke than in playing chess." But such a being as Lafcadio does not draw back when danger threatens. He " goes all lengths "; he leaps into a void.

This feeling of complete availability gives Lafcadio so

---

[1] I think Lafcadio goes too far when he says: " I might just as well have strangled this poor old woman whose sack I have taken on my shoulders." If through a free action he has passed beyond social morality, it does not follow that he should be able to act indifferently. He remains subject to his individual morality.

much assurance that he succeeds in all he undertakes. The ordinary mortal speaks of his " chances," but chance in this connexion is but the faculty of grasping every propitious opportunity for action.

Henceforward free activity becomes a game. If the child seems to be the very image of freedom, it is not because he is *morally pure* (on the contrary, he is " pitiless," full of vanity and deceit), but because he *plays,* because he seems *free.* If children help to cure Michel, it is because they represent for him the ideal of freedom. And if he prefers Moktir to all the others, it is because the theft of the scissors represents another free activity. . . . The rusty, worthless scissors are stolen by Moktir for no other reason than the fun of the deed. Lafcadio, himself little more than a child, has also indulged in " petty larceny," not for the sake of acquiring things, but for the pleasure of making them disappear as if by sleight of hand.

But we must not deceive ourselves. The child is only the *symbol* of freedom, he has no self-mastery and perpetually relapses into slavery. He weeps, abandons himself to misery, is the prey of fear and desire. His freedom is spontaneous, but frail and unstable because it is not the result of a slow and persevering acquisition of consciousness.

Even games demand an apprenticeship. Only after long training can the diver make easily and naturally his trajectory through space. To act for the joy of action, of expressing oneself, of being, does not mean, we must repeat, to make just any sort of gestures, but to act according to one's deepest nature, and this cannot be attained save at the cost of laborious and painful effort.

". . . If you do not lovingly succour your eagle," explains Prométhée, " he will be grey and miserable . . . one must devote oneself to one's eagle . . . love him so that he may become beautiful. . . ." To begin with, Prométhée's eagle " was grey, ugly, stunted, surly, resigned, and miserable . . ." and Prométhée shed tears of pity over him. . . . " — Faithful bird,' said he, ' what is the matter with you? ' — I'm hungry,' said the eagle. — Eat,' said Prométhée, uncovering his liver. And the bird fed. — You are hurting me,' said Prométhée. Yet he continued to give daily more and more of himself and soon saw the eagle leave off fluttering just above the earth and learn to fly. — We will be off one day,' said the eagle. — Do you mean it? ' cried Prométhée. — Because I have become very strong, you very thin, and I can carry you.' — Eagle, my eagle . . . carry me away! ' And the eagle flew off with Prométhée. . . ."

Our personality is our *raison d'être*, but only on condition that we sacrifice it to ourselves. This is the price of creation and of liberty. " It is not people I like," says Prométhée, " but that which devours them." Therein lies the meaning of all individualist morality.

THE ROLE OF ART AND THE ART OF GIDE:
HIS STYLE

IF liberty opens to us the door of a marvellous life, it seems at first to impose upon our reason the necessity of choice. At every moment of time we can act only once. The whole of our vast and various wealth of feelings and imaginations can attain, at a given moment, only *a single form of action*, which will never be repeated. " Let all that can be [for me] be! . . ." cries Lafcadio. But all, alas, is reduced to one. The gratuitous action is unique. But our minds, placing themselves *before* or *after* the action, imagine its thousand other possible forms and regret them. . . .

" Choice," writes Gide, " seemed to me not so much selection, as repulsion of that which I had not chosen. . . . I never did anything but *this* or *that*. If I did this, I immediately regretted that. . . . With amazement I recognized the restrictedness of time. . . ." The necessity for choice is never more painful than in adolescence. The youthful Proust, faced by his bunch of grapes, *les jeunes filles en fleur*, wanted to possess them all at once and did not know which to choose. At the age of twenty Gide made himself miserable over the impossibility of undertaking every kind of study at once.

It is here that art comes to the rescue. It enables us to live, imaginatively, the forms of life we have been obliged to renounce. " I speak," writes Gide in *Les Nourritures terrestres*, " of countries I have never seen, of perfumes I have never breathed, of things I have never done. . . ." At this time Gide had just discovered Algeria, but this is only *one* of the countries he would have liked to know. So he writes his book: Naples, Malta, Granada, Damascus, Biskra, Peru; he is everywhere at one and the same moment. Art multiplies the journey he has undertaken, enlarging its possibilities almost to infinity. . . . Poetry gives him the gift of ubiquity.

But art, like day-dreaming, has its dangers. Under the influence of Symbolism and of his religious scruples, Gide, during his youth, came to prefer the possible to the actual. Hence the unvarying reproach of the critics: Gide had done nothing but look on. " What one does," he writes in his Journal [1] at the age of twenty, " is unimportant. What one can do is worth more than what one does." The state of " availability " immediately preceding action, the moment during which we believe that what we are about to do may acquire a thousand unforseen aspects — this exceptional moment seemed to him so fine, so exalting, that he would have liked to prolong it indefinitely. " O moment, remain unspent . . ." implores Faust. " O time, suspend thy

[1] Unpublished.

flight . . ." cries Lamartine at his moment of supreme happiness. But only God can transform the instant into eternity. Man lives in time, which has only one dimension and flows ceaselessly. His duty therefore is to act. And this is what Gide has increasingly affirmed the more fully he has entered into life. " One *must* choose . . ." says already *L'Immoraliste,* and in *Les Nourritures terrestres* he writes: " It is action that makes the splendour of mankind. . . ." In growing older, Gide has striven more and more not to spare himself either direct action or the explicit answering of questions.

Yet, if an action cannot be *lived,* it can be *dreamed,* and this dream, if it gives birth to a work of art, is itself an activity.

Thus it is that the artist will attempt to embody in his work those actions which, whether through fear of public opinion or by idleness or incapacity, he is prevented from carrying out in life. If he be a novelist, he will *make* the children of his spirit *act* on his behalf, he will intervene in their existence and speculate on their possibilities. If in his books Gide sometimes seems to be a kind of " voyeur," following with passionate curiosity the result of the experiments he has tried on his characters, it is because, while operating their destiny, he frees himself of his own temptations, his own remorse. Art, above all, has played for him this moral role. Like every authentic artist, he has allowed to blossom in his work the secret instincts, the occult desires and subversive ideas driven down into the unconscious by conventional ethics. Our books, he writes in the preface to

La Tentative Amoureuse, will have been " aspirations to-wards other lives, for ever *forbidden.*"

Moreover, art offers the same kind of compensation to the public. The spectators of a great drama believe that they are really sharing the violent, unbridled, or sublime passions of the hero, and when the curtain falls on the final act, they feel disappointed in returning to ordinary life. They once more become their social selves, but those wonderful hours of *freedom* have enabled them to give rein to some of the instincts repressed in the unconscious — large, dangerous emotions which have no place in daily life.

Although these awakened desires usually exhaust them-selves in the course of the spectacle, it sometimes happens that they later become active in daily life. It is then that we hear of the injurious influence of plays and books. But the result of this influence is unpredictable. In some cases it will extinguish these instincts, in others it will encourage them.

Proceeding from these considerations, Gide further de-clares that the more man is able to satisfy his passions *in life,* the more will they be bridled *in art* by formal rules. " Restore freedom of manners," he says, " and artistic re-straint will follow." He refers particularly to the Renais-sance, a period of free, luxuriant living wherein Shakspere, Ronsard, Petrarch, and even Michelangelo made so much use of the stern formality of the sonnet.

But this example would not appear to be a test. Is not

the essential art of Shakspere and of Michelangelo characterized rather by its free, romantic quality?

As a matter of fact, it is constraint rather than freedom of manners that seems to produce constraint in art. Rigid tradition gives birth to strict forms of expression. Never have writers been so restrained as during the conventional seventeenth century. To this Gide assents, but elsewhere, and in apparent contradiction to what has already been said.

What he maintains, then, is that hypocrisy in life, in withdrawing itself from art, *favours* art. It matters little, he says, that society and the artist should be subject to a common religion, however *severe*, and to a common morality, however narrow. But it is essential that society should give birth to a *small* group of cultivated persons serving an ideal they recognize *in common*. The artist belonging to this group will seek the sources of his art in a common fund of sentiments and ideas. He knows for whom he works, and what he produces will have style. This was the case with the Greeks and in the great classical centuries. Never, Gide maintains, has art blossomed under better conditions than in these great periods of history.

To-day the public is heterogeneous and comes from anywhere and everywhere. Its members have neither culture, tastes, nor *duties* in common. Therefore the artist is obliged to break with his time. He is to be seen either in isolation, " ideally flattering " a group of unknown future readers, or taking his chance with the vulgar crowd. In either case he risks perdition.

Undoubtedly a *more or less* orderly society is necessary

to art, and it can hardly flourish in periods of anarchy and social revolution. But it surprises me that Gide should seem to regret the order of the past, and that apparently he does not recognize in the inferiority of to-day's public the fact of a bourgeoisie that no longer has any actual ideal, and a proletariat (as those on the Left very rightly remark) which is not yet sufficiently educated to create one for itself.

The greater number of these thoughts on the subject of æsthetics were written during his youth. Though already, in the domain of morals, he denied to the aristocracy, and particularly to the bourgeoisie, the right of regarding themselves as representatives of the elect, he regretted at the same time the absence, in the world of art, of an elect few, a group of " good people," a bourgeois or aristocratic caste. Both his attachment to the French genius, considered, measured, and reasonable,[1] and to the writers of her great century, and his passion for traditional form seem here to have carried away this writer, who in other questions has always afforded such an admirable example of " the unprejudiced mind."

For indeed Gide is deeply classicist. " Art requires a certain temperance," he writes, " and repudiates enormity." In the midst of the unvarying Congo forest he delightedly took refuge with La Fontaine. He has always believed in the necessity for art of restraint, clarity of outline, and

[1] Gide recognizes, however, the existence of a second French tradition, the romantic tradition, represented by Villon, Nerval, Hugo, Baudelaire, Lautréamont, Rimbaud, and the Surrealists. But he maintains that it has always remained aside from the main current of our literature.

strict rules. " The great artist," he writes, " is he who glories in being hampered and for whom an obstacle serves as a spring-board." It is true that writers such as Valéry and Edgar Allan Poe claim to have found inspiration in the very difficulty of their chosen forms. But if the ready-made rules imposed by tradition have served certain temperaments, they have hampered others. We know that Corneille suffered all his life from the law of the three unities, dominating the drama of his period. The only defensible rules are those imposed upon an artist by himself. And these may be, amongst others, those of tradition *freely* accepted. It is curious that Gide, who in the matter of morality has been such a thoroughgoing individualist, should have been moved, in that of æsthetics, to generalize upon the principles that apply to his own case,

Nevertheless this tendency has not prevented him from being one of the first critics of the day: a critic who is the more remarkable in that he understands those whose genius is the most opposed to his own, exactly those who are " *énorme*," such as Michelangelo, Shakspere, William Blake. And if amongst the writers of his own day he has been secretly attracted by Moréas and the " beauty " of his *Stances*, he nevertheless discovered Claudel, Péguy, and Proust. . . .

While desiring to remain a classicist, Gide has always repudiated false classicism, simple, reasoned, shallow clarities. It was in his polemics with the disciples of Moréas, Maurras, and Clouard, after the appearance of his first essays on æsthetics, that he so admirably set forth his point of view. Neo-classicism, he maintained, appeals only to "the self's . . . most superficial part," only to ready-made sentiments, well known and outside ourselves. Anatole France is an example of apparent perfection due to poverty of temperament. If in a period less highly evolved than our own one could be satisfied with the cultivation of "lean acres," to-day, in a literature that has already passed through romanticism, the author who would still move mankind must bore down into the depths of human personality, into the "savage and feverish lower regions" which it is exactly the business of art to *set in order*. They are undoubtedly more rebellious regions, but "upon what should our discipline exteriorize itself if not upon that which resists?" "Oh, alluvial soil! New, difficult, dangerous, and infinitely fertile regions!" These are they which must be submitted to the restraint of form, if we are to achieve the truly classical works of our century. Thus does Gide perfectly define not only the ideal of contemporary art but also the character of his own, and particularly that of his style.

The genius of Gide resides in the marvel of his form, enclosing and dominating passion. A form tending entirely, as he has said himself, towards the classic ideal, to litotes: "the art of expressing the most by saying the least." What seems to be lacking in this phrase, owing to its conciseness, is compensated by its suggestiveness.

But suggestion itself is inoperative unless the author has

freed himself both of rhetoric and of preciosity. Those are Gide's two grand temptations. He easily escaped the first and, in *Les Cahiers d'André Walter*, denounces emphasis: " the word greater than the thought." Preciosity, however, has been more dangerous for him. For Symbolism yielded to this tendency in its search for the musical and the inexpressible. And the so-called modern style of to-day reproduces this defect in its use of inventions and of startling images. Gide has always endeavoured to retain only so much of preciosity as shall serve to increase *precision*. Certain of his obvious oddities arise from his use of words in their etymological sense. His archaisms and his unusual elliptical constructions are intended only to break the movement of a period and reduce it to the fewest possible words.

Thus it is that the rather stilted, ascetic, early style soon acquired the firmness of a prose narrative that makes straight for its aim. The blurred, abstract wording of the *Cahiers* gives place in *Les Nourritures terrestres* to words which evoke clear and precise sensations of skies and cities and landscapes. In *Œdipe*, one of his most recent works, he does not recoil even from the familiar and the crude, so long as they serve his purpose. In the *Voyage au Congo* even the commonplace has no terrors for him and he speaks of the *defects* of a friend, the *beauty* of woman, and the *happiness* of love. " To become banal," he writes courageously, " is to become as human as it is possible to be " — that is to say, to rid oneself of the encumbrance of all the redundant or merely offensive elements which falsify the expression of personality.

Henceforward he needs, for the purpose of evoking the unconscious, only a few words, a brief appeal, a simple juxtaposition of images. With a single phrase, all clarity and purity, he reaches down into the dim equivocal depths of the ego. Such a phrase will bring back in its fine mesh the most troublous sentiments. The remarkable starkness of his style releases an intense fervour, its economy an overwhelming emotion. An increasing, rising, emotion flows forth and yet is held in its place in the fair framework of style by a perfect technique. It is this moral contrast, this deceptively flowing style, and this disquieting purity that make Gide's writing unique.

Doubtless there are other classical styles more compact, or more complex, like that of Pascal or of Saint-Simon. But within the apparent " banality " of his form Gide expresses his whole personality, maintaining exactly the right note, without either forcing or lowering the tone. And this it is that gives him his distinctive value.

At the present time Gide can go on writing and leave his books to their fate. His style will retain its remarkable characteristic quality. The author has attained to naturalness: to the saying of what he must say without either divergence, inflation, or affectation. " Everything is simple and everything to the purpose." He is sincere. Art has restored his freedom.

PART III

HIS ETHIC

THE FIRST ASPECT OF INDIVIDUALIST
MORALITY, OR MAN IN SEARCH OF HIMSELF

" What was it that drew you outside? "
" Nothing. . . . Myself."
LE RETOUR DE L'ENFANT PRODIGUE

Gɪᴅᴇᴀɴ psychology, which we have already outlined, brings
us to Gidean ethics. It was in becoming aware of the great
laws of the inner life that Gide was led to draw up rules
of conduct. Starting from man himself, from his deepest
nature, egoist *and* altruist, individual *and* social, he has
attempted to build up a morality.

This ethic may not be regarded as a complete, co-ordi-
nated system, but rather as a work upon which he has been
occupied throughout his life. Incessantly evolving, it moves
by a series of apparent contradictions, proceeding for a
while entirely in a given direction and then, quite suddenly, taking the opposite path: but from these very oscil-
lations there comes forth a unique and powerful line of
thought.

We are not here concerned with tracing the history of

163

this evolution, but only with the essential movements of his mind; with seeing how, starting from egocentric individualism, he has reached the evangelical morality of self-giving, and then how these *two* aspects of his thought, after having been in conflict within him, became reconciled in the living synthesis which, for Gide, is true individualism.

*   *   *

It is towards the age of fifteen that the thoughts of the adolescent, unless indeed he has no sort of inner life at all, are most keenly at work upon his situation on earth. At this age he feels his loneliness in the midst of his family, who seem long ago to have solved the great problems of life. Yet if he questions serious-minded people, he is aware of making them uneasy; the feebleness of their replies astonishes him. His doubts increase. . . .

He then asks himself why he has been taught religious and moral principles which waver as soon as reason awakens, why he should be obliged to unravel, piece by piece, the network of arguments that has enwrapped him from his earliest years. To free himself from religion he must engage in long and painful labours.

From the day he begins keeping his " Journal " André Walter debates with himself: how it is, he writes, that devout people do not understand the " impossibilities " of believing? " They imagine willingness is enough! . . . And, most wonderful of all, they think they are believing with their reason."

He is forbidden, moreover, to examine dogmas, which have been made sacred with this end in view. If one of them totters, it is said, the whole edifice falls, and this is calamity. Naturally superstitious, the youth tries to save at least a living God, the traditional proofs of whose existence he goes over and over again in his mind. One by one he sees them vanish. Later on, Gide will write a " round " for voices,[1] but at present he is afraid of his own thoughts. . . .

Yet when adolescent sensuality awakens, the whole edifice of his faith crumbles away. Sensuality is a terrible test for religion, which is exactly what claims to control it. Most men give up the confessional from the day their sexual life begins. It is then that the majority of them insensibly detach themselves from their beliefs and accept, for the rest of their lives, a compromise which more or less consciously, but systematically, they refrain from thinking about.

But it sometimes happens that when the adolescent has been brought up in a closed traditional sphere, he will reject the occult principles only at the cost of a complete spiritual upheaval. . . . The book-filled room wherein his studious years have been passed is suddenly stifling. Outside beckons the unknown, liberty, endless perspectives. He is emancipating himself. This is rebellion: a moment of joy and pride during which he believes himself to be stronger than society, sees all others as the dupes and slaves of prejudice, while he, he alone, has broken free. His soaring enthusiasm sweeps away restraints, petty laws, conventional morality. The curb is broken. I have " cleaned

[1] In *Les Nourritures terrestres.*

the slate," writes Gide. "I have swept everything away
. . . I stand naked upon virgin soil, with the sky to
repeople."

Confronting a God who has always held him in a state of
pupillage, the individual raises his head and proclaims his
coming of age. This, no doubt, is the gravest of crimes, the
crime of pride, for the God of Christianity exacts from His
creatures a perpetual humility. Even for the great believers,
humiliation of mind and body is a large part of religion.
Equally formidable is the audacity of those heroes of literature who, from Job and Prometheus to Maldoror and Zarathustra, have attacked the gods of Olympus and of heaven.

It is only towards the end of his life that Gide, speaking
through Œdipe, has dared openly to defy divinity. But the
whole of his work, even that part of it that is apparently the
most religious in feeling, is a movement towards this definite negation. Already in *L'Immoraliste* Michel says to his
wife: — You must not pray for me, Marceline." — You
spurn God's help? " — [Yes] for then He would have a
right to my gratitude. I don't want Him." It is true that the
word " God " frequently appears in *Les Nourritures terrestres*. But in human language there is no vaguer term, none
that is more often empty of meaning, or that wears a more
deceptive mask. " To everything I love," writes Gide, " I
have given the name of God, and I have wanted to love
everything." This fervent synonym has nothing in common
with God the Father and Legislator of the faithful.

Yet Gide's character is anything but that of a rebel.
Indeed, it is the absence of rebellion that gives his thought

its peculiar tonality, so different from that of Nietzsche, even when he seems to approach him most nearly. The attitude of universal challenge was no more than a youthful gesture. But if he has had insufficiently complete experience of rebellion and its creative destructions, he has at least escaped its gravest pitfalls: lassitude, pessimism, renunciation. Rimbaud, having rejected everything, returned, in the second half of his life, to acceptance of everything: work, the family, morality.

This sudden retrogression frequently occurs amongst those who in youth were held captive by a stern religious education, and is the result of their failure, when at about the age of twenty they cease to believe, to build up another morality. All hope, and any aspiration towards ideal good, they feel to be irremediably lost. They can conceive nothing beyond a utilitarian and materialistic morality, in the vulgar meaning of these words. Willingly would they declare with one of Dostoievski's characters: " If there is no God, then everything is permissible! " It seems to them that only the fear of the police can curb man's antisocial instincts. Life appears to them to be a horrible desert. And it is to escape from this desert that they soon return to God.

In their youth Claudel and Maritain were disciples of Le Dantec. It was disgust with this scientist thought-system that induced in them a nostalgia for religion and paved the way for their conversion.[1]

Gide, on the other hand, has never been able to live with-

---

[1] When man abuses the use of reason (as is the case in " scientism "), he will soon reach a complete contempt for it.

out a legitimate sanction for his actions. When traditional morality failed him, he at once found it necessary to create another.

*   *   *

But in this new ethic the individual has become his own master. He creates *his own* good and *his own* evil, without considering established rules. He draws up his own scale of values, and even allows these to vary according to circumstances and times of life.

Kant seems already to have proposed an analogous method. But, as a matter of fact, in Kantian ethics, the individual is merely his own executive agent and not his own law-maker. It is he who rewards or sanctions an action, but the lawgiver is *Universal Reason*, and its laws are the same for everyone.[1] Traditionalists have always thought it necessary to place a system of sacred spiritual ideas outside and above the individual: the laws of God, of Society, or of Pure Reason. The originality of Gide's ethic, as of Nietzsche's, is the handing over of this power to the individual considered as a separate entity.

Are not men all different from each other? Is it not monstrous to apply the same code to each one? Nature protests against such uniformity. The prime betrayal, writes Gide, the greatest sin, the sin against the Spirit " which shall not be forgiven," is to deprive anyone of his characteristic " savour," " his precise, irreplaceable significance."

---

[1] No doubt one may claim that according to Kant each individual is determined by his noumenal personality. But it is none the less true that in his view the individual, in society, is subject to universal laws.

Already Goethe had written: " The highest aim of man, and the one most difficult to reach, is that of becoming conscious of his own thoughts and feelings; in other words, of himself." For, in order to realize what he has in himself, he must first know his qualities and his weaknesses, his powers and his limitations. The point of departure for individualism is the determination by the individual of what will be fruitful and what will be noxious for him: here are his good and his evil. Nothing is more important than to fashion one's aspirations according to one's nature. How many intelligences have been wrecked through seeking for a perfection that is unrelated to their abilities? And how many creators, only moderately dowered by nature, but aware of themselves, have succeeded in producing valuable work?

It is not enough, however, to adapt one's morality to one's consciousness and to life. One must also be faithful to it. " The most difficult thing in this world," declares Dostoievski, " is to remain oneself." " It is not ascent that is difficult," writes Michelet, " but, in ascending, to remain oneself." And Gide in his turn has written: " Nothing is more tiring than to realize one's dissimilarity."

Does not everything enlist our idleness, the idleness which incites *L'Enfant prodigue* to return to his own people? " I wanted to stop," he confesses, " to attach myself somewhere. I was tempted by the comfort this master promises . . . yes, I know it now; I have failed." This is the underlying error of very many lives. The deformed, dessicated existences to be found in the provinces, the wistfulness of spinsters when spring returns, the recriminations of embittered mediocrity, the lamentations of isolated adolescents vainly striving to exhaust the indwelling monster — are not all these expressions of renunciation, fear, and prejudice? It is so much easier to let go one's hold.

Stranger than all the rest is the fact that the individual does not dare to give way in the minor concerns of everyday life, does not dare to let his beard grow and neglect his appearance and the duties of the toilet. For such things he finds strength longer than for anything else. But when it comes to great actions, he gives in. Thus it is that at the moment when unhappiness descends, round about the twentieth year, when courage is needed for the plunge into life, the greater number of religious vocations are decided. So easily, moreover, does a man grow accustomed to his own cowardice that he ends by even finding happiness therein: nearly all bourgeois happiness is based on self-renunciation. When Alissa visits her sister Juliette and finds her " happy " in the midst of her numerous children, she experiences an actual " malaise " in face of " a happiness so perfectly *equable* as to be stifling and oppressive."

Thus do the forces of inertia ceaselessly draw mankind towards a dead point. In order to be oneself, one must engage in ruthless warfare against one's conscience and against the world. One must take up an attitude of real " hostility," as did Michel at the time when he was trying to get well. More often than not, it is actually by means of destruction and denial that the individual comes to create. To acquire a mastery in art or in sport, is it not necessary to repress unsuitable reflexes and consciously acquire those that fit the occasion? In order to exercise imagination, must we not put away from us all ready-made associations of ideas? To live is perhaps, above all things, to get the better of our reflexes, to dominate and disintegrate matter.

Individualist morality demands that one shall contend with nature, with environment, shall try to divest oneself of everything that does not properly belong to one. It is an enterprise in which one must be ceaselessly prepared for all risks. It matters little whether society calls desires good or evil, so long as they are the expression of the depths of a personality. It may happen that the instincts which are the most severely condemned will be the most fruitful. It is not by chance that one finds, existing side by side in the strongest personalities, the worst and the most sublime instincts. Evil instincts are those which the individual has not succeeded in elevating and making creative, but they are of the same nature as the others. " The comfortable and reassuring idea of the good, beloved of the bourgeoisie," writes Gide, " invites humanity to stagnation and slumber. I believe that what Society calls evil [is] often [a] manifestation of energy . . . of an educative, initiating virtue . . . capable of leading indirectly . . . to progress."

The accursed instincts are rooted in humanity. According to the Bible, the first death was the result of a crime. Great must have been the rapture of Cain in discovering that he was capable of revoking life as well as giving it. In descending to the primitive sources of being, we find love associated with the dark need to destroy. Michel, having engaged in a furious hand-to-hand struggle with a driver, returns to his wife full of exultation. " What a kiss we exchanged! " he remarks afterwards.

Yet soon he is to cause the death of this adored woman by dragging her with him upon a desperate journey to southern Algeria, which she will be unable to resist. For this crime, committed under conditions which put police investigations out of the question, Michel feels no kind of remorse.

It is his failure in self-knowledge that has brought him to this point. He had not the courage to admit to himself that the near presence of this woman, even though he loved her, was hindering the evolution of his deeper being, the free realization of his desires. As a result of his inability consciously to sacrifice his love, he has unconsciously killed the woman who is its object.

His failure to find the courage to break away from Marceline, earlier, was exactly the result of not following his individualist morality. He gave way to indolence, the enemy of decisions, and also, no doubt, to pity.

This illustrates Nietzsche's estimate of pity as one of the forces of perdition, running counter to human development. Pity, he says, is the worst temptation, and poisons the whole of the society of our day. To acclaim pity is to give the one who inspires it the means of " harming " him who is in pity's toils. Nothing is easier than to yield in face of the suffering Christianity has exalted. " To know how to suffer," writes Nietzsche, " is a small matter. Weak women and slaves are past masters in this art. But not to succumb to the assaults of distress . . . when one inflicts great suffering, that is greatness. . . . Resist this perversity," he adds, " harden thyself. . . ." And Gide: " O my heart, harden thyself against ruinous sympathies, suggesters of all the compromises,"

Without promulgating, as did the author of *Zarathustra,* a new law, Gide nevertheless understood that duty frequently demands the sacrifice of individual pity to a work that in the end will be useful and fruitful for all. Perhaps the best service we can render to those who seek to move us to pity is direct opposition. When the adolescent must emancipate himself, assert himself, and choose his career, his whole life, and the lives of those near to him, will be poisoned if he gives way to the tears and exhortations of those who wish to turn him from his path,

There is nothing more serious, nothing more moving and terrible, than the moment when the individual must go on his way. In thus putting himself forward he must become aware of his own value, a burden so heavy that few can undertake it. Far from being an expression of egoism, as is so often believed, this undertaking implies the most painful duties. For there is parental pressure to overcome, and the pressure of friends and environment, the past to be rejected, and, worst of all, an inexpressible anguish to be vanquished. The moment of liberation is a tearing away of the whole being, analogous to that which is produced by some great setting forth. A moment's hesitation, and the entire future of a life goes under.

This is exactly the subject of *Isabelle.* The young girl has for months been preparing for a clandestine flight with a young squire in the neighbourhood, whom her parents have refused to allow her to marry. Everything is ready. The date of their departure is fixed. But suddenly she is seized with anxiety. She draws back . . . and also refrains from informing the young man who is to carry her off by night. With supreme cowardice, she lets events act for her. Her fiancé is killed by one of the family servants, and the scandal for herself, soon to be a mother, becomes irreparable. Henceforward she lives in debauchery and misery. She has mismanaged everything, lost everything.

In this way does a pang of " remorse," at the last moment, bar the way to action: the individual falls once more under the sway of society and is recaptured by his " bad conscience." And the stronger the individuality, the greater the risk: the higher a man reaches in his own counsels, the more unstable is the equilibrium of his consciousness, the more urgent the necessity for a constant testing of its bearings and redressing of its balance. In the same way in social life insecurity and precariousness increase in the lives of genuine creators in proportion to the growth of their potency: it is when the man of action, who has overwhelmed whole societies and countries, is at the height of his power or his wealth that the smallest slip will land him in prison, in ruin, or in obscurity; no doubt he will have reached a point when any further progress was beyond his strength. That, however, is the point: " To undertake beyond one's strength," says Philoctète to Néoptolème, " that is what is called virtue."

There are, in fact, two stages in individualist morality, and this is what constitutes its greatness: *It is not merely a question of liberating one's instincts, but also of impelling them beyond themselves. It is not enough to be oneself; one must rise above oneself; the end, once reached, must be surpassed.* . . .

" If God does not exist, everything is permissible. . . ." No, there remains an enormous obligation, and a hope as great. If we consider the transformation of humanity itself, every kind of progress, for centuries past, has been made externally to man himself, in manners and in civilization. By seeking to maintain himself at the extreme point of his consciousness, man may perhaps attain a more powerful physique, a new kind of intelligence. Then indeed he will have passed a stage in his evolution. In order to rise above oneself, one must be oneself.

*   *   *

If, so far, Gide's thought, although upon a different level, has run parallel to that of Nietzsche, from now onwards it will take a different direction. In order to plumb individualist morality to its depths, Gide has successively espoused all its tendencies. Having glorified man's will-to-power in *L'Immoraliste*, he drives to their utmost lengths, in *Les Nourritures terrestres*, his longings for pleasure.

Pleasure, Gide tells us, is also a duty, for it is natural to man to be happy. " Every perfect action," according to the teaching of Ménalque, " is accompanied by pleasure; thus thou knowest thou wast right in doing it."

But pleasure also is to be attained only by an effort which

in the beginning is painful. Laws and religions represent it as forbidden fruit. Wise adults and the whole of society restrain the adolescent from his own inclinations. What bracing of our courage is usually required if we are to respond with an affirmation when life offers us splendid adventures! Each of these is unique and should not be allowed to pass by. " I fear," writes Gide, " that every desire, every potentiality I shall not have satisfied during my life will survive and torment me."

Moreover, it is always the same obstacles that arrest us: shame, fear, convention. Yet the worst danger is within us: our own lassitude, the satisfaction of the flesh itself. " When my body is tired," writes Gide, " I blame my feebleness." All fatigue is guilty. " Regrets, remorse, repentances, these are former joys seen from behind."

Doubtless man's senses are miserably limited. All joy is ephemeral. Everything passes, says the believer, all is fragile and crumbling. But Gide, who has made an admirable analysis of pleasure, has adapted it to the perpetual flowing away of things. It is to its transitory character that happiness owes its inestimable value. " If you knew, eternal idea of appearance, what value the near expectation of death gives to the moment! " The Romans made their slaves bring a skeleton into the midst of their feasting, their wine, women, and roses, in order that the sight of it should increase the intensity of their pleasure.

Man has never been able to represent happiness as other than ephemeral and terrestrial. In paradise, where, according to the painters and the poets, soft-limbed angels blow celestial trumpets,[1] the ears of the elect must soon weary of this uninterrupted melody. Weariness is the apanage of all that lasts. It is, indeed, a psychological law that every sensation is blunted in being prolonged and that prolongation will transform an agreeable stimulus into actual physical pain.

Therefore Gide falls back upon the " moment." " Moments, who shall understand how powerful is [your] presence! " Every moment of even the most ordinary day can bring joy: the sight of a fence, the mystery of a shop, the oddity of a passer-by; or still more simple emotions, such as the intoxication of speed in driving; or, more direct, more animal: the sight of a pure, luminous sky, the sensation of sunlight on the skin, of lying on the sand, of water, the feeling of the warm towel against the face at the barber's; every kind of sensation. The human body, the moment we know how to be aware, is an admirably sensitive receptacle.

It is strange that the hedonist systems culminate almost necessarily in sensation, to the detriment of passion. The Marquis de Sade sternly forbids love to all his partisans: the only thing that matters is pleasure. " Not love," says Gide, " but fervour." Love is a troubled state wherein are mingled many strange images weighing down pure sensation, preventing it from reaching the consciousness, or deadening its shock.

Therefore the hedonist must try to free his soul from

---

[1] The ideal beatitude of the soul is thus represented at any rate throughout the ages of deepest faith, the Middle Ages as far as the Renaissance.

those encumbrances which come between himself and the external world: intellectual complexities, memory, the past, traditions. No doubt to abolish all our memories is to impoverish ourselves. What does it matter? Let us travel lightly whatever we do. Let us burn our books, says Gide, and sell our goods; leave our rooms and our surroundings. Every possession is a burden, every attachment painful. The passions are evil because they tie us to people or to things.

In the end it is desire itself that is true joy. The setting off is more marvellous than the journey, hunger than being fed, thirst than drinking. Thirst itself becomes intoxication. Fervent desire is supreme voluptuousness. . . .

Thus what is important is not to satisfy desire, but to aspire to satisfaction; not sensation, but the image one makes thereof. By a kind of implacable logic, the systematic pursuit of what is *material* in pleasure leads the hedonist to the most perfect idealism.

And this is characteristic of Gide's morality. The ignorant have always believed epicureanism to consist in wallowing like a pig in the mire. From few books, however, do we receive as strong an impression of purity as that which emanates from *Les Nourritures terrestres*. The voluptuous ardour of the foreground ought not to conceal from us the background of the picture, comparable to the far-away, divinely clear skies to be found in the pictures of the Fra Angelico or Fra Filippo Lippi. In the centre of this dream-landscape appears the hero, not unlike *L'Enfant prodigue*, most gentle and tender of countenance, wrapped in a linen robe, holding out empty hands, that yet are full of joy and happiness.

Setting out from the most violent rebellion, the adolescent reaches the ultimate point of his ascent — ecstasy. That eternity he had rejected he recovers within the moment; that absolute in which he no longer believed is brought to him by sensation: " powerful, complete, immediate " sensation " of life [in] forgetfulness of all that is not itself." Nature is restored to her primitive elements; the unburdened and, as it were, emptied soul communicates with her in a fervent, carnal pantheism.

The spirit, freed from the contingencies of daily life, feels rising within it an immense tide of joy, which is like the floating ecstasy of a spring morning. This ecstasy is strangely like the intoxication produced by drugs. Differently pure, however, for it is the sudden reward given by nature to the available soul, the soul that has known how to win its freedom.

In ecstasy pleasure takes the final form of an adoration. " Through everything," writes Gide, " I have been lost in adoration."

WHATEVER the grandeur of this first aspect of individualist morality, it embraces only part of the inner life and of life in general.

He who adopts it becomes, sooner or later, aware of its limitations, particularly in the moments of relaxation following powerful activity or the frenzied acquisition of pleasure. In vain does he say: " Nothing wearies me," for fatigue is the stronger, or ". . . every joy is always waiting for us," for joy turns to ashes. If he looks back along the way he has come, it is the oppressive sense of the uselessness of everything that forces itself upon him. What is the good of it all? Nothing is of any avail.

Released from the family and its conventions, he is more uneasy than ever. Is this remorse? When he is amongst his own people, in the midst of humanity, his heart is dreadfully oppressed, he comes to envy united families and is ready to weep over the spectacle of a mother, full of love, lulling her child to sleep. It seems to him that he has acquired freedom only at the cost of uprooting in himself the great primitive human feelings. When he is no longer able to endure his condition of loneliness, forsakenness, and hopeless aridity, he catches a glimpse of another morality: the morality of self-giving and sacrifice. . . .

" Give me reasons for existing," implores *L'Immoraliste* at the end of the book. Reasons? Then his whole life is crumbling into ruins.

After having written *Les Nourritures terrestres*, Gide was already frightened by his own audacity. Has he, after all, merely reinvented the hedonist system as a " screen for [his] sensuality "? A man can always discover " good reasons " to justify his actions. With words, he is capable of anything. " Words! Words! Words! " Words are also the Devil's retreat.

It was just at this time that Gide drew the portrait of Saül. With what ferocious irony does he make game of the pretentions of this individualist, this King who gives way to all his desires and never engages in activity! Poor Saul, declaring that " his value lies in [his] complexity," whilst admitting to his tent a troop of young demons, who push each other aside to reach and prostrate themselves upon his knees. " Wherewith shall a man console himself for his downfall," cries Saul, " if not with that which has brought him low? " Yet at the same moment he admits: " I am completely cut off."

Henceforth, Gide seeks for another rule of life. Where shall it be found if not in the heart of religion, and perhaps even of the family? For it was there, in his childhood, that he saw certain of his relatives give him the example of self-giving. He turns again to God. Relinquishes the pride that only yesterday gave vehemence to his joy and to-day, in the eyes of God, is his " shame." He kneels. He prays. In a mystical transport he writes, in *Num Quid et tu:* " I submit my heart to thee. . . ." Suffering shall take the place of joy. For glorious sunlit gardens shall be exchanged the dark and heavy forests of repentance. " What! For the sake of a little pleasure shall I deny the death and the mercy of Christ? " Not yet does he realize the deep significance of this strange reversal. He repudiates everything he has adored: beautiful faces, the bodies of women and adolescents, all forms of life that have captivated his senses seem now to be " horrible impurity," the " soilure of sin." The resplendent flesh is now only " corrupt " flesh. He fears that this corruption may have reached his very soul.

Then, all at once: " Forgive me, Lord! I know that I am lying. The truth is that I still love the flesh I hate, more than Thyself."

For Gide was not able to maintain himself for long in this purifying state of grace. If he is aware of some truth hidden within traditional religion, he finds also too many dogmas to thwart and shock him; too many objections arise and prevent him from finding his place there.

In addition to all this, he finds the " domestication of the instincts," as taught by Christianity, unjustifiable. Nature is pure, declares the pastor of the *Symphonie pastorale.* It is man who has made desire guilty. " Life would be beautiful . . . if we contented ourselves with real evils." It is religion which tortures life.

Pain undoubtedly helps the development of the individual, but does it not lose all its grandeur the moment it becomes an imposed " duty "? In drawing the portrait of Alissa, Gide has tried to get clear with himself in regard to the systematic character of this religious ethic of sacrifice. It is enough for Alissa to become aware of a desire, immediately to refuse to give way to it; experiencing love for Jérôme, a legitimate love which she herself respects, she at once condemns this emotion. If she is proud of her beauty, she tries to make her appearance unpleasing. One is necessarily led to inquire, as does Alissa herself at one point, why the dark spectacle of suffering should please God, whilst human pleasure, on the other hand, would be offensive in His sight? By what curious process of thought has man arrived at the belief that wrongdoing must be effaced by suffering? Gide also shows us how Alissa, who all her life has tried to enter heaven by the " narrow gate," is in the end derided by God. . . .

Nevertheless — and this is an important consideration — he could not bring himself to depict the gentle figure of this young girl otherwise than with the tenderest emotion, with a most pious and fervent love.

And, indeed, throughout his work, beside the Ménalques and the Nathanaëls, the individualists and the hedonists, there are resigned, obedient women whose self-effacement is an active, quivering self-giving. " *O Femme, monceau d'entrailles, pitié douce . . .* " [1] wrote Rimbaud. . . . When Gide depicts a fatal woman, such as Lady Griffith in *Les Faux-Monnayeurs,* she is too heavily drawn, too heavily laden with gems and demoniac vices. But Emmanuèle or Laura, Rachel or Gertrude, seems to emerge from the very depths of the author's own soul, to be fashioned from his own flesh. Marceline too, in *L'Immoraliste:* whilst Michel, in order to be able to give himself up to his pleasures, deserts her when she is ill, then returns to her weeping, and then, when he finds her entirely given up to God, wounds her afresh with hard words, she submits to her lot with a wonderful and increasing strength of soul. So much so that in the end, when Michel drags her with him far away into the desert, where she is to meet her death, he seems never to have loved her more deeply. The spectacle of her fills him with a respect that is stronger than himself, and it is as if now he dare only kiss the hem of her garment, fervently. . . .

Thus for long was Gide tormented — hesitating, in particular, between two apparently contradictory moral attitudes; and it is this uncertainty that was the very basis of his disquietude. . . .

On a sudden he emerges from this disquietude by once more returning in a " transport of love " to the Gospel, which he reads with new eyes, seeing " both the spirit and the letter . . . become luminous. . . ."

*　　　　*　　　　*

[1] " O Woman, cluster of entrails, tender pity . . ."

He then understood that its moral teaching as to self-giving has been so much disfigured by the religions as to be hardly recognizable. Never did Christ systematically teach the seeking of pain in order to please God. In Gospel morality there are no prohibitions, no " railings " or " strait-jackets," no interdiction of desire nor any perpetual domestication of instincts. " Woe unto you also, ye lawyers," Christ says, " for ye lade men with burdens grievous to be borne. . . ." And he adds: " Your laws have been invented by men and are not of God." [1] Jesus said there are no other commandments but to love God, and one's neighbour as oneself. The only sin, wrote the pastor of *La Symphonie pastorale,* is " that which makes an attempt upon another's happiness or compromises one's own."

The more deeply Gide studied the sacred book, the more distressed and indignant did he become over what the churches have made of it. In the course of the centuries every line of this pure text has been clothed in commentaries and interpretations that are the very antithesis of truth. And thus it is that our whole civilization, professedly Christian, has become that which is " furthest from the teachings of the Gospel " and the most " opposed " to them. To-day, looking for Christ, one comes upon the priest and, " behind the priest, Saint Paul." Religion is nothing more than " a cross of lies to which . . . [Christ has been] so securely nailed . . . that the wood [can] not be removed without tearing the flesh."

[1] Isaiah had already spoken thus. Christ cites his name and uses his words.

Christianity versus Christ is to-day so commonplace a theme that Gide has hardly thought it worth developing in his work.[1] But the question has nevertheless played an essential part in his life. It was in returning to the Gospel itself that he discovered the full splendour of the morality of sacrifice and was intoxicated thereby. Doubtless this doctrine has found equally beautiful expression in other sacred books (in the Bhagavadgîtâ, for example), but it is in the Gospel that we Occidentals find perhaps its truest and purest expression.

It is, moreover, rather remarkable that the grandeur of the Gospel should receive some of its finest tributes from the heterodox and the unbelievers. Gide, first of all quoting Rousseau, makes his own commentary: " It is not so much a question of believing Christ's words because He is the Son of God, as of understanding that He is God's Son because His words are . . . infinitely above and beyond anything propounded by . . . the wisdom of men." But it is not only Rousseau who has attributed divinity to the Gospel morality. We find at his side in this respect all those who have made the liveliest attacks upon the dogmas of the Church: Renan, Spinoza, Nietzsche. " What an abominable abuse," writes the last, " is committed in the application of this *sacred name* [the name of Christ] to such degenerate formations as . . . the *Christian faith, Christian life!* " And it is the Voltaire of *Écrasons l'infâme* (Let us crush the infamy!) who also said: Christ's moral teaching " is so

---

[1] Gide has made on this subject a number of notes which might form the substance of a book, but have not so far been published.

pure, so holy, so universal and luminous and ancient that it seems to come from God Himself. . . ."

What, then, is the vital secret drawn from the Gospel by men of such diverse genius? What, for Gide, is the true meaning of this wisdom?

What Christ offers us is the Kingdom of Heaven. But it is of prime importance to be precise as to the meaning of these words, from which so many misunderstandings have been born. For the greater number of believers, to enter the Kingdom of Heaven means to go, after death, to a paradise situated above the celestial vault and to be in the presence of God enthroned in glory. According to this view, Jesus indeed created a new *religion* by announcing survival, the rewarding of the good and the punishment of the evil.

For Gide, the eternal life proposed by Christ is something quite different. " There is nothing future about it. It is completely present in us, here and now." It is the consciousness of eternity at every moment. The " nature " of this state is " inward and spiritual." Yes, there is no doubt about it, it is the faithful who obscure these words that are so clear. At every moment, at every turn of his thought, Christ comes back to it: " The hour is coming . . . *and now is.* . . ." He who has not known this hour during his life expects it in vain after death. . . . It is " *now, in this present century* . . ." that you will have the Kingdom of Heaven. " Verily, verily, I say unto you," Christ repeats, " he that heareth my word *hath* eternal life." [1]

[1] Gide himself did not at once reach this concept. Held back by final scruples in regard to his relations and friends, by a last superstition, he did not dare to wound the traditional belief in a future life. Later on he

It follows thence that the whole of the traditional interpretation of the Gospel needs modification, as Nietzsche so
admirably explains: " The Kingdom of God is conceived
by [Jesus], not as a chronological and historic event, but as
a transformation of the perceptible being. . . . Beatitude
is not a promise: it exists here and now when one lives and
acts in a certain way. . . . To daily life Jesus opposed a
real life, a life according to truth." And Spinoza: " Beatitude is not a prize for virtue, but virtue itself. . . ." The
Kingdom of Heaven is but the result of a *moral* attitude.

Neither Buddha nor Jesus, each of whom was the founder
of a religion in spite of himself, has promised survival.[1]
They have created mythical terms, the Kingdom of Heaven,
Nirvana, susceptible of a variety of interpretations. But
when Buddha's friends pressed him to tell them whether
Nirvana is nothingness, he replied: — It may be, it may
not be. And when the disciples kept asking Jesus when the
Kingdom of Heaven would come and where it would be
and what would be the sign of its coming, the Master answered in parables, using all kinds of images to represent
the Kingdom, notably a grain of mustard-seed, the smallest
of seeds, which yet produces a plant " greater than all
herbs." Similarly, the Vedic scriptures tell of the " little

wrote: " One of the gravest mistakings of the mind of Christ results from
the confusion which often establishes itself in the mind of the Christian
between future life and eternal life." Gide is no longer troubled in regard
to a future life. In *Robert*, one of his most recent works, Éveline declares,
at the moment of the last sacraments: " I do not believe in eternal life."

[1] Doubtless it is impossible for anyone to affirm survival save in the
dubious terms once used by Bergson: — The immortality of the soul is a
possibility in which there is nothing contradictory. . . .

man " in the smallest cranny of the heart of each of us, or smaller than the smallest hair upon our heads split into innumerable parts. And yet the " little man " is larger than the whole of the celestial sphere. In reality it is at once that which is smallest and that which is greatest; it is without dimensions, a state of the soul. All those images and all those answers have a single aim: to prove to us that everyone can attain, by himself, to this joy which carries the soul by a sort of *ascesis* to the summit of itself. " The Kingdom of Heaven," said Christ, " is within you." It is within your heart.

Properly, it is an ecstasy and is described in the Gospel in marvellous terms as a sublime inward resurrection: man actually passes from death to life; he becomes capable of all undertakings; yet all his needs are satisfied; he is as free and light-hearted as a child; he recovers his laughter, his freedom, and his " gratuitousness." He is above all law.

At this point we may remark that the quality of this ecstasy is not very different from that of the pantheistic carnal communion of *Les Nourritures terrestres*. The extraordinary purity which seemed so characteristic of the happiness of the hedonist indeed appears to be of the same nature as the extraordinary innocence of supreme happiness in the Gospel. Is this resemblance fortuitous? Is it possible that the ultimate culmination of genuine hedonism brings the individual to a state of consciousness resembling that which is produced by geniune self-giving?

This possibility we shall now try to elucidate by inquir-

ing *by what means,* according to the Gospel, we may reach
the Kingdom of Heaven.

Through charity, said Christ. But, here again, the Gospel meaning of this word has almost nothing to do with
that commonly attributed to it to-day. Before visiting the
poor it would be needful, according to Christ, to be poor
oneself. Nothing could be more abhorrent to him than the
spectacle of the richly dressed wealthy, giving alms to some
wretched person from the midst of his luxury and believing that by thus depriving himself of a fragment of his own
superfluity he makes God his debtor. Indeed, most devout
people, wishing to follow the teachings of the Gospel and
lacking the courage to be faithful to them, are content with
making gestures which are nothing more than caricatures of
real gestures.[1]

Yet Christ said: " A rich man shall hardly enter into the
Kingdom of Heaven," and, in answer to the astonishment

[1] The comedy has been pushed so far that to-day the word " charity "
is prefixed to dinners, balls, and shows of all kinds where the wealthy enjoy
themselves in a small way, and also help the poor. The cream of the jest
is the fact that this system has actually acquired the status of a sociological
theory, hitherto approved by a considerable proportion of the clergy: the
industrial employer claims that he " *supports* " his employees, the fashionable woman that she " gives a living " to the retailers, the master that he
" keeps " his servants. Because the produce of their spending goes to the
poorer classes, this spending comes under the category of " good works."
The fact that they are simply a return, often an inadequate return, for
labour, is forgotten. Thus it is that all claims on behalf of the worker are
regarded as scandalous and unjustifiable, since the whole of the money
which goes to him takes on, in the eyes of the rich, the character of a kind
of gift. Thus it is that the owning classes still justify their opposition to
social reforms and their belief in the necessity of " safeguarding " their
fortunes.

of his disciples, he repeats this phrase and adds: " It is easier for a camel to go through the eye of a needle than for a rich man to enter into the Kingdom of God." This is not just an image, or rather, as Gide explains, not just a monstrously absurd image. *To pass through the eye of a needle:* these words prove that for the rich it is for ever impossible to attain eternal life. For to those who have great possessions, to the prime possessors, Christ said: " Ye cannot serve God and mammon. . . . That which is highly esteemed among men is abomination in the sight of God."

The rich man must divest himself, not of a little of his superfluous wealth, nor even of a great deal of it, nor even of all of it, but of both the superfluous and the necessary; of the whole of his fortune. " Sell all that thou hast, and distribute . . ." says Jesus. Then: " Take no thought for your life, what ye shall eat; neither for the body, what ye shall put on. . . . Consider the birds of the air. . . . Consider the lilies of the field. . . ." Yet it is not only material goods that man must renounce, but all his habits and his ties, his heritage and his family, his father and his mother, his brothers and his sisters. . . . Then and then only will he be able to follow the way of the Gospel, and, devoid of all things, be at last joyous and free. . . .

From now onwards the similarity between this doctrine of charity and the ethics of individualism is accentuated. Ménalque, having been for some time engaged in collecting the rarest of treasures, suddenly gets rid of all of them. " It is my experience," writes Gide in *Les Nourritures terrestres*, " that everything I covet on this earth . . . becomes opaque exactly because I covet it." Possessions burden the soul; they are all perishable, they deteriorate and fall into ruin; they bring us anxiety; all ownership is a source of trouble. The only goods worth having are those which we can carry away with us. . . . And the hedonist, too, urges us to get rid of everything which encumbers the spirit, if we would attain to joy. Leave thy town, he tells us, " thy family, thy room, thy thoughts," and then, " with neither wife nor children . . . alone before God on earth," like Ménalque thou canst cry out in the intoxication of thy joy: " My heart, having no attachment . . . has remained *poor!* "

The fierce pride of the individualist seems here to respond to the pure humility of the Gospel.

How is this approach possible? The terrible dilemma against which Gide flung himself for so long, and by which all his ideas were obscured, was the necessity of choosing between the rule of religion and the rule of individualism, between the ethic of pain and the ethic of pleasure, between discipline and liberty. Is it possible that the choice can have become useless?

It is characteristic of one of these two ethics to affirm man's egocentric forces and of the other to affirm self-sacrifice. They therefore roughly correspond to the two primitive tendencies of consciousness: egoism and altruism.

Our ideas are constantly falsified by the error of assuming that individualism is *solely* the expression of egoist tendencies, that to be oneself means to develop *only* these tendencies. *But altruism is also a part of the individual.* A mother's devotion to her child is as real an innate instinct as the instinct of self-preservation. If a mother abandons her new-born child, we call her, very justly, *unnatural* or *inhuman.* When a man sees another drowning, he is spontaneously moved to throw himself in the water and attempt a rescue. The desire to succour one's neighbour lies deep in one's being and, like the superficially contrary desire for personal continuance, demands satisfaction.

But if altruist tendencies are really a part of personality, then *the ethic of sacrifice, in its entirety, is nothing less than an individualist ethic.* In devoting himself to others or to an idea, man develops an essential part of his inner life; he is performing a genuinely individualist action, and the greater his sacrifice, the clearer his sense of the uplifting of his whole personality. . . .

" For whosoever shall save his life shall lose it; but whosoever shall lose his life . . . the same shall save it," says Christ. Yes, Gide explains, it is the individual who triumphs in renouncing the individual; it is in abandoning his life, his soul, that he acquires the power of saving it and being born anew.

Gide reproduces this phrase from the Gospel again and again. It corresponds, for him, with one of the summits of his thought on the subject of ethics. In the end the two parts of his being, the self-attracted part and the part that was drawn towards his fellow-creatures, were reconciled in a moment of supreme joy. . . . The doctrine of renunciation here reaches the same point as the doctrine of self-affirmation, which equally demands that the individual shall surpass himself, sacrifice himself, in order to recover that self further on.

"There are in everyone," writes Baudelaire, "two simultaneous postulations: one towards God, and the other towards Satan." Then Gide quotes Dostoievski: "I may experience a desire to do good, and it gives me pleasure. But at the same time I desire to do evil, and that also gives me pleasure." Good and evil, God and Satan, Heaven and Hell — all these images are perhaps mistaken in regarding one part of our being as superior to the other. Nevertheless they indeed show us that there are in every individual antagonistic aspirations which meet when they are pushed to their extreme limits.[1] This is not a figure of speech, but a psychological reality. We are saying that altruism and egoism are complementary forces; to exalt the one is to exalt the other, for they meet in infinity. It matters little, therefore, that in moments of relaxation, in everyday life, two beings are at war within us, if we know that in enthusiasm, in moments of rapture, the only real moments, they are but one. . . .

Genuine individualist morality is now about to enlarge itself without changing its nature. We have, it is true, presented it under two successive aspects which we have seen developing along parallel lines. These two aspects are, however, a single whole, which is still individualist morality.

[1] Cf. William Blake: *The Marriage of Heaven and Hell*, of which Gide has made a fresh translation.

Whether the forces of his ego spring outwards or concentrate themselves within, the individual's most pressing task is that of using all his forces in the acquisition of the intensest possible self-consciousness.

He will begin by ousting foreign elements from his personality, by getting rid of all that is not *sui generis*. This first effort of detachment will almost always take the form of a struggle between the individual and society with its inert forces: routine and tradition. Even Nietzsche fought against his environment no more ardently than did Jesus, who was all gentleness, against His own brothers, against the law, the rabbis, and the scribes. It is then that his voice swells and that this hero of resignation cries: " Suppose ye that I am come to give peace on earth? I tell you nay, but rather division. . . ." " Those," writes Gide, " who believe in peoples, races, families, and do not understand that the individual perpetually gives all of them the lie, are they who refused to believe Christ when He came! . . ."

But the individual will fight also against himself, against everything in his consciousness that is ready-made and matter-of-course, against everything mechanical and static, against indolence and fear. Doubtless all these efforts will be painful, but there is in this case no seeking of pain for its own sake; pain is inherent in effort, is merely the inevitable means of raising the level of the inward life. It is active and not negative, is fruitful and not punitive. Above all, it is not the result of impeded instincts and desires; for forbidden desires become hypocrites taking indirect paths, concealing themselves behind " bad reasons " or in neuroses. Thwarted, they become diabolical and engender "pestilence." [1] In order to find himself, a man must search along various paths, often strange, sometimes dangerous: voluptuousness may lead to charity, the will-to-power to self-abnegation. On his way he must liberate his instincts and his desires, even those regarded by religion as the most deadly sins, but on condition, only on condition of lifting them to a higher plane, detaching himself, by becoming aware of them, from those which do not correspond to his deepest nature. [2]

In the parable of the Prodigal Son, Christ teaches us that the just man who has never sinned will be less well received in heaven than the one who has strayed and recovered the path. This scriptural precept, writes Gide, is undoubtedly the one the believer has the greatest difficulty in admitting, the one against which his spirit cannot refrain from rebelling, exactly as did the brother of the Prodigal when he said to his father, weeping with rage and indignation: "Lo, these many years do I serve thee, neither transgressed I at any time thy commandment: and yet thou never gavest me a kid, that I might make merry with my friends: but as soon as this thy son [the Prodigal] was come, which hath devoured thy living with harlots, thou hast killed for him the fatted calf. . . ." But the father answers: "This thy brother was dead and is alive again; and was lost, and

[1] It was William Blake who said that Desire not followed by action engenders pestilence. "Beatitude," writes Spinoza, "is not to be obtained by the reduction of sensual appetite. . . ."

[2] To become aware of a desire is not merely to take note of its nature and its consequences for the individual, but, above all, to put it in its appropriate place in the inward harmony of one's being.

is found." An answer that recurs again and again in the Gospel, like a leit-motif with all kinds of variations: " For whosoever exalteth himself shall be abased; and he that humbleth himself shall be exalted "; and again: " But many that are first shall be last, and the last first."

From those who are content to obey the Commandments, to refrain from murder, theft, and adultery, there is not much to be expected. Those who live normally, pay their tithes with regularity, count their steps and their money, those who invite friends to dinner in the hope of receiving invitations, the Philistines and the Pharisees, those whose lives are arid and whose joys are stifled, those who are " neither hot nor cold " and to whom even the " cold " are preferable — none of these will Christ accept as followers. They are undoubtedly His worst enemies. He consorts with outcasts, with publicans and sinners, and the outraged Pharisees murmur amongst themselves: " He eateth with them! " He associates with prostitutes and with the vaga-bonds to be found along " the highways and hedges." For these, in a sudden awakening of energy, in the extremity of evil or of pain, may be capable of exercising true charity and attaining to complete deprivation.

We must not reduce the individual to a single model. Each one, in following *his own* bent, should attain his limits and pass beyond them. In Dostoievski, Gide explains, it was the sense of suffering and failure which at certain mo-ments enabled him to reach the summit of his soul. " Do you understand what it means ' *to have nowhere to go* '? No, you do not yet understand that." That is to say that this cry is not to be expected from the honest man who believes he stands well with himself and with society, but only from one who has dared to risk all and who, like Raskolnikov, has lost all, and yet, in the moment of loss, has been nearer to God than ever before. . . .

In the life of a man who has *dared everything*, there are sometimes certain secret and horrible actions which are choking him like something stuck in the throat. During the day, amongst others, his friends and relations, he conceals his agony; the air thickens about him; in his smallest gesture he feels upon him the whole weight of human misery. In order to break through this enclosure, he rushes forth at last, going headlong as if panic-stricken. . . . In the same way, when a pack of ferocious dogs chases a hunted beast, hems in and surrounds it and puts it at bay, the beast indeed does not know where to go. . . .

Yet at this very moment, the moment when man has nothing before him but the perspective of death, the miracle occurs. When at the end of *Faust* the soul of Marguerite is to become the prey of the Evil One: " Saved! She is saved! " Such is the formidable cry one hears sounding in a superior voice in the midst of the celestial music. Marguerite has killed her child and allowed her mother to be poisoned, but " she has greatly loved." " Saved! She is saved! " This supreme appeal seems to reverberate from summit to summit across some of the greatest works of literature, for the justice of the Kingdom of Heaven has little to do with that of society and the laws of man, and it may well be that those upon whom society has laid great burdens of guilt will be first amongst the elect. Souls will not be weighed in a balance; but perhaps those who have fallen lowest will find in the abyss the greater power of soaring to the " first place," the " highest place," in heaven.[1]

Thus, through heaven and hell, wretchedness or rapture, pleasure or pain, self-giving or egoism, thought or action, he who uses the whole strength of his being to the point of losing his life recovers that life in the Kingdom of Heaven.

Each century, every race, and perhaps every great individual, have conceived of this ideal state of consciousness in its own particular way: Eden, the Golden Age, the Garden of Ideas, the State of Nature, the World of the Third Stage of Knowledge. And this vision of absolute happiness has always been placed, whether in time, at the beginning or the end of history, or in space, in the lowest or the highest sphere, at a point infinitely distant, so that man may reach towards it only by means of unlimited effort, and that the aim shall always be retreating and the effort ceaselessly to be begun anew. . . . " Everything is to be done over again, eternally to be done over again," writes Gide, because man is heedless, because he is recaptured by submission to convention, because he again desires to possess, because " whilst the Passion unrolls itself, the covetous soldiers cast lots for the garments [of Christ] and divide

---

[1] This mystical interpretation of suffering and failure becomes dangerous the moment these things are sought *for their own sakes*. The same truth holds good in relation to those who seek only victory and conquest. For the individual, suffering and joy alike should be but the means of self-education.

them." The moment of sacrifice cannot be other than exceptional.

*   *   *

The moment man falls back, the duality of his nature throws him once more into a state of division. "On earth," writes Dostoievski, "there will always be these two contrary postulates, at enmity with each other."

Nothing, therefore, is more dangerous than to develop only a part of oneself; for thus does a man falsify his nature, turn it from its path, and disfigure it. The great outcasts, the rebels who, supported only by their own pride, have rebelled to the uttermost, have almost always been constrained to abdicate. The great ascetics, cultivating renunciation alone, have driven themselves into a tragic impasse. If in nearly all Gide's novels the principal character is pulled up in the end, it is because, in the person of nearly every one of his heroes, he has driven to its extreme one or the other, only, of these two individual tendencies. Michel relies only upon the urgency of life in himself and presently does not know what to do with his freedom. Alissa lives only through renunciation and in the end " is dispossessed of herself."

In everyday life man ought therefore to resign himself to accept the existence, side by side within him, of these contradictory tendencies. Here again it is the Gospel which tells us: " Lest while ye gather up the tares, ye root up also the wheat with them. Let both grow together until the time of the harvest." One cannot unify one's consciousness by force.

After the intoxication of re-reading the Gospel and Dostoievski, after a last intense period of mysticism, Gide realized that he would never entirely succeed in reducing the antinomies of his nature. Where is the powerful personality who is not aware of the existence within himself of mutually inimical desires and ideas? Frequently the internal conflict becomes dramatic. Do we ever know whither life is taking us?

Meanwhile, as time passes, life alone can bring near to each other the mutually opposed ideas, every day a little nearer, after the manner of pebbles which strike against each other, but whose angles are gradually rounded and softened under the sway of every tide. By means of this slow, continuous, painful process the forces of attraction and repulsion, struggling together in a human personality, will be reduced.

This is the pathway, not of exaltation, but of equilibrium; it demands a more constant and equally painful, if less violent, effort; it leads, as does the other, to a deep happiness, but one that is less intense and more durable, that of serenity.

3

AMOROUS PASSION AND PLEASURE

PASSION has an important place in Gide's novels. How does he assess its moral value?

He never describes fleshly *grande passion*, that fatal life-disorganizing malady. Only once does he introduce this theme, and then it is for the purpose of demonstrating its egoistic, ravaging nature. Lady Griffith is entirely possessed by her physical love for Vincent, and this mad passion, vehemently expressed, seems to Gide monstrous. She is a fatal woman and a frenzied Nietzschean, living in almost demoniac luxury — an exceptional character in this author's work. What she seeks is not the moral perfection of her husband, but merely his social success. The unhappy Vincent discovers that " from the complete satisfaction of desire can be born, accompanying joy . . . a kind of despair." So their love soon turns to jealousy, jealousy to " ferocious " hatred, to personal violence. Whilst their yacht is sailing up an African river, Vincent is to throw Lady Griffith overboard and himself become insane. . . . To such an abyss does passion lead whose source is purely sensual.

The love described by Gide is man's pure adoration for woman, his longing to devote himself to her and compel her esteem by heroic action. Such is the love of André Walter for Emmanuèle, of Jérôme for Alissa, of Bernard for Laura, and also of Édouard for Olivier (for the sex of the adored person is immaterial). Yet the lover does not remain chaste; he seeks pleasure, apart from his passion, in casual encounters. . . ,

This dissociation, so characteristic of those we meet in Gide's books, between tender affection and physical attraction, between the love that is of the soul and the love that is of the body, would seem due to Christian influence. Once having placed the soul so high and the body so low, man can no longer reunite them. . . . The flesh is for him so abhorrent, so contemptible, that he is incapable of experiencing desire for a beloved and esteemed woman. He no longer dares, says Bernard, to touch her with the end of his finger. It would seem like " profanation." He has been educated into fear and an invincible timidity, into an inferiority complex. He is at ease only with those he need not respect, lads or prostitutes, who are socially his inferiors and with whom he can give rein to his bodily desires. The Algerian boy whom Michel prefers is " as supple and faithful as a dog."

Seen thus, the apparently contradictory attitude of Gide's heroes in regard to carnal pleasure is more easily understood. For a long time the adolescent is not aware of his inner duality. " You will *disgust* me in advance, both with myself and with life," cries Bernard when Laura, the

woman he venerates, tells him of the needs of her body.
When Olivier tells his friend about his first night with a
girl, " Well, old chap . . ." he says, " [it was] horrible. . . . It left me wanting to spit, be sick, claw off my
skin, kill myself." Held back by all kinds of inhibitions and
unconscious moral prejudices, adolescent desire wanders
seeking, hesitating. Yet when at last he finds a passive creature in whose presence he has no fear of giving himself up
to the joys of the senses, it is an intoxication. How wonderful is Bernard's night with the provoking and dissolute little
Sarah! What intense emotion is Michel's when he meets the
youths of Biskra; his great and noble passion for his wife
Marceline had not prevented him from meditating suicide,
but the passive and submissive creatures with whom he can
experience pleasure restore him to the joy of living.

This sensual pleasure is in no sense that pagan pleasure
which is associated with sentiment and with intelligence.
Michel's pleasure is that of having overcome sin, of having
freed himself therefrom, of having conquered the scruples
and apprehensions within him. Henceforth his liberated
consciousness floats in an ocean of delight. An ephemeral
delight, however: Bernard leaves Sarah at dawn after their
first night; Lafcadio leaves Geneviève in the morning. " Not
love, Nathanaël, but fervour." In fact, any kind of lasting
relationship with these insignificant creatures seemed to
the hero impossible. His heart and his spirit are turned
towards a woman for whom he burns with so-called " platonic " love.

This duality in love, so characteristic with Gide, dominates, however, the whole of Christian society. Such was the love of the mediæval knights for their Dulcineas, such the love of Dante for Beatrice whom he met on a single occasion when she was eight years old, and that of Petrarch for Laura, half-seen one day in church, and whom, it is said, he refused to marry so that he might reverence her the more. Nerval's romantic love for Laura retains its character. Musset suffers in being unable to escape from debauchery and therefore from smirching the idealized object of his passion. And this, again, is the subject of George Sand's *Elle et Lui*. The poet of the period sighs despairingly for the well-beloved while carrying on with a grisette. Baudelaire addressed to Madame S——, whom he had met in a salon, his most splendid poems: *" Je t'adore à l'égal de la voûte nocturne. . . ."* Nevertheless, when she offers herself to him, he escapes, like Joseph, and turns to a Negress, a prostitute, one of those with whom alone he dared to experience pleasure, enjoining " silence," so that he might dream of Madame S——.

> *" Une nuit que j'étais près d'une affreuse Juive,*
> *Je me pris à songer près de ce corps vendu*
> . . . .
> *A la triste beauté dont mon désir se prive. . . ."* [1]

Gide has a deep sense of the sadness of this inward separation which compels a man to divide between several that which he would wish to give to one alone. On the one hand

[1] " One night, having with me a frightful Jewess,
I fell a-dreaming at the side of this bought body . . .
Of the sad beauty my desire forgoes."

he is driven perpetually to change the creatures of his pleasure; on the other, and this is more serious, his platonic passion remains perpetually unsatisfied. . . .

Such is the love of André Walter for Emmanuèle, a tender boyish attachment trying in vain to prolong itself. It is true that in spite of the too ethereal style of his writing at this time, Gide has depicted this love with a rare delicacy of touch. It is nourished by reading together or by response to the beauty of nature; it is full of effusive outpourings, hand in hand, cheek against cheek, down which flow sweet tears of joy. " Real life," declares André, " holds no such transports." But " real life " is soon going to fail these two children. In order to draw nearer to each other, they pursue the same studies, try to store up the same memories and become exactly alike. An illusory similitude; for love, as Schopenhauer has so justly remarked, unites only two beings who are so completely opposed that they must fight one against the other for pre-eminence. In the *Cahiers d'André Walter*, the two almost identical souls do not succeed in fusing; " they collide and cross each other," or move like parallel lines into the invisible distance. In the same way will two friends ask of friendship that which it is unable to give. Their only medium of interchange is conversation, which they uselessly prolong. One of them sees the other home and cannot bring himself to leave him: in a state of artificial intellectual excitement, he seems to be hoping and waiting for some kind of shock, some real emotion which does not come, which cannot come. It is then that friendship seems a kind of impotent love.

When Emmanuèle marries a stranger, Walter is not jealous. " Jealous of what? " he admits. When she dies, he does not appear to suffer. " She is dead; *therefore* he possesses her." He seems, indeed, glad to be able to cry: "Lord, I am pure, I am pure, I am pure! " Yet in the *Cahier Noir*, which follows the *Cahier Blanc*, the hero tells us of his hard struggles with the call of the flesh. . . .

In *La Porte étroite* the love between Jérôme and Alissa becomes entirely chivalrous. By means of heroism and asceticism the two souls seek to attain to a purely spiritual embrace. In spite of the passion linking the young people one to the other, they compete in the art of escaping each other, and this novel reaches at certain moments to a tragic grandeur.

Reading more closely, however, we may find ourselves disappointed. If these lovers fly from each other, it is because when they are together they feel intolerably embarrassed, they are afraid of remaining alone together and " finding nothing more to say." The disquietude of Jérôme in the presence of Alissa is so great that the moment he leaves her he feels relieved, tranquil, almost happy, and able to set to work again. Your " love was, above all, cerebral, a fine intellectual obstinacy of fidelity," the young girl writes spitefully, and without believing her words, which are nevertheless true. In the later part of the book the mirage of this love is dissipated. We learn from Alissa's Journal that the girl had had but one genuinely deep desire: to fall into the young man's arms and yield to him.

Édouard's passion for Olivier, again, is of the same kind.

If it seems to us to be more real, it is because the author is himself attracted by the young man. Their very first meeting acted upon Édouard like a " flash of lightning." — " I felt as *he* looked at me," writes Édouard, " that he took possession of me, and my life was no longer my own." But in his nephew's presence Édouard's desire is inhibited by so much embarrassment, felt by them both, that from the first their love seems to be transformed into an ideal or, more exactly, into a moral passion. Édouard longs to bring the young man to surpass himself; Olivier to win Édouard's good opinion. It is for this reason that the words " esteem," " disesteem," " judge," and " misjudge " are so frequently in the mouths of both these characters. . . .

There is, however, in these pure passions, notwithstanding their sentimental and intellectual nature, a single moment wherein the two lovers experience the perfection of joy, a joy as complete as that which may be reached by means of simple carnal pleasure. In each case consciousness is suddenly released from moral constraint: timidity, modesty, and fear, which can arrest sexual desire as well as the pure desire for self-giving, suddenly fall away. The individual allows the deepest aspirations of his being to flow forth, and these, in a state of exaltation, become contagious. In the passion of the heart such a moment occurs when the lover perceives that his devotion is understood, recognized, and accepted by the beloved. When, during a dinner-party, intoxication has helped Olivier to conquer his shyness, he flings himself, in his gratitude, " quivering with tenderness and distress," upon Édouard and, " pressed against him," sobs out: " Take me away! " Having in his turn attained to self-forgetfulness, he has reached a state of lyrical inspiration, of supreme enthusiasm, of, he declares, " divine visitation," and henceforward dreams only of self-destruction.

The day after the dinner-party Édouard finds him half-fainting in the bathroom with the gas turned on. " I understand how one can take one's life," Olivier had said the evening before, " but it would be after having experienced a joy so great as to make further life seem pale by comparison, a joy of which one can say to oneself: It is enough."

In *La Porte étroite* Jérôme and Alissa, too, reach a moment of supreme satisfaction in regard to which they know that there can be " nothing further," and they say to themselves: " It is enough. No more. Already it is not so sweet as it was just now. . . ."

Perhaps nothing is more dangerous than ecstasy. It takes us to the very verge of life and deprives us, thenceforth, of the desire to return. Human joy is so negative that the perfect ecstasy of the mystics, and notably of the Hindu mystics, carries them straight into death.[1]

However, after this great and beautiful scene of supreme love, the passion of Édouard and Olivier is brought to an end in *Les Faux-Monnayeurs*. The novel goes on, but we do not again meet these two together. Has their love ceased to exist? Or have they, too, " nothing more to say " to each other?

Here again appears the incompleteness of such a love. " Sublimated " from the first, it reaches, after the first real meeting of the lovers, a height that makes return to earth

[1] *La Vie de Ramakrishna*, by Romain Rolland.

impossible. The dinner-party scene is, in fact, for both Olivier and Édouard the scene of the avowal of their love, but it is also, apparently, that love's final scene.

Passion born of physical desire, satisfying it, then idealizing it, can acquire fresh depth. Carnal intimacy will subsist through the tender affection which succeeds desire. The lover will first affirm his personality by winning the beloved woman and will then surpass himself in self-forgetfulness on behalf of this same woman. Thus are fused his egoistic and altruistic aspirations; thus does passion collect around it all the images and the sentiments of the ego and allow the individual to be himself.

Doubtless all human love is sadly imperfect. It is while watching Albertine asleep that Proust calms his jealousy and finds his greatest joy in love. Édouard experiences his greatest happiness at the moment when, in his desperate need of self-giving, he brings the half-asphyxiated Olivier back to life, as one might rescue a drowning man; when he washes the young man's " chest and face," covered with vomitings. One must devote oneself, says Rimbaud's *Vierge Folle*. " Although it may not be exactly tempting . . . dear Soul." There is indeed always a strange disproportion, an absence of coincidence, between our inward exaltation and the poor, material gestures wherewith it is expressed. But if, in Gide's work, love sometimes gives us so disappointing an impression of sadness, if the moments of joy seem so very ephemeral, it is doubtless because the author has not succeeded in finding in passion the deep unity of his consciousness.

CORYDON

In the preceding chapter we considered love between two persons, sometimes of the same sex and sometimes of different sex, as it appears in Gide's novels. In either case the psychology of love is one and the same. If this were not so, we should immediately detect what has been done wherever, as not infrequently happens, an author changes the sex of a character in order to avoid shocking the public. What appear to us unlikely in Proust's love for Albertine are the circumstances of time, place, and social surroundings, but the analysis of the great laws of passion (crystallization, jealousy, etc.) are of such general application that some even of those who are well-informed have refused to believe that the original from whom Proust was inspired to create the character of Albertine must be of the masculine sex.

Thus it is that the question of inversion presents itself to Gide essentially from the moral point of view. We have shown already, in the earlier part of this book, with what rare courage Gide was led not only openly to discuss this problem in *Corydon*, but also to speak of himself in *Si le*

211

Grain ne meurt. Substantially his attitude may be summar-
ized thus: Since I consider that inversion is not immorality,
why should I not venture to speak of the life of my senses
without subterfuge and make-believe?

Of Wilde, Krupp, and Eulenburg Corydon declares:
" They all denied; everyone will deny. . . . People have
the courage of their opinions; but of their morals, no. They
will accept suffering, but not disgrace."

Yet Gide's admission was looked upon as a challenge, or,
what is worse, as the result of an obsession. What has
scarcely been realized at all is that what Gide claims is
simply the right to be natural — the aim of his whole life.
" What I long for," adds Corydon, is " someone who . . .
would endure reprobation and insult without boastfulness
or bravado; or, better still, someone whose value, honesty,
and uprightness are so well known that reprobation would
hesitate at the outset. . . ."

Actually, there was no hesitation: reprobation was almost unanimous. Yet did Gide fail altogether in what he
undertook? Not only is this author not " dishonoured," but
he has never been more eagerly admired than he is to-day.
How is the attitude of the public to be explained?

There are no prejudices more powerful than those dictated by our " modesty " and sexual disgust. " We are
always at a loss to understand other people's love-affairs
and their way of fulfilling them," writes Gide. And this, no
doubt, is why " misunderstandings on this point are so
thoroughgoing and stubbornness so ferocious." They were
so, before the war, to such a degree that it was impossible,

in a work of literature, to handle the question of inversion in any manner whatever, and even Zola the audacious, tempted to try his hand, withdrew from the enterprise; while a doctor who made an effort to study the subject as a man of science lost his objective detachment and constantly permitted himself the expression of his contempt and horror for the very subject of his investigations,

To-day the ideas of the public on this subject are to some extent modified. The ephemeral outbreak of frenzy in certain circles during the post-war period, the influence of psychiatry, and, in literature, the works of Proust and of Gide have brought a considerable section of the public to regard inversion no longer as a vice, but rather as a sort of fatal disease. Thenceforward the writer may mention " sodomites," provided that he regards them as the children of an accursed race and depicts them as the victims of their own desires and of society, which hunts them down. Society loves to sympathize with its victims (hence the success of books on convict-prisons). For this reason Proust's dolorous accents in *Sodome et Gomorrhe* made the subject acceptable. And here there is an indication of the progress of public opinion: inversion has lost its character for immorality and is entering the domain of pathology. And this exactly explains why the public, in spite of the appearance of *Si le Grain ne meurt*, is able to value a writer such as Gide and why a few even go so far as to admire his courage.

But Gide has gone much, much further than Proust. Inversion for him is not only not a vice, but does not appear

to be against nature; it is, for him, as natural as heterosexuality. Thus, at the end of *Corydon*, he evokes the splendid loves of the ancient Greeks, the ephebes whose virtues
were often even heroic, who were to be met in the gymnasia,
who inspired the poets, philosophers, and sculptors of the
day and were the source of some of the greatest works of
art. When *Sodome et Gomorrhe* appeared, Gide did not
recognize this love in the tragic and repulsive Proustian
pictures. In the course of a friendly conversation with the
author, he reproached him with having made his picture of
Sodom too black, and Proust, with his customary amiabil-
ity, immediately declared that in his travesty of young people in "*jeunes filles en fleur*" he had exhausted all the
lively colours on his palette: grace, charm, youth.

How is it possible that there should be such a difference
of outlook? Is the inversion of which Gide speaks something quite different from that described by Proust? One
shows us unhappy victims of obsession; the other some of
the finest human types. Yet if we remain within our own
period, in Paris itself, if we visit one of the resorts where
inverts habitually gather together, in the promenade of
some music-hall, for example, it is Proust's descriptions
which seem the nearest to reality. Uneasy are the eyes of
these figures brushing past each other in the half-light.
Glances, from eyes which seem to glitter and gleam in the
obscurity, meet and cross each other. Here a giant of a man,
bulging enormously, with a huge moustache, seizes the arm
of a tall, slender, fair young fellow who smiles sanctimoni-
ously, keeping his eyes on the stage with a simulated in-

terest. There, sitting on a secluded bench, an old gentleman, with greying hair, the respectability of whose appearance is accentuated by pince-nez, is surrounded by three diminutive youths laughing and squealing. A pair of inverts creates the grotesque impression of being a parody of a normal couple. Their appearance of youthfulness is deceptive. With many of them it is no more than an appearance, which may be due either to rickets or to arrested development. Meanwhile, here is someone all at once taking flight for fear of being recognized in this resort by spectators in the orchestra. At the entrance of the music-hall sundry young bounders, shop-salesmen in their Sunday best, with hair glistening with pomade, are waiting on the pavement. . . . In face of such a spectacle, it seems difficult to evoke the beautiful Greek adolescent. . . ,

How does Gide arrive, in *Corydon*, at his defence of his conception of inversion? The book is certainly regarded by critics as his weakest. It was looked upon merely as a piece of special pleading on the part of the author. The whole of the second part is, indeed, a defence of inversion. But the earlier part is a generalized, objective study of the sexual instinct. Here Gide, who has always been interested in natural history, reaches, as a result of reading and personal observation, remarkably exact and cautious conclusions, coinciding in more than one particular with those of Freud, whose work was then unknown to the French public.

The sexual instinct, he explains, is not a simple, unique, definite tendency attracting, in the animal kingdom as a whole, one sex to the other. It is not an instinct which re-

leases itself with the precise categorical imperative of a reflex. Supporting this statement by a number of valuable
facts, Gide points out on the one hand males considerably
outnumbering females, and, on the other, females in rut
only for a few days a year. Thus there is nowhere in nature,
he says, an *absolute* relation between sexual pleasure and
procreation. The species seek solely voluptuous pleasure,
by whatever means. The act of procreation " amidst the
most disconcerting profusion is, more often than not, a
fluke."

Going on to consider sexuality in mankind, he observes
that it is at first without a definite object. In order to attract man, woman uses " artifice," " veils and adorn-
ments." Civilization does the rest. It is only by means of
" advice, example, invitation, incitement, and excitement
of all sorts " that society succeeds in " maintaining the desired coefficient of human heterosexuality." If a young
man, once he is adult, seeks love only with a woman, it is
because the whole of his education has urged him towards
the feminine sex; because it has been nothing but a series
of " injunctions " and " prescriptions " whose effect is to
bring him to consider woman as the only possible object of
love.

Strikingly enough, the Freudian theory reaches the same
conclusions. " You make the mistake," writes Freud, " of
confounding sexuality and reproduction." The nature of
the sexual instinct is " complex." It does not, at the age
of puberty, spring fully formed from the individual, like
Minerva from the brain of Jupiter, but develops slowly

from birth to maturity under the influence of modifications of the organism and of psychic inhibitions (transferences, sublimations, etc.). Now, there is, says Freud (and a large number of present-day psychiatrists are in agreement with him), in every individual, up to the time of the full development of puberty, a period during which the adolescent is attracted towards either sex *indifferently*. And it is essentially the unconscious constraint of moral laws and of public opinion that leads him, at maturity, towards heterosexuality.

From this point of view inversion in Greek social life, where women were shut up in the gynæceum and only men were considered of importance, is easily understandable. But how in our own time can an adolescent escape the powerful influence of education, drawing him, as Gide has so ably demonstrated, by every possible means towards the cult of woman? How is it possible that he should be sufficiently attracted towards his own sex to be willing to brave public opinion?

Gide has not solved this mysterious problem, and his failure to do so is the great gap in his work. Freud himself admits that psychoanalysis can do no more than offer a few suggestions on the subject. He thinks that in the case of the invert the sexual instinct has suffered a kind of arrest in its development, has remained at the primitive stage wherein, still diffused, it attracts the individual towards himself or towards his own sex. If heterosexual education has failed to influence this instinct, it is because, in his unconscious, the individual has not known how to break with his childhood; he is too closely attached to it, and this attachment itself, Freud adds, is to be laid to the account of the mother's love, either too tender or too austere, for her son. And it is curious to note that in the childhood of Gide, as in that of Proust, the mother played a very important part.

Is inversion, as it appears in our own day, " against nature"? The expression is meaningless, since everything that exists is within nature. It would be more exact to inquire whether, to-day, inversion is a perversion of the sexual instinct. And it is under this head that Freud has dealt with it.

Yet can a mere arrest in the development of an instinct be regarded as a disease? No, Freud replies; there is no neurosis unless inversion is accompanied by other deviations, unless the totality of the functions and activities of the individual has also undergone serious modifications.

Even to-day, therefore, inversion is not in itself pathological. It is indubitably no more abnormal than is the dissociation between the senses and the feelings produced in the individual by the influence of Christian society. Doubtless the larger number of inverts are to-day actually damaged beings because their sexual perversion is accompanied by other perversions (fetishism, sadism, impotence . . .) and by other physiological disorders (rachitism, etc.). It is such as these one meets in the promenade of a certain music-hall, and the sad and painful impression they create when they are gathered together is thus explicable. Yet it is impossible to ignore them, for they probably

constitute the vast majority of inverts in contemporary so-
society,

It is because he has not mentioned them (save inci-
dentally, in a note) that Gide has not succeeded in convinc-
ing his readers. They do not grasp his remarkable analysis
of the sexual instinct. It is a matter for regret that, after
having spoken of the " bisexuality " of the adolescent —
instead of explaining how it occurs that in spite of current
education certain individuals are attracted by their own sex
— Gide should immediately have criticized this heterosexual education, against which he has set up ancient Greece.
He has too rapidly transposed the problem from the psychological to the social plane. Doubtless these two aspects are
closely allied. It is none the less true that to the question
as to whether inversion is to-day a perversion of the sexual
instinct, he has given only the beginning of an answer.

But since in certain respects his work has anticipated
some of the great conceptions of modern psychiatry, these
may help us to complete our study of Gide. Psychoanalysis
recognizes an infinite variety of inversions, the extreme
forms being on one side morbid, and on the other merely
the emergence of one of the two bisexual tendencies of man,
which, in an unprejudiced society, can find free expression,

Gide ends *Corydon* by evoking Greece. But the inversion
of antiquity, founded solely upon a contemptuous estimate of woman, can scarcely be regarded as an ideal. Contemporary society has released woman from an unjustifiable slavery and inclines towards giving her back her
personality. Can woman become man's equal? Thencefor-

ward a Plato would no longer exclude her from love.

What Greece can teach us, on the other hand, is the splendid platonic union between body and spirit, or, more exactly, the progressive elevation of vulgar passion to celestial passion, the transport love brings to the soul being directed and controlled, the inspiration of the heart leading to virtue, the madness of desire to wisdom, delirium to a veritable initiating ectasy.

Two prejudices would seem, for long, to have imprisoned passion: the antique prejudice against women, and the Christian prejudice against the flesh. Loosed from these preconceived ideas, love would at last be free, and the problem of inversion merely a social problem.

PART IV

HIS SOCIAL CRITICISM

THE INDIVIDUAL AND SOCIETY

" POLITICAL questions," wrote Gide in 1923, " seem to me less important than social questions; social questions less . . . important than moral questions. . . . It is fitting to blame institutions less than men, and . . . it is they, first and foremost, whose reform is of importance." Nevertheless, in his novels as in his essays, he has often been moved to criticize some of the great institutions of contemporary society.

This criticism arises naturally from certain general ideas which Gide has not developed; and we should like to attempt to reconstruct them in order the better to understand the bearing of each of these special criticisms. The word " reconstruct " is no doubt ambitious: there can be no question of anything more than a few very brief statements indicating the general orientation of Gide's thought,

*   *   *

The formula of the individualists, " the individual *versus* society," seems to me to be in opposition to Gide's social ideas. It implies an entirely Rousseauesque conception of history and prehistory and sees man, at the beginning of

223

time, as a good savage living perfectly happily in splendid isolation and an ideal state of anarchy. But one day he accepted civilization and lost his liberty. From that moment the individual became " the enemy of law." In the present state of society, therefore, laws are regarded as an inevitable evil whose range should be restricted as far as possible. Along these lines a whole series of writers, from the eighteenth century onwards, have arrived at " liberalism ": believing that in a completely liberalized society the individual would in fact approach his original, lost state of anarchy.[1]

To-day, however, liberal individualism rests upon ruined foundations. Spinoza has already most justly declared that a man left to his own resources alone in a forest is less free than in a prison. The individual needs society. Without it he would lose not only his liberty but his life. However far one goes back into history, one fails to meet good savages living like Robinson Crusoe. Studies of the primitives have confirmed this truth. Society is never found to consist of a collection of isolated, autonomous, and independent individuals, but rather of a company of social beings. In itself it is a collective being and is reflected *as such* in the consciousness of each one of us. Thus there are, in everyone, individual tendencies. The real question,

---

[1] In various post-war numbers of the *Nouvelle Revue Française* are to be found articles expressing the views of the group on this subject. While certain of the newly-converted (such as Ghéon) inclined towards the social ideals inspired by the *Action Française*, Jacques Rivière, in a long article, set forth the insufficiency and powerlessness of liberalism and has been interested since that time — with certain reservations, it is true — in Russian collectivism.

therefore, resolves itself to this: how can a man reconcile the two?

Here is Gide's answer to this difficult problem: "*It is in being the most particular that we best serve the most general interest.*" But this truth, he adds, should be strengthened by the following: "*It is in renouncing oneself that one finds oneself.*"

An immensely far-reaching answer, whence we have seen Gide draw his ethic, and from which a sociology might be drawn. In developing whatever is most " particular " to himself, in *specializing,* the individual will play, in the social group, the irreplaceable part assigned to him by nature.[1] In putting his personality at the service of all and forgetting himself the individual will indeed co-operate in the collective work. Thus one is led to consider the division of labour, and co-operation. It is true that I am deducing these ideas from Gide's thought, but it seems to me that indeed they are implicitly contained therein.

One might say, further: to be individual means to become conscious of oneself. " Social life," writes Valéry, " would indeed be transformed if all demonstrations and

[1] True specialization is the pathway to generalization. The man of science, specializing in a single branch and making a thorough study of it, becomes aware of the great laws of life. There are, however, two kinds of specialization, the one tending to augment and the other to reduce personality. Thus, in industry, division of labour ends by creating on the one hand *specialists* and, on the other, *specialized* workers. The first have acquired, by virtue of a more or less prolonged apprenticeship, a *particular* technique enabling them to retain a sense of the *general* bearing of their work; the second, " chain-workers," simply carry out certain automatic movements learned in a few days or even in a few hours. They have become parts of a mechanism.

all external actions, words, etc., were judged according to the presumed degree of consciousness on the part of their author, if everything escaping into action without self-control were considered shameful." I would add: were considered the sole crime of humanity, the one that necessarily includes all the others.

In this sense individualism is clearly no more than a *limited tendency*, for only a god could be completely conscious and in perfect collaboration with other gods. But if society set this ideal before all its members, we should witness an amazing revolution.

Society, however, regarded historically (and with due allowance for periods of decadence and of reaction), does seem to be gradually evolving towards this form of individualism.

In the primitive tribe all the members were subject to the *same* religious laws. To this cohesion, attained by a group of individuals more or less identical with each other, has added itself an organic cohesion, still very imperfect, of *differentiated* individuals co-operating towards a single social end.[1] Formerly crime was punished as crime in itself and, generally, without consideration of the degree of consciousness on the part of the individual. To-day individual responsibility has been added to this objective responsibility, though so far only in a very rudimentary fashion.[2]

[1] This new cohesion appears in the division of labour, a development not more than a few centuries old.

[2] In law it is represented by the recognition of attenuated responsibility, the play of attenuating circumstances, only fairly recently admitted.

Perhaps the foundation and the unity of Gide's social criticisms are to be found in his struggle against the extraordinary slowness of social evolution towards true individualism.

Most contemporary institutions seem to us to be *very* ancient monuments, underpinned by a few reforms. Education, the family, religion, justice, and patriotism still rest upon the principle of authority, on an ancient dogmatism originating in religion, on spiritual submission and a whole system of punishments and rewards. Whoever stands out, says the brother of the *Enfant prodigue,* is " the product of madness and of pride." Blood-relationship, attachment to the same soil, and the cult of ancestors will turn the individual, by a process of successive reductions, into the average social type. The old morality of similitude still holds good; everyone must resemble everyone else. Need one do more than consider our forbidding-looking schools, our barracks and prisons, and all our large State buildings in order to understand that the individual is there called upon to lose his soul and his *raison d'être?* It is through these that we have come to believe that the military régime is the model of social life.

Nevertheless these ancient institutions are defended, to this day, by certain classes of society. In no other way can their survival be explained. If Gide has not directly attacked them, he has sometimes vehemently, more often ironically, denounced the attitude of mind to be found wherever they are supported. " Crustacea " is the name given by the young Lafcadio and his friend Protos to all these respectable people enclosed in their shells, nationalists, defenders of the cult of the dead, judges imbued with their omnipotence, husbands living on the idea of conjugal honour, fathers leaning on their authority. . . . The " crustacean " is the man who subdues reason to rule, is afraid of the critical spirit, drills the individual into imitating what has already been done and what is being done all round him. He is the traditionalist, the " conformist," always ready to bow to public opinion. Well provided for, at ease in his house, in his profession, in life, he runs no risks. He has sacrificed the spirit to the letter, the man to the uniform, and inward development to the outward aggrandizement represented by honour and decorations. His egoism remains intact because he does not know the meaning of the word " self-renunciation "; for, in order to renounce himself, a man must first have a self to renounce, and this he has suppressed once and for all.

In politics, the " crustacean " is nearly always conservative. " The conservative parties," writes Gide in a study on *L'Avenir de l'Europe,* " deceive themselves if they reckon they can lodge the future in institutions belonging to the past, for old forms cannot be fitted to young forces." In our society, where the industrial and economic aspects of life are changing with so great a rapidity that nothing which lacks the power of movement seems able to maintain itself, there are still those who can believe that the form of the State, of the family, and of the administration of justice ought not to change and that their structure must be maintained at all costs exactly as in the past.

It is true that the transformation of social institutions is a risky undertaking. Movement towards collectivization doubtless frees mankind from the oppression of the ancient forms, but will the new be any less tyrannical?

So far Gide has not considered this danger. Yet to-day every one of our institutions is doubly threatened: thus the individual is no longer to be suppressed by the family, but it is possible he will be stifled by the State. At present the adolescent is often obliged to use the best of his strength in revolting against his own relatives, but what if he is constrained to fight against the pressure of the whole collective social group? The ideal education will be that which seeks to make of the child, not a slave of the family or the State, but a living being, unique and irreplaceable.

*   *   *

Gide has interested himself in social questions only in so far as they have directly forced themselves upon him. It was while he was serving on a jury that he gave his attention to the administration of justice; and while travelling in the Congo that he discovered the abuses of colonization. . . . As regards the family, he felt himself hemmed in thereby from childhood onwards.

Yet he has always tried to avoid questioning the great principles.

Nothing seems to him easier than to throw down everything: but this is to suppress problems rather than to solve them.

Nevertheless, the further he enters into any matter, the bolder he grows. The facts themselves seem to provoke him.

Without either outcry or violence he breathes a destructive doubt into our belief in institutions. He suggests suspicions, scruples. Nothing is more dangerous than the disquietude he awakens, so much more efficaciously than by savage denunciations. Woe to " conclusive books "! In Gide's belief, the novel with a purpose, weakened by its intention, has no power of demonstration. He wishes a book to retain " a question without an answer." What people cannot endure is uncertainty as to things they regard with religious reverence. It is only when they are detached from their tranquillity that reforms become possible. Socrates, with the help of his daimon, was content to ask questions. But these questions were so terrible that he was regarded as a perverter of youth and condemned by his city. The title accorded to Gide is that of " evil-doer." [1] The scandal he provokes, without seeking it, proves that his method is good.

*   *   *

Thus Gide has been able to engage in criticism of society without entering the political battle-ground. In order to reach the crowd, one's voice must carry without inflections: the writer must become a journalist. No doubt it is sometimes painful to be obliged to resist the desire for a more direct, more physical attack upon the errors and abuses of society; it is, however, by remaining in his proper domain, in that of thought, that the writer, by nature the destroyer of conventions, will most effectively operate with greater force.[2]

[1] See page 78.
[2] Romain Rolland made an eloquent defence of this point of view in the course of his stirring controversy with Barbusse.

There are nevertheless times when public events are so urgent, when the iniquity of a spectacle presses so immediately upon a writer, that he cannot rest. At such times he must fling himself valiantly into the struggle, as did Voltaire and Zola. After his return from the Congo, Gide fought for almost a year in the hope of crushing the despotism of the great concessionary companies. But as soon as the case was at an end, he regained his self-possession and refused to respond to further appeals.

But from this time forward he attended more deeply to social questions, not so much to this or that particular aspect as to their bearing on life as a whole.

To-day he appears to believe that he has finished his imaginative work. And it is in order to give this work a more precise and a wider application that he observes, with keener interest than ever, the social problems that have preoccupied him from the first. A vast, terrible, painful investigation. Everywhere, under the shelter of law, man exploits man. Is it possible that the civilization of which he is so proud should be resting on a ruined foundation?

Gide seems to be led into taking up a more and more exact attitude towards these great problems. It is for this reason that he watches so sympathetically the development of the Russian experiment in " a society without the family and without religion." If, some little time ago, he thought that the way to improve institutions is to reform the individual, to-day he is perhaps ready to believe that the renovation of institutions may likewise renew the individual.

THE FAMILY AND EDUCATION

" The family, that social cell."
PAUL BOURGET
The family, " cellular régime."
ANDRE GIDE

ONE may regard the family, as it exists to-day, from many points of view. Gide saw it primarily as a patriarchal institution. The father, occupied outside the home, knows nothing of the inner life of those near to him. The mother is absorbed by household cares, wherein she is supposed to find all her happiness. The eldest child, " sententious," keeps guard over the traditional spirit of the house. The adolescent listens, uneasily, to the call of distant spaces. The youngest, " precocious and awakened," secretly cherishes thoughts that are hostile to his family. Meanwhile, gathered round the table in the evening, they are strangers to each other. Every kind of spontaneity is falsified by compulsory association and the constraint of family duties; the love which relationship might create is crippled; and the ruling forces are the sentiments of conjugal

232

honour, filial respect, and obedience: embarrassment and treachery. . . .

The " *grande chose fermée* " (great shut-in thing) that is the family rests upon the fidelity of the married couple. " Of all branches of human knowledge," wrote Balzac, " that of marriage [is] the most backward."

Amongst the severe, devout bourgeoisie, the class most often depicted by Gide, the young girl has scarcely evolved and is in many respects exactly what she was in the nineteenth century. The old apparatus of social precautions, set up for the purpose of protecting her innocence, is still in place. The girl herself, if she belongs to the upper classes, has, more or less consciously, a single preoccupation: a husband. The rest of her unemployed existence is merely a pastime. When Éveline is trying to persuade Dr. Marchand to let her friend Yvonne work for him, he replies ironically: " And the elegant arts? . . . Why were they invented, if not to occupy the idle? . . ." Men who regard the young girl as one of the world's marvels are apt to forget the drama going forward in her consciousness beneath her " futile preoccupations ": the young girl's drama of husband-catching. " It is atrocious . . ." says Éveline, " that the desires of this creature, her virtues, and her gifts should be dependent upon the more or less good will of a man; it makes me indignant! " Éveline pities her friend Yvonne. She thinks of the old maid, that product of the half-freedom the West accords to women: " To feel within oneself all that is needed for helping, for succouring, for spreading joy about one, and to be unable to find the means of doing so! "

The young man, too, often encounters equally disturbing difficulties. If social and moral laws are to be observed in a society such as our own, where adultery is condemned and girls must remain virgins, with whom, if not with prostitutes, can he satisfy his normal desires? " Degrading liaisons," writes Gide. . . . Should the young man remain chaste until he marries, as do undoubtedly certain pastors and provincials in Gide's novels?

Such, then, is the couple, so little prepared for marriage, that is bound by society " in indissoluble bonds," consecrated by religion " for all eternity." Gide has most happily described certain of the nuptial ceremonies. " Drives," " receptions," " visits," punctuate the engagement period, a " comedy of happiness," allowing the newly-made pair no time to collect themselves. The couple are disguised as married people. " Crowd," " heat," " refreshments," bridesmaids. And, amongst the puritans, the pastor, in his address, sows " the good seed," with an " indescribable something, ineffably high-flown, paradisical, and inane."

In the end, however, everything is more or less of a compromise. Juliette, in order to sacrifice herself for her sister Alissa, marries a business man, outside their circle, a great hearty creature, bald and rubicond. In giving him, for the first time, her icy hand, she faints away. " That marriage may turn out pretty well," is the confident verdict of her people. And they are right. For Juliette, away on her honeymoon, writes home " enthusiastically." Some

years later, Alissa will see her again, surrounded by children, happy, and with all the emotional disturbances of
her youth forgotten.[1]

When Gide explores the intimate life of a couple, he
usually comes upon adultery. Almost all nineteenth-century
novels turn upon this theme, and most contemporary plays.
In *Les Faux-Monnayeurs* Gide describes the family lives
of two magistrates, each of whom may be called average
citizens. In one case it is the wife who disappears from
home, and presently returns. In the other the husband em-
barks on a " little adventure " and is obliged to " trick " his
wife, to " dissemble " and " lie." Pauline even believes it
her duty to be her husband's accomplice, society having
taught her that men are subject to urgencies that morality
is ashamed to recognize and that yet it is dangerous to leave
unassuaged. Upon the surface of these " false situations "
life goes on, goes on. . . .

Nevertheless Gide has shown us faithful couples: in the
École des Femmes there is a Catholic pair. After a few
years Éveline, who was altogether in love with her husband
when she married him, comes gradually to see him as he
is. This is the law of love itself: when passion is at an end,
one no longer recognizes the beloved. But marriage, as conceived of by the Church, *ought* to last. Éveline, thenceforward, is unhappy with Robert, but her father and her confessor, the conscience and the director, advise her above
all things to " hide " her husband's deficiencies " from

[1] It is in the face of this happiness that Alissa experiences the discomfort we have already alluded to.

all eyes " and to pray to God for consolation. The duty of the " Christian wife " is resignation.

"To what a point," writes Gide, " can two beings who are living on the whole the same life, and who love each other, remain (or become) enigmatic and immured one for the other! " Marriage becomes an invitation to indolence. The man gives up all efforts to attract: his wife belongs to him. She, too, moreover, has given up. It is in relation to an elderly Protestant couple, the La Pérouses, that Gide shows us how " abominably " a husband and wife, while still remaining attached to each other, can make each other " suffer." " Any casual stranger one passes in the street," cries La Pérouse, " would understand one better than the woman to whom one has given one's life." Amidst the friction of a joint existence, " married life is nothing less than an inferno."

* * *

In *Corydon,* written over twenty years ago, Gide made a kind of return to the past; observing the part played by the woman enclosed in the gynæceum, devoting herself, as nature orders her to do, primarily to maternity, and ennobling herself exactly by means of this sacrifice. It is because the women of antiquity were hardly ever lovers, he wrote, that the Greeks were able to create the " admirable figures of Andromache, Iphigenia, and Antigone." Nearly all Gide's early heroines are akin to these. They live only through devotion and self-giving.

But in *Les Faux-Monnayeurs,* published in 1926, there appears, in the midst of a family wedded to tradition, a young girl, Sarah, who, with the vehemence of youth and the intransigence of a rebel, claims complete emancipation. Sarah sees, both in the " pious resignation " of the old maid and in " conjugal devotion," nothing but " deception," and, in marriage, nothing but " a dreary bargain." She declares herself ready to " face all the scorns and all the reproaches." She is rather like those English and American girls who, reacting against puritanism, frenziedly give themselves up to pleasure. But brutish impulses annihilate passion as surely as asceticism. Every reaction begins with an excess.

The feminine characters since created by Gide demand the same liberty, but with a firmness born of thought. Éveline, brought up in bourgeois surroundings, rebels in her mind, but does not dare to free herself. Her daughter Geneviève, however, declares that she will never submit to marriage as it exists to-day and that she is determined " to make *an associate, a comrade*, of the man with whom she [shall fall in love]." Man's equal, she will live, " as he does, a life of her own." There will be one slave the less in social life, and one more individual: woman.

Geneviève goes still further: she dares to say openly to her mother: In renouncing love outside marriage, " you have made yourself the slave of your duty . . . an imaginary duty . . . I cannot be grateful to you for this." And in her heart, without admitting it to her daughter, Éveline approves.

Doubtless, she might reflect, a Princess de Clèves can stir our feelings by carrying resistance to the point of heroism. But what is the meaning of her " sacrifice " if it is " *useless* "? Balzac has very justly remarked that a wife injures her husband, not by giving way to, or by curbing, her passion for another man, but from the moment she feels this passion to be *involuntary*. For the husband, his wife, even if she *remains faithful,* becomes, from this moment, a stranger obsessed by thoughts that are entirely out of his reach.

Gide has been struck by the fact that in traditional jealousy, and especially in that of the husband, there is always present the idea of conjugal honour, a species of legal right based " upon self-love " and on this account, he says, " ceasing to interest [me]." " That an Othello should be jealous is understandable; he is obsessed by the image of the pleasure taken by his wife with another." Yet I have often heard Gide declare that even this instinctive jealousy appears to him to be a feeling made of violence and hostility that it would be fine to be able to dominate. It is not love, not the generously blossoming passion of the individual, that should be vanquished, but jealousy, the dangerous, constricting passion. There is in real love such a spontaneous desire to give that he who loves, desiring nothing but the other's happiness, will accept his inconstancy as a painful opportunity of proving the self-sacrificing strength of his love.

It is along these lines that Gide, if he had developed the question, would propose to liberate marriage and the married. " The evil is never in love," says the pastor in *La Symphonie pastorale*. It is the idea of the sinfulness of the

flesh that, by imprisoning love, has perverted all the sentiments, even friendship and affection; has created " our
doubt and the hardness of our hearts " and made men less
generous. The idea of the sinfulness of the flesh was one of
the reasons for the subjection of women.[1]

But though Gide finds the root of the evil in our belief
in the malignity of love and desires greater freedom for
love, he does not by any means conclude that the individual
should be invited to do as he likes, but rather that he should
achieve self-mastery. What is needed is not the prohibition
of desires, as the orthodox Christian would have it, but
their education. So that man may struggle no longer against
his passions, but rather against their tendency to oppress

---

[1] According to the Fathers of the Church, woman should be " ashamed
of her beauty "; for this it is that incites to fornication and is the " mother
of human ills " and " the gateway of hell." " Marry," said Saint Paul . . .
" that Satan tempt you not for your incontinency." But it is not only the
idea of the sinfulness of the flesh that for so many centuries has driven
men to insist that women shall be virtuous: the question of paternity has
also played an important part. It is the child that to this day introduces
into the problem of feminine emancipation and the liberation of married
couples so many serious and complex difficulties. As a novelist, Gide has
never been called upon to consider the matter, because, for him, the family
is always, or nearly always, injurious for the child. Does this mean that the
family should be suppressed, or merely reformed?
In *Marriage and Morals* the English philosopher Bertrand Russell suggests very reasonable solutions. He claims that in gaining considerable
control over procreation we have, in a sense, conquered nature. He would
therefore give the married complete freedom — so long as there is no child.
He even believes that " trial marriage " is necessary for the moral, and still
more so for the physical, welfare of the partners. — But the moment a child
appears, everything is changed. Russell regards divorce, and particularly
repeated divorce, as only less disastrous for the child than temperamental
incompatibility between the parents. Yet though stable marriage is desirable, it does not follow that there must be absolute fidelity between the
parents. Like Gide, Russell believes that the conquest of jealousy is a finer
and more difficult achievement than the conquest of passion.

others. Husband and wife would cease to be police-officers charged with mutual surveillance. Freedom would put an end to the petty lies of the adulterer. And since it is the nature of love to diminish as soon as it ceases to grow, it would the more naturally evolve into an affectionate intimacy.

*   *   *

Yet more serious, in Gide's opinion, than the situation of the married couple is that of the child in the " family circle."

Jacques appears to have been so much reduced by fear and by respect that he says when his father (the pastor in the *Symphonie pastorale*) opposes his love for the woman of his choice: " Father, I am resolved to *obey* you." He only just dares to ask: " May I know your reasons? " And thus it is that he is soon moved to join a religious order.[1]

Now and again the child revolts: his early puritan education left in Armand " an incurable resentment "; it made him for ever rebellious, despairing, bitter, and cynical. He regards all that is called virtue with " horror " and " hatred." [2]

[1] Jacques had been converted to Catholicism.

[2] The child, it would seem, has only recently been discovered. Hence the novelty of *Émile*. Hitherto the child had been supposed to have no personality. Education was a sort of training; the rod was the schoolmaster's indispensable instrument. Jules Boissier tells us that the howling of children could be heard coming from the Roman Catholic schools. English village schoolmasters in the eighteenth century were in the habit of flogging the boys' hind quarters publicly in class, says John Carpentier. At this time young princes were symbolically beaten in the persons of children who were specially attached to them. Must we believe, as certain historians assert, that the son of the Marquis de Boufflers died as a result of a flogging too zealously administered by his teacher? Many things contributed to the unhappiness of the child's lot: even in the following century it is enough to read *Petit Chose, Jack, David Copperfield,* and *Poil de Carotte.* . . .

In the middle-class conditions described by Gide, education seems hardly more successful. " The children of opinionated parents will be still more opinionated." And he adds: " Some who are indignant with the alcoholic who teaches his son to drink act, along their own lines, no differently."

The child who wants to escape is bound to rebel. When little Georges comes to work at his mother's side under the lamp in the evening, " It is not," she says, " affection that I meet in his glance; it is defiance." Like *Le Prodigue,* he stiffens himself against the pressure of the family. In his turn, the younger brother of the *Prodigue* exclaims: " How should one of my own people be my friend? "

At the age of twenty, however, the child is thrown on his own resources. Alexandre Vedel and Vincent Molinié behave like country bumpkins suddenly let loose in Paris.

Nevertheless Gide believes that parental indulgence succeeds no better than severity: " The most lamentable are those who are the victims of adulation," an adulation that can so easily become an irritating, misplaced solicitude, or take the form of " advice . . . admonition . . . reprimand."

In the end, the parents themselves pay the price of their mistakes. The child soon escapes. " One loses hold," says Pauline, " the tenderest love is helpless." Gide does not forget to reveal the situation from the mother's sorrowful point of view. Deceived by her husband, Pauline is still more deceived by her sons. And it is Olivier she most regrets. " His confidence . . . ? I have lost it! . . . He hides himself from me." The child prefers any stranger to his parents, if only because the stranger is unlike them. The father, too, may be a victim. Even Profitendieu, the least sympathetic of bourgeois, never fails to move Gide. When Bernard leaves the " House," Profitendieu, hiding " his face in his hands " and " all shaken with sobs," says indistinctly: " You see . . . you see, sir, that a child can make one very miserable."

Such, for Gide, is the " cellular régime." The story of little Boris is, I cannot but believe, symbolic. This fragile, gentle little soul is sent by Édouard, who in the end admits his own blindness, to the *pension* Vedel, to breathe the " poisoned air " existing there " under the cover of religion and morality "; and before long is driven to take his own life. . . .

Over against these adolescents, all more or less deformed by education, Gide sets up the triumphant bastard [1] — according to Euripides, " the son of transports." Everything succeeds with him. The " future belongs to him "! " He alone has a right to the natural." See with what assurance Bernard and Lafcadio advance towards life; with what assurance and with what supple gestures.

Doubtless the illegitimate child was " imprudently begotten." According to Œdipe, he is the " unwanted " child and is " compromising." Lafcadio calls him the " product

[1] Evidently, for Gide, a symbolic image. As a matter of fact, in contemporary society, the illegitimate child usually shares the ideas of his own circle. He is ashamed of his origin and sometimes suffers all his life from an inferiority complex.

of an extravagance, a kink in the straight line." Molinié, the grotesque magistrate, calls him the " fruit of disorder and disobedience," who " necessarily carries within him the seeds of anarchy." But Gide delights in him exactly because he is a check on the traditional principle of the family. The framework of family life is cracked. Gide himself suffered too much within it. He is too certain of its evildoings. " Amongst forty families personally observed by me," he writes, " I know hardly four wherein the parents do not act in such a manner that nothing could be more desirable for their children than escape from their control." So much the worse if the " crustaceans " proceed to " exclaim at the scandal "! Without hesitation he takes, at this point, a revolutionary attitude. Truth is at stake, and the existence of the individual.

A rejuvenated society may arise. Is it a dream? Perhaps. We are beginning to live it. For indeed, though slowly, very slowly, the family is evolving towards new forms. . . ." [1]

*   *   *

One may regard as fantastic the education of Lafcadio as it is presented by Gide in *Les Caves du Vatican*. This child, " to whom his mother gave five uncles," has from his earliest years been accustomed by them to " the free disposal of himself." He has known nothing either of punishments or of rewards and has been at liberty to go about just as he liked. Taken across Europe from one country to an-

[1] So far we see only the simple disintegration of the family, notably in Germany and in America.

other, ceaselessly transplanted, he creates his personality. " All instruction," writes Gide, " is an uprooting." Wonderful hygienic measures were taken: Lafcadio went " with head and feet bare " in all weathers, always in the open. He is taught entirely by means of games. In order to make the child active, is it not necessary to inspire in him the desire for activity? One of his uncles teaches him to reckon by allowing him to " get into difficulties " with " foreign coinage." Another teaches him physics with the help of the tricks of conjurors, jugglers, and prestidigitators. Later on, Lafcadio will say: " I profited greatly by this teaching."

In spite of the irony of the narrative, I find there some of the more important of the principles underlying the most modern educational theories. In these new schools, situated in natural surroundings, quite young children are at work on material objects: boxes, frames, colours. The taking of places in class, and examinations, have been abolished together with immobility. The old system, founded on compulsory attention and memory, has disappeared in favour of one whose method is not unlike that of the teaching of Lafcadio. It recognizes the primary necessity of getting the child to think, imagine, understand, and create, for himself.

But the difficulty of the problem lies in deciding by whom instruction shall be given. To this, so far, Gide has no answer.

To-day everything shows that it is the State which inherits the functions of the family in proportion as the latter disappears. The evolution began, moreover, several centuries ago,[1] and seems, unhappily, to be leading us towards a very menacing future. The liberation of the child is in danger of being brought about less in his own interest than in the interest of a new collective oppression and a uniform system of ideas established by the State. We need to discover how to avoid stifling the original personality under the weight of collectivism, how to escape the danger of conformity, perhaps to-day threatening humanity more seriously than ever.

To be sure, if the influence of the State did not deviate, if, in its educative capacity, it would keep within its proper role, the experiment would be interesting to follow. It is likely that the social group, being larger than the family, might be less tyrannical. The State is less likely to concern itself with the intimate personal life of the child. In the classic conflicts between two generations concerning the choice of a profession, marriage, etc., etc., the State has no interest in opposing the child. The father usually wishes his son to follow either his own profession or the one which he himself would have liked to follow. The State will merely

[1] From the inception of the *pater familias* down to our own day the family has ceaselessly evolved towards individualism. Industrial development has favoured this evolution. The State has begun to teach children. It also attends to their health (laws as to medical care for the children of poor parents, laws as to cases of paternal destitution, etc.). There is even a tendency towards State intervention, under the influence of eugenics, in sexual life. In a negative sense eugenics are already practised in certain of the American States where " degenerates " who are also professional criminals are sterilized. But how can authority, to-day, prove degeneration?

aim at so placing each individual that he shall give the best that is in him.[1]

Are there any educators beyond the State or the parents? Gide has remarked that the adopted child is often more pampered than the legitimate child. The feelings of Bernard's father for his son " are by so much the stronger " in that they are free from the " call of the blood."

Can one imagine individual teachers who, while enveloping the child with a truer, purer love, would expand his intelligence? Most of the Greek philosophers were surrounded by young folks whom they tried to raise to their own level. In the finest of these schools, which one might call " liberal," the aim of the teaching was the progress of the interior life.

In *Si le Grain ne meurt* Gide declared that if he had not been a writer, he would have chosen to be a professor. No task seemed to him more generous than that of awakening a young mind to thought. A difficult task: " the implacable Persephone," desiring to give young Hercules a divine education, exposed him in his cradle on live coals surrounded by flames. True teaching exacts, from master and pupil alike, a certain hardness towards themselves; abnegation even, for, in proportion as the pupil develops, the master must detach himself: " Nathanaël, throw away my book. . . ."

[1] It is with this end in view that the investigation of occupational aptitudes tends to become a science that shall enable the educational authority to allocate to the child the branch of study for which he has the most aptitude. But this science, which seems to rely only on psycho-physiology, may bring many errors in its train.

If teaching is still too often a system of misunderstanding, if the family remains a closed circle, if husband and wife are deformed by jealousy, it is because self-giving has not in any real sense entered the home.

"Family egoism is hardly less hideous than individual egoism."

3

JUSTICE

In 1912 André Gide was called to serve on a jury at the Rouen assizes. " It is one thing," he writes in his *Souvenirs,* " to hear justice administered, and quite another to help in administering it. . . . The extent to which human justice is a doubtful and precarious thing is what, for twelve days, I have been realizing to the point of anguish."

Yet Gide was full of goodwill when he made his way to the Palais de Justice. Each of the jurors, magistrates, and lawyers is also going to try to perform his duties conscientiously. Why, then, does the judicial machinery emit such " horrible creakings "? . . .

Before coming to the law-courts the members of the jury had already been submitted to the pressure of public opinion: the Bonnot case had roused the country. The fiat of the newspapers had gone forth: " Above all, no indulgence! "

During the whole course of the trial collective opinion controls justice. After a pitiless verdict " hideous applause breaks out in court," and shouts of " Bravo! Bravo! " — " it is delirium." Has nothing changed since the days of an

248

eye for an eye? A crime has been committed. The community, stirred to the depths of its consciousness, demands reparation. To be sure, society must intervene. But in answering crime with punishment, does one efface the crime? Does this system of retribution restore its prestige to the violated law?

— The court! The case is opened. Gide, attentive, is going to devote all his powers to discovering the truth. — Accused, stand up!

Every time I have attended a case, I have been struck by the distance separating the judge from the accused: the latter, confined in his narrow box, between two police officers, is fighting for his life. Opposite to him is the judge, enthroned, imposing by reason of the prestige of his solemn robes, with his counsellors on either side: much as the Trinity is pictured in the popular imagination. And if the judge assumes the appearance of a kindly paterfamilias, if, by introducing jests into his moralizings, he makes the public laugh, let the accused beware. The interrogation is indeed a perilous test!

Gide declares that the accused often does not understand the questions of the judge, which are put in a language that is too learned for him. But the judge goes on. The judicial machine continues to revolve. He has noticed nothing. And now, in the course of the explanations of the accused, who is growing confused, he pounces on a compromising word and expatiates upon it. If the inculpated man tries to justify himself, occasionally he interrupts and often hustles him. He tries, possibly without knowing it, to " make him appear guilty," to get him to contradict himself. If the accused is emphatic, he is lying; if he is timid, he is insensible; if he has a reputation for being " sly," he is suspect. — What do you mean by " sly "? inquired Gide of a witness. " I mean that he never drank or enjoyed himself with others." A commentator of the *Grande Ordonnance* of 1670 declared that the " bad name " of an accused man could be charged against him. In our own days an unsociable person, or one who is for some reason " objectionable," is at a disadvantage. If his reputation is " deplorable," he is almost as good as lost. The fiction that the accused is presumed innocent until he is proved guilty is powerless in the face of law which is administered only in the interests of repression.[1]

With aching heart, Gide does his best to prevent mistakes. But how is this possible in regard to proceedings based entirely on bringing the passions into play? The prosecutor evokes the horrors of the crime, and demands vengeance in the name of society. Counsel, in his turn, begs for pity and indulgence.[2] Having been swayed this way and that, each juror is now thrown on his own resources: his unverified, unverifiable conviction will be dictated to him by the voice of conscience, such a fallible voice. As a

[1] An official circular by M. Chéron, then Minister of Justice, sent out after the assizes, congratulates the judges on the way they have accomplished their duties — and particularly for having obtained from the juries such a small number of acquittals.

[2] Gide is surprised that the lawyer makes so little of the facts favourable to the accused. Mauriac, in the *Favre-Bulle* case, records the same impression. Moreover, lawyers themselves admit that their pleadings are not much use, especially in the case of small misdemeanours.

matter of fact, remarks Gide, the opinion of the jury is almost always that of the judge. . . .

Whenever a writer endowed with sensibility has been brought in recent times in contact with the administration of justice, he has endured the agony suffered also by Gide.[1] This feeling is provoked in the modern consciousness by the very nature of judicial research, with its reliance on analogy, appearance, presumption. In endeavouring to see a man as the *cause* of a crime, justice is preoccupied with human causality, and this bears no relationship to scientific causality. To connect two physical phenomena with each other is a very different matter from connecting a criminal action with its *author*. The connexion between a man and his actions remains almost incomprehensible. "We are the fathers of our actions as we are of our children," wrote Aristotle long ago.

The terrible difficulty, however, arises from the fact that justice seeks not so much a link between cause and effect (Who did it?) as the establishment of guilt (Whose fault is it?). All rigorous methods are consequently excluded and justice reduced to uncontrollable intuitions. Uncertain witnesses, vague indications, susceptible of contradictory in-

[1] M. Maurice Martin du Gard, editor of the *Nouvelles Littéraires*, recently conceived the happy idea of asking several literary men for a report of a great criminal case. Most of them were attending a court of law for the first time and were unanimous in expressing feelings of astonishment and anxiety. I believe that, without going too far, one may speak of a crisis existing to-day in the administration of justice, which seems no longer to correspond with what we demand of it. One has, moreover, only to open a text-book of criminal law for the use of students, to realize how fragile, and how much the subject of controversy amongst competing schools, are the theoretical principles upon which this administration rests.

terpretations, which for a savant could never constitute *proof*, suffice a judge, not merely to identify the culprit, but also to determine the degree of his culpability. It is exactly because real proofs are lacking that magistrates are obliged, willy-nilly, to try to obtain confessions. These confessions seem so necessary that public opinion tolerates the methods often employed even to-day by the police in order to obtain them.

Meanwhile the case draws to a close. After it has been debated for several hours, or several days, the accused awaits the verdict. All is over. The warders open, at the back of his box, the door through which he will pass to his dark fate. The die is cast. . . . Amongst all the accused persons who passed before his eyes, Gide was particularly struck by one Cordier, an honest young sailor of twenty, something of a moral weakling, who, when in a state of intoxication, had been drawn into crime, almost in spite of himself, by a pair of professional cut-throats. Gide felt that he was almost guiltless. But how make sure of this? Truth escapes through the confusion of details and the complexity of human feelings. Only patience and precision could reach clarity in each particular case.[1]

— The proceedings are over, announces the judge. Gide is full of " consternation " over their rapidity, for he is still uncertain. Nevertheless the jury reaches a decision. In a loud voice the judge gives sentence. No, this solemn truth is not the truth for Gide. Cordier's five years' sentence is

[1] When several accomplices are judged together, it is still more difficult to estimate culpability. Frequently, in such instances, one is a victim; this was exactly the case with Cordier.

an error of judgment. But the judicial machine revolves, irreversible. The warders take Cordier away. . . .

That night Gide could not sleep. " I am ashamed . . . to feel safe." He is haunted by the memory of the recent hearings. On another day a witness described the sound made by the murderer's knife within the flesh of the victim: " crrac." With the result that the accused was sentenced to penal servitude, with hard labour, for life. Nevertheless this detail must have been a fabrication. Is justice perhaps the expression of fatality? So little is needed to bring one within her grasp: " It is enough," says Protos to Lafcadio, " to leave one's home, or be forgetful . . . have a gap in one's memory." When I open the Penal Code, I perceive that there is not a single movement of our activities that is not in danger of being transformed into a misdemeanour or a crime. If these laws were literally applied, the smallest deviation would be enough to condemn a man. Once within the toils, " unless heaven helps you," writes Gide, " it is the very devil to escape."

* * *

Nevertheless the flaw in construction tends to-day to become irremediable: justice not only seeks, for every crime, the responsible party, but also professes to give a sentence *exactly proportionate* to his guilt. Judgment, wrote Kant in his mania for equity, should be pronounced " *proportionately to the inward wickedness of the criminal*."

With the development of individualism, particularly during the last century, the interest of society has centred more and more upon the personality of the accused and has increasingly endeavoured to estimate the degree of his responsibility. Thus has the law successively created, for the same offence, first a variety of penalties,[1] then aggravating, extenuating circumstances and, finally, suspended judgment. Henceforth, therefore, the judge must estimate the *degree* of the delinquent's perversity, must penetrate his consciousness.

It is for this reason that such prolonged questionnaires are addressed to the jury.[2] The latter, often unaccustomed to mental labour, are confused by the legal procedure that to-day has grown so complicated. Gide saw them, in a case where the sentence threatening the accused seemed to be too severe, decide not to vote " aggravating " circumstances, and nevertheless constrained to vote them in order not to deny the material facts, so that they would have liked afterwards to vote " extenuating " circumstances, in order to reduce the sentence. Poor jurors! They come away from their consultations " with haggard eyes, overwrought and furious with each other. . . ." For the problems put to them are, by their very nature, almost insoluble.

The questions addressed to the doctor in court are equally perplexing. He must determine in what degree the intention to do harm is present in an insane criminal. He is asked whether the lowering of the sense of responsibility is " slight, great, or very great." [3] Here again, this discrimi-

---

[1] The Penal Code of 1791 fixed an exact penalty for each crime. That of 1806 indicates only the maximum and the minimum.

[2] As is known, upwards of a hundred questions are sometimes required.

[3] It is noteworthy that a ministerial decree, and not the law, has created " attenuated responsibility." A decree of 1905, interpreting Article 64 of

nation leads to almost insurmountable difficulties. Although, for example, an epileptic delinquent may not be a lunatic, the expert, in order to save him from prison, is constrained to throw " over his shoulders the cloak of insanity." [1]

There is indeed a flaw in the system based on the idea of responsibility. Gide saw it clearly and, with his notion of " gratuitous action," has demonstrated the absurdity of the whole procedure.

Substantially, Gide says to the tribunal: — You do not wish to punish a crime until you have estimated the intention of the criminal. So be it! But if the criminal shows no sign of any intention, what will you do? You will be estopped. — There are always intentions, replies the judge; there must be. — Not at all, responds Gide, or at any rate, and this amounts to the same thing, there are cases in which one cannot see them. " A gratuitous action. . . . Let us be clear about this. . . . The words ' gratuitous action ' are a convenient, *provisional* label. . . ." But there are " actions which elude ordinary psychological interpretations, gestures which are not determined by simple self-interest." Let us call them " disinterested acts." And let us take, as an opportune example from the " general news," the Redureau case.

In 1913 Marcel Redureau, a fifteen-year-old agricultural labourer, murders his employer, by whom he had been reprimanded, and then cuts the throats of six persons

---

the Penal Code, pronounces as follows: " There is neither crime nor misdemeanour when the accused is in a state of insanity."

[1] Legrand du Saulle.

remaining on the farm: wife, children, and servants. Neither money, love, nor jealousy is the motive of these murders. Yet the medical consultants certify that young Redureau is neither insane nor a degenerate, and the court decides that he is perfectly able to discriminate (a decision resulting, for him, in twenty years' imprisonment). But if one does not know his motive, the interest that drove him to the seven-fold crime, how can one affirm a conscious intention to kill? And if one does not perceive the intention to do harm, why should one condemn?

Thus by the simple account of a typical *dossier* Gide drives a wedge into the antiquated system of regulating the punishment by the crime. Nor is this an exceptional case. If Gide has collected " general news " items,[1] it is exactly because these items jog prejudices and bewilder the mind. They would be more numerous were it not that the trans-mitting agencies modify them in order to rid them of their more disquieting elements. A young girl of twelve, " ani-mated by a spirit of mischief," throws a three-year-old child into a well. But the quoted words were added by the jour-nalist as conveying " the only possible explanation. . . . At such an age one does not commit murder." Gide wit-nessed the trial of an incendiary who " manifestly had started the fire simply because he wanted to burn some-thing." — Why did you do it? asks the judge. — I had no motive. — Had you been drinking that evening? — No, *monsieur le Président.* — Was it through jealousy? Covet-ousness? . . . Then you don't want to say why you lit

[1] In a collection entitled: *Ne jugez pas.*

them [the fires]? — *Mon Président,* I tell you I had no motive." Faced with his Code, the judge ought to suspend his verdict. Innocently, by means of his " disinterested action," the accused was doing him a good turn, like a sick man who survives after having been given up by the doctor. . . . " And the judge [should] take his head in his hands, giving up [the hope of] understanding."

The apparent absence of human causality is as terrifying to man as is the mystery of infinite space.

When an unmotivated action is coupled with insanity, one ceases, it is true, to be uneasy. And can one be sure that a Redureau is not acting under the influence of " a naïve and summary impulse " *whose pathological character we have not yet discovered?* . . . There are cases where doctors fail for a long time to recognize a neurosis. In certain forms of epilepsy, writes Dr. A. Cellier, there is *not a single sign,* amongst those upon which diagnosis habitually rests, that may not be lacking.[1]

To be sure, no confusion is possible between a healthy man and a violent lunatic. But nature hardly ever makes *precise* demarcations, corresponding to our mental classifications. It is as difficult to find a *frontier* between the nor-

---

[1] Cf. Dr. A. Cellier's report on the " Penal Responsibility of Epileptics." This remarkable and courageous report appeared in the *Annales de Médecine légale* (1929).

In regard to schizophrenia, M. Minkowski holds that medicine ought not only to " label " the exact external symptoms, but also to make a " penetrating " diagnosis, by means of sympathy with the patient and of general intuition. This indication is interesting as revealing that psychiatry is losing its inflexibility and tending towards psychology.

mal and the abnormal as between the animal and vegetable kingdoms. One passes from one domain to the other by insensible gradations. Now, nearly all criminals belong to a category that must be placed in a dim and uncertain region between the sane and those proved to be insane.[1] As it evolves, psychiatry, far from confirming the discrimination between the responsible and the irresponsible,[2] increasingly discovers that all the so-called normal and the so-called pathological tendencies exist side by side in the same person, whose behaviour is determined only by the relatively stronger development of this or that tendency. Doctors called upon in court to answer almost unanswerable questions desire nothing more than to see disappear from judicial inquiries the idea of culpability. In his analysis of the inexplicable criminal action, Gide reaches the same conclusion: the problem of responsibility linked to that of liberty appears to-day not unlike that of squaring the circle.[3]

" Surrender, judge," writes Gide, " give place to the doctor." Can one fail to be impressed when one learns that nearly all the accused who appear in the *Souvenirs de la Cour d'Assises* display more or less marked signs of degeneracy or are born of defective parents?

[1] This is exactly why one could " count by hundreds," as has been noted by the psychiatrists Pactet and Colin, " the insane persons shut up in prison."

[2] The introduction of one or two intermediate classifications has aggravated rather than lessened the difficulty.

[3] Gide, moreover, has very justly remarked that the laws founded on the idea of responsibility are but a poor protection for society. Actually they ought to be less hard upon " a predestinate who cannot not kill than upon one whom a *dementia brevis* has accidentally blinded. . . . "

At one time syphilitic prostitutes were severely dealt with, nowadays they are compelled to undergo treatment. Why, therefore, should imprisonment be considered better for an epileptic criminal than medical treatment?

The fact is that the public still hesitates to follow the doctor because, as the law stands to-day, to recognize one's malady is to recognize one's irresponsibility and, *in consequence, to be restored to the world,* and, what is worse, without receiving treatment. Yet Lombroso, who was the first to fight the principle of responsibility, explains that to *care* for the delinquent, if he be dangerous, is to *eliminate* him from society. If this idea were better understood, it would escape the public protests always to be heard as soon as there is any talk of reforming justice.

*   *   *

" Judge not," writes Gide, but adds immediately: " I do not in the least persuade myself that society can do without law-courts." The two statements are in no way contradictory: do not judge the crime, but do protect society! If the idea of defending society had more closely penetrated our legislation and our customs, it would have changed the nature of penalties, which are still regarded as punishments.

After the unjust condemnation of Cordier, Gide asked for and (after great difficulty) obtained a reduction of his sentence. " If we give him a helping hand, perhaps we may save him! " But he adds: " After prison, it will be the African battalion [for him]. And, coming out at the end of these six years, what will he be? What will he be? " For the régime of repression actually corrupts the prisoners.

Children who have been through correctional institutions, and delinquents who have been imprisoned, are almost invariably more dangerous to society than before their detention. There is no longer anyone who dares to deny the truth of this. One is therefore driven to a paradoxical conclusion: society would be safer if those delinquents, who in due course will be released, were never apprehended.

To-day sentences make primarily for the humiliation of the condemned man, forcing him to conform to fixed rules, depriving him of his personality, and reducing him to a mere cipher, a number, a thing. And not merely in law, but also in religion, as in education, chastisement is of the nature of excommunication and depersonalization — when it should rather be attempting the exact opposite if it would reform and save the individual.[1]

Scarcely a hundred and fifty years ago the law made use of torture. Three centuries ago lunatics, children, animals, and inanimate objects were sentenced. Perhaps less time will be required to make our current administration of justice appear equally anachronistic. Thus will the walls

---

[1] If one could arouse a criminal at the moment of his crime, the totality of his self would be far from approving his action; he would discover, repressed within his unconscious, numbers of ideas and images which, had they taken part in the action, would have completely transformed it, would have made it another action. But he acted at the bidding of an obsession, under the influence of an isolated desire, *and therefore with only a part of himself*. To teach him to act from the whole of his consciousness would be to enable him to avoid the crime. This idea naturally presupposes a society whose aim is the free development of the individual. The crimes at present suppressed by law are committed in the kind of hallucinatory condition so well described by Dostoievski. Hence the traces almost always left even by the most astute criminals. Since they are not in a state of self-possession, the smallest unforeseen item throws them out completely.

of the law-courts collapse. Judge not! No, God has not rele-
gated to man the right to judge and punish! No, man is not
the centre of the universe.

Doubtless the evolution of justice would be more rapid
if judges were not wedded to the principle of authority,
which is their *raison-d'être*. In *Les Faux-Monnayeurs* it is a
magistrate, the president of the Molinié law-court, who declares that " prejudices are the props of civilization."

VIEWS ON WORK AND COLONIZATION

IN 1925 Gide left France for the Congo. He went for pleasure, armed only with butterfly-nets and hoping to enjoy, in "voluptuous delight, forgetfulness," nature, blue skies, virgin forests. But at the first halt the "enchanting" country revealed other aspects of its being. At Libreville there was a lack of provisions. Supplies forwarded from Bordeaux had suffered on the way. At Brazzaville there was a complete absence of sanitation, and epidemics were raging: it was the prologue.

Almost as soon as he entered the Ubangi country, where Europeans rarely venture, he saw coming to meet him a little group of natives, the most lamentable human cattle it would be possible to imagine: "Fifteen men and two women attached by the neck to a single rope . . . scarcely able to walk . . . escorted by two guards armed with five-thonged whips." In other districts they met further columns, still more wretched. Questioned by Gide, none of these unfortunates dares to reply. Terror rules. These are the blacks who are flying from *portage*. There are neither railways, roads, nor adequate waterways. The authorities,

to ensure transport, are obliged to recruit the natives; since
the administration of the recruiting system is abused, the
blacks are mobilized by force. The militia, sent to fetch
them, engage in a veritable man-hunt. The natives take
flight, leaving the land they have cultivated. Families are
dispersed. Everyone takes to the bush. The secret administrative reports [1] say that they go to earth " like wild beasts."
Of rich lands and flourishing villages there is often nothing
left but a ruined desolation. This picture recalls that of the
mobilization of the natives in 1914, as described to me by
a colonial administrator. Each village was obliged to fur-
nish a contingent, whose number was fixed in advance. A village failing to supply the required number was regarded as
insubordinate and surrounded by a squad which would
open fire on the cabins. If the blacks did not appear
quickly enough, the cabins would be set alight. Hunted and
terrified, they would give themselves up. The herd would
be sent, well guarded, to the nearest administrative centre.
The infirm and the bandy-legged were sent home; the
others, after a short interval, to the front. The front to-day
is the timber-yard of the route which is intended to connect
Brazzaville with Pointe-à-Pitre. At Fort Archambault, in
the heart of the country, Gide watched the departure of
boat-loads being sent by river to the coast: the transport of
" pieces of ebony," like those of former days. So crowded
on the decks of the cargo-boats that some of them fall into
the water and are drowned; they are burned by the cinders
falling from the funnels; they are unclothed, and many die

[1] Quoted by Gide in his *Voyage au Congo* and *Retour du Tchad*.

of fever.[1] Gide did not see the timber-yards on the coast. They have been described by Albert Londres. Since there is no equipment, he says, the Negroes take the place of the machine, the lorry, and the crane. " Either," said Monsieur Antonetti, the Governor-General, " we must accept the sacrifice of from six to eight thousand men, or give up the railway." By 1929 the sacrifice had risen to seventeen thousand men and there were still three hundred kilometres of railway to be constructed.

The material difficulties, in this country that is three times as large as France, will doubtless appear to be almost insurmountable. But this fact takes nothing from the horrors of the picture revealed by Gide. Exaggerating nothing, he puts before us the plain truth.

Since, however, he did not wish to raise the question of the principle of colonization in itself, it is primarily the wretched errors of its administration that he contests.

Gide tells us that the black is often aware of his backwardness as compared to the European and is desirous of rising to his level. He calls for collaboration. But the white man replies only with contempt and cruelty. That is the first stage in the drama of colonization.

It is the old principle of authority reappearing, but this time in all its brutality. Lost in an enormous territory, of which he knows but little, having as almost his sole charge the collection of taxes, the requisitioning of food-stuffs and

---

[1] *Voyage au Congo*, page 195. It is interesting to compare this page of Gide's work with *Aventures d'un Négrier* (*Choses vues*, published by Plon), at the beginning of the nineteenth century.

men, the administrator believes that force and forced labour are the sole possibility. Any other method he regards
as chimerical.[1] "Don't worry," a colonial told Gide,
" *those fellows* won't let themselves die of hunger." Therefore there is no need to feed them. Those fellows " are all
cheats, liars, and thieves." Therefore there is nothing to do
but to hustle and ill-treat them. " The less intelligent the
white man is, the more does the black seem to him to be a
fool."

In his personal relationships with the natives Gide almost invariably met with honesty, faithfulness, friendliness, and the " desire to learn and thereby draw nearer to
us." Hence his indignation: " What! So much devotion
. . . so much goodwill . . . and capability of affection,
meeting almost always nothing but rebuffs. . . . I feel here
a whole suffering humanity, a poor, oppressed race." The
longer he stays in the country, the more powerfully does
wrath rise within him: " What perseverance in misunderstanding, what a policy of hatred and ill-will has been necessary to secure justification for . . . the exactions and
the severities! " Gide rebels, and his book, by reason of its
prudence, its precise truthfulness, and its moderation, becomes a terrible indictment of European methods of colonization.

And Gide has spoken only of the Congo and only of facts
he has personally observed. Yet this tragedy is repeated
everywhere. Wherever he has settled, the European has

[1] Cf. the naïve admissions of M. Jean Bénilan, administrator of the Congo
at the time of Gide's visit (*Revue de France*, November 1, 1930).

promised the benefits of his civilization. And the native, accepting the accomplished fact, has generally approached him with respect and confidence. In India the " great builders," as far as Gandhi, have held out their hands to England.[1] In Indo-China, Tonkin, and Annam the sons of noble houses have looked hopefully to France. Nevertheless Gandhi is in prison; hundreds of Annamite nationalists were beheaded — notably students mostly under twenty years of age — two years ago, as malefactors; airplanes have bombarded native villages, killing women and children.[2] Everywhere, the colonial exclaims: Dirty nigger! Dirty yellow! Dirty black! And under the sign of racial contempt a life-and-death conflict, no doubt involuntary, goes forward between the colonist and the colonized. One is finally drawn to the conclusion that for the white there is no choice between seeing the native disappear and himself being driven out by him.[3] To-day, therefore, Gide is asking

[1] In his profound studies of *Ramakrishna, Vivekananda*, and *Gandhi* Romain Rolland shows how much the "great builders" of India in the nineteenth century owe to England and what a desire they then had to collaborate with her.

[2] Cf. M. Louis Roubaud's record of these facts in a courageous and moving report on Indo-China (*Viet-Nam*, published by Valois).

[3] It seems to me that hitherto colonized countries have been unable to escape this alternative: Certain races, as formerly the Aztecs and the Incas, to-day the Polynesians, the Australian natives, and the blacks of the Congo, have disappeared completely or are in process of disappearance. The Negroes, writes Gide, " as soon as they are ill," become " limp " and " remain motionless in a corner." It would seem as though the life in them were but a feeble flame which goes out on contact with the white man. Other races, however, for example in India and Indo-China, have multiplied, thanks to the prophylactic and economic measures early introduced by the white colonists; but then they have driven out or are about to drive out these colonists.

himself whether it is not the principle of colonization itself
that is indefensible.

I believe that colonization has been from the first irremediably vitiated by the fact that the European has always
behaved amongst the black races as a conqueror and de-
spoiler (it is his role of persecutor that has engendered
his race-prejudice, and not his prejudice that has led him
to persecution); it is because one treats a man as a slave
that one despises him. If such horrible abuses come to be
generally tolerated and regarded as normal, it is because
violence is the very basis of all colonial enterprise.[1]

Yet to despair of the principle of colonization is surely
to despair of all *rapprochement* between peoples. The earth
is nowadays too small for anyone to live isolated. The
Great Wall of China has become a motor-track. Little by
little the old civilizations are awakening from their ancient
lethargy. Meanwhile a fresh peril is arising, of which Gide
has not needed to speak, because it appears principally in
Asia, amongst more resistant peoples who do not go under
in contact with the white races.

These peoples are transforming themselves into modern
nations, but, alas, into warlike nations jealous of their
sovereignty. Nothing, we know, is more difficult than to
turn one's mind towards true individualism, the individual-

---

[1] It is interesting to note that M. Albert Sarraut (Colonial Minister in
1932) courageously recognizes the fact that every fresh colonizing enterprise is, at its beginning, a system of " spoliation." (Cf. *Grandeur et Servitude
coloniale*, Sagittaire publications.) He considers, however, that the white, by
bestowing material and moral benefits, redeems the initial misdeeds. But
in order to succeed he would need to have the self-abnegating power of a
god. Alas! " He who takes the sword shall perish by the sword."

ism that leads to co-operation. Yet for nations, as for individuals, it is only by developing their own qualities, by
bringing to the world something unique and particular,
that they can move towards an equilibrium that shall be
founded neither upon reciprocal assimilation nor upon an
opposition of forces.

If, on the other hand, we see to-day the ancient countries
of Asia evolving in so menacing a fashion, slowly escaping
from their motionless racial framework to place themselves within the separatist framework of nationality,
it is doubtless because they are trying to imitate Europe,
it is because, in awakening them, Europe has instilled into
them the poison of her own egoism.

*   *   *

Thus does the problem of the colonies oblige us to return
to the organization of European society; as did Gide when
he wished to take action against the Congo concessionary
companies.

I have so far made no mention of these companies. Yet
the worst exactions practised in the colony have been much
more their doing than that of the administration. Two or
three large societies share these vast regions for the purpose of gathering rubber. The blacks were conceded to
them, together with the territories, by the State, " absolutely." [1] They therefore fix their pay as they choose, giving
them just enough to keep them this side of starvation: 1 fr.
50 per kilo of rubber, which they sell at 20, sometimes at

[1] The " specifications " contain, it is true, certain clauses which should
protect the natives, but these are largely ignored.

30, sometimes at 40 francs.[1] In order to gather ten kilo-
grammes a native must spend a month in the forest and will
earn 10 francs, 120 francs per annum. The smallest agent
of the company receives 60,000 francs per annum. It was
in the Congo that Gide saw worked out the famous bronze
law of Karl Marx. Initiating himself little by little into the
details of prices, exchange, and dues paid in kind, he saw
in their full proportions those " agonizing social questions " which hitherto he had only " glimpsed." Behind
colonization he discovered capitalism.

A régime whose principles are everywhere the same, but
in the colonies are more directly evident. Gide was re-
volted by the deductions made by the agents, on account of
delayed transport, from the sums paid to the natives, who
are thus often obliged to work one or two months without
remuneration.[2] He saw the way the companies wangle con-
tracts by promising overtime pay under " certain favourable conditions " (if the price of rubber rises in Europe;
if the rubber is sufficiently dry . . . etc.). But those conditions are never realized and the black does his extra work
in vain. Picturing the life of a *pagayeur* (the paddler of
a native boat) who died while they were going up the
Lagone river, Gide writes: " What a wretched existence he
had known! . . . Kara was about forty years old. He was
the eldest son of a numerous family. . . . He leaves life
without hope, and during his whole life never had any cer-

---

[1] In a neighbouring province, where the companies are not in power,
rubber is paid for at 7 fr. 50. All these figures are supplied by Gide.

[2] In many European businesses the employé's wages are docked if he
is a few minutes late.

tain hope of being able to earn more than one franc fifty per day." It is the destiny of many proletarians that Gide thus evokes.

It was only by chance, however, that he was to discover the worst abuses of the companies. Shortly before he passed through the country, twenty blacks had been tortured by the agents of the Forestière; five children deliberately burned to death in a cabin; whole tribes oppressed and bled white by reprisals. The administration, an accomplice, in this case, of the companies, had demanded the delivery of " the ears and genitals " of the dead Negroes, whose number amounted to a thousand.

Why these victims? Because a few of the gatherers, without even refusing to work for the company, had returned for a few days to their village or had produced an insufficient quantity of rubber. The company had ordered their agents to force the production. To what excesses such measures can lead, Gide saw for himself. He was horrified. A few years before, the sight of the sailor Cordier, as a victim of injustice, had deprived him of sleep for several nights. But this time the injustice is more vast, more general, more terrible. His consciousness undergoes a revolution. A new reality opens before him. It is no longer a matter of a few more or less responsible commercial agents; " it is a régime that is at fault," he says, " an abominable régime . . . enslaving and enfeebling a whole people. . . ." The country can never recover " until it is delivered from the leeches that are the concessionary companies." How is he to divulge, in a manner that will secure a hearing, the facts known only to himself? What will be the most effective way of exposing them? He makes it his first care to refrain from generalizing, in regard to " the abuses peculiar to " French Equatorial Africa. He believes that his cause is worthy of bringing together " all the honest men " of all parties. But his effort to reach beyond politics will be vain. Nevertheless, he decides to speak and, if necessary, to fight.

Even before he reaches France, he learns that his book ought to be " torpedoed." [1] The moment it had appeared, the companies began to recruit allies in the press. In one big newspaper Gide is treated as a hypersensitive *littérateur*. Who is the author of this article? A relative of one of the managers of La Forestière. In another organ the company is represented as a benevolent society to whom the blacks are indebted for medical assistance, a savings-bank, an orchestra, and a cinema. Which company is this? A society that has no connexion whatever with the concessionary companies. [2] About this time, I met a friend of one of the managers of the Forestière. This business man, believing that my present book was almost ready to appear, gave me to understand that it would be to my interest to defend the Forestière company. [3]

In one paper only, in *Le Populaire*, where M. Léon Blum

[1] His *Voyage au Congo*, wherein the abuses of the companies are revealed.

[2] Moreover, this same newspaper puts matters right in a later number.

[3] I was of course to be furnished with a full and exact report of all the facts of the case. This report was doubtless made use of by the manager himself in the replies to Gide and to Léon Blum which we are about to consider.

had come to the support of Gide's campaign, did M. X., the
manager of La Forestière, use the right of response in a
very lengthy letter, wherein the company poses as both innocent and kindly. Negroes have been shot and burned and
tortured? What can the company do beyond assuming the
attitude of Pontius Pilate? It has no powers, and it is the
government agents or the blacks themselves who have engaged in these atrocities.

Gide, however, will not allow the tragic situation to be
whitewashed. The official inquiry set on foot by him gives
rise to judicial action. Meanwhile the affair has reached the
Chamber. In 1927 the Colonial Minister, keeping faith with
his personal interview with Gide, makes a declaration:
" All the large concessions expire in 1929. I can assure the
Chamber that not one of them shall be renewed or prolonged. . . ." Is this victory? Has Gide helped to " deliver
a hundred and twenty thousand Negroes from slavery? "
Six days after this sitting of the Chamber *L'Information*
announced that La Forestière was proposing an augmenta-
tion of capital in order to carry out a plantation program
" in connexion with the renewal of the concessions in 1935."
An astonishing piece of sleight-of-hand. La Forestière,
whose lease does not expire until 1935, was not included in
the promise made by the Minister, who had referred only to
the renewals due in 1929.

By what right does Gide abandon his novel-writing in
order to make a protest? Are things going so badly in the
world of capital? Who dares to speak of the enslavement of
blacks who have " voluntarily enrolled themselves "? Are

there not regulations, with clauses framed to protect the natives? Where these are not adhered to, is it not because such adherence is not always possible?

La Forestière enlarges not only upon the *benefits* of colonization in general, but also upon those the company confers " upon its black employees by making them appreciate the material satisfactions procured [by labour]." [1] Large concerns and their directors like their profits to have the appearance of disinterestedness: Lœwenstein in diffusing electricity sought the happiness of mankind; Michelin, its fecundity; Ford, its " prosperity." La Forestière has similar aims: the people are to be " more numerous, more prosperous, happier." To desire the abolition of the big companies is therefore to desire a " solution that fails by being too simple " and offers nothing but " considerably to retard the valuable exploitation of vast regions " (in the Congo) " and the increase of the well-being of the natives." Tragically enough, those who support this kind of thesis do so in good faith.

" The *primary* cause," explains the manager of La Forestière, of the harsh treatment of the black is the terrible condition to which he has sunk " during thousands of years " of inertia.

---

[1] Reply of the manager of La Forestière to Léon Blum. In his book *Épopée de Caoutchouc*, M. G. Le Fèvre, in speaking of the coolies, writes: ". . . the dual formula of life: labour and poverty."

In the United States the directors of Standard Oil pronounce as follows: " Our administrative organization is the application to big business of the Sermon on the Mount." That is to say, runs the explanation, " He who forgets his own interest in the joy of doing his work well is the one who, finally, will be the most enriched thereby."

If the blacks rebel, writes Galliéni to Madagascar, " it is owing to the mentality of those savage tribes and to [their] . . . inability to discern the benevolence with which we have always treated them. . . ."

Therefore, without intending to criticize an economic and social system, Gide has been obliged to testify to " the hidden power of these societies organized solely for the profit, solely for the enrichment, of a few shareholders." No doubt he had the Congo companies in mind when he wrote these words, but he adds: " The evil begins in Paris . . ."; in Paris are to be found the administrative chiefs and the rulers of the press and of politics: a small group of men, controlling the principal social organs, works only in its own interests, to the grievous detriment of the masses. A growing number of voices begins to-day to denounce these abuses, which are still astonishingly secret. With his vehement campaign against the Congo companies, Gide has certainly contributed towards a clearer understanding of this hidden state of affairs.

At the moment of taking action he certainly had no idea of questioning the régime itself. But as soon as the problem of capitalism had stated itself in his mind, his sincerity prevented him from shutting his eyes to its defects. In recently written articles he turns to Russia: " I should like to cry, to cry aloud my sympathy for U.S.S.R., and have my voice heard; and that it should be of importance. I should like to live long enough to see the success of this tremendous effort, a success I long for with my whole soul, and for which I should like to be able to work. . . ."

Whatever may be the dangers in any case attending a
new experiment — dangers inherent in life itself — Gide
to-day prefers these to the forms of oppression to be found
in our own society. For the march ahead is capable of leading us towards a state of free human relationship in place
of the old bourgeois society; towards a veritable association of individuals, " wherein the free development of each
[shall be] the condition of the free development of all." [1]

[1] Communist Manifesto of K. Marx and F. Engels.

5

THE IDEA OF PROGRESS

THE PRESENT work was nearly finished when André Gide rallied to the cause of Communism. This startling adhesion comes therefore as a confirmation of the views I have set forth in the course of this book. What has captivated me from the first, in studying Gide's thought, is his growing attachment to the individual, not to an isolated, theoretical, abstract individual, but to the individual in his place in the society from which he is inseparable. Therefore from the outset I decided to reserve an important place for Gide's social ideas. For although, up to the present, these ideas have hardly been directly expressed, I felt that they were to be discerned in the author's most diverse writings: if Gide has so often concerned himself with the family, religion, justice, patriotism, it is because he was already more or less consciously preoccupied with the question of society.

In spite of its indirectness and its many apparent contradictions, Gide's mind has evolved continuously in a single direction: more and more away from the idea of God, a traditional God who rewards the good and punishes the evil, and more and more towards the idea of man. His inward struggle against religion was undoubtedly long and painful. It is no easy matter to be obliged to reconstruct one's universe, and it is so convenient and comfortable to accept revealed truth, a ready-made system of morality, of life and of after-life. And Gide's pious adolescence, so full of marvellous exaltations, had laid up for him such a number of pathetic memories!

No matter. He has thrown off all this past. "For me," he writes, in his Journal: "God is the grand Stop-Gap. And I can indeed shout, with Hugo: 'He is! He is! He is! He is, frantically!' But how much further am I if I don't know *what* he is? Our adoration remains at the level of humanity. . . ." Henceforth, whatever be the riddle asked by the Sphinx of Gide's Œdipe, Œdipe has decided in advance to reply: Man, for to all life's great questions "there is but a single answer, the same. . . ."

Nevertheless, exactly at the moment when after so prolonged a period of disquietude Gide makes this first affirmation, a fresh conflict begins within him. He seems to be approaching serenity, to be reaching the goal. But what of a tranquillity he must enjoy *alone*? No, he cries, I don't want a " pitiless happiness. . . ."

Is this because he desires to make converts? Does he wish to impart the new certainty inhabiting him to his friends and to those who are nearest to him? Does a profound generosity move him to communicate his joy? His whole moral being urges him to consider more attentively those who are all about him: — A morality wherein there would be no need for me to devote myself, he declares, could not in any way satisfy me. . . .

It was at this time that Gide was seized with real anguish when he thought of the restriction of the simple material conditions of happiness. For one can hardly say that these exist even on a small portion of the globe, and there, at best, only for a small circle of the privileged. Everywhere else there is famine, oppression, the invading vision of the most shocking human misery.

It is true that in his earliest writings Gide often calls up the haunts of poverty, the " sordid houses " inhabited by " sickness, prostitution, shame, crime, and hunger." But now these miseries have become for him a reality so immediate and so pressing that it gives him no rest. Everything brings him back to it. Everything in contemporary social life, its injustices, masked under high-sounding, meaningless, democratic words, its barbarous militarism, its powerlessness to distribute the riches it creates — all this he finds revolting. No longer can he command the serenity of spirit necessary for writing fiction. The traditional little novels seem to him to be laughable. Can the artist work only by interposing a sort of screen between himself and the world? There are moments, constantly recurring, when he feels impelled to go down, as it were, into the market-place and speak. . . . It was under some such imperious prompting that Gide published, in the *N. R. F.*, his notes on Communism. . . .

There can be no doubt that for some time past Gide's

evangelical fondness for genuine deprivation, his complete indifference to the sense of property, his hatred of possessing goods, naturally drew him to conceive of a state of society wherein labour should be less closely connected with money than it is to-day, and acquisition no longer the main motive of human activity. Nevertheless, it is his own individualist morality, rather than any sentimental aspiration, that has drawn Gide into Communism. This it is that has led him to study social problems: once within this domain, he sees only one issue, cherishes only one hope. . . .

Is it not remarkable that another fine intelligence, one whose literary work has not always been appreciated by Gide, should have arrived almost at the same time at very much the same conclusion? In terms very similar to those used by Gide, Romain Rolland has declared himself in favour of the great Russian experiment. " I believe," he has written, " in the work of U.S.S.R. I shall defend it as long as I have breath." And further: " My friends in U.S.S.R., you have free consciousnesses and are therefore, without knowing it, true individualists. . . ." And according to Gide: " Individualism, properly understood, should be at the service of the community. . . . I hold that it is a mistake to regard it as opposed to Communism."

It is not by chance that two such widely separated writers find themselves in agreement. There is hardly a thinker in the Western world to-day who is not inclined either to an entirely tragic pessimism, to rebellion, or to regarding social reform as a last resource. Valéry despairs both of Europe and of a humanity that seems vowed to a war of extermination. Einstein has reached the point of advocating the most serious of rebellions: the refusal of military service (but has individual insurrection ever had any chance of success?). Writers and savants, essayists and philosophers, all those who lucidly contemplate our civilization, feel it to be threatened from within and believe in the necessity of renewal.[1]

Does not the whole of history demonstrate the perpetual evolution of life, and, notably, of social forms? The moment one accepts the idea of evolution it seems that the natural movement of societies is drawing them, more or less quickly, but of necessity, in the direction of Socialism. One notes that for a century or more the ideas of the front-rank thinkers have, at any rate in part, been turned towards customs and institutions: in 1789 we have the doctrines of the Encyclopædists, in the course of the nineteenth century the so-called reform program of the Socialists. A period of only fifty years was sufficient to shift a parliamentary party from the extreme Left, little by little towards the Centre.[2] Perhaps at no very distant time we shall see the

[1] Particularly striking is society's inability to distribute the products of labour. M. Caillaux has justly pointed out that if science and industry succeeded in producing a single machine, run by three workmen, which could supply all the needs of mankind, everyone would die of cold and hunger, since without work there would be no money and therefore no means of acquiring the goods produced by the machine. He therefore suggests (as Duhamel has also done) that for a certain period all fresh inventions should be held up and progress to some extent arrested, in order to avoid the greater catastrophe. . . . If it be true that present-day society, whose chief merit so far has been its encouragement of scientific and industrial development, is incapable of continuing to play its part, then it becomes difficult to defend it. . . .

[2] In to-day's Chamber of Deputies, parties sitting on the Right have

Communist Party itself being gradually pushed in the same direction by a much more extremist party. If life, and, above all, social life, affords us the spectacle of perpetual advance, is it not our duty to help this forward march?

The idea of Progress is to-day one of the dominant preoccupations of the mind of André Gide, the one which gives to his adherence to Communism its true significance. It is both serious and dangerous, this idea of Progress! Those who, in the eighteenth century, were the first to voice it, appear to have been so much intoxicated thereby that they drove it, too quickly and too simply, to extremities. It is for this reason that those who to-day believe in Progress are so often called " elementary." Whence this contempt? Generally it comes from the believers and the orthodox, who feel the necessity of attaching themselves to a static conception of the universe, to a definite and eternal belief given by God.

Gide, moreover, has no hesitation in rehabilitating the discredited idea of Progress. Even in the present state of our civilization, even if one ignores the increase of material power, one must indeed recognize that knowledge is in a perpetual state of becoming. Philosophy is therefore obliged incessantly to revise her criticism of intelligence and to indicate the value, always more relative to mankind, of the results acquired by experience. Negative progress? Possibly, in a sense that it takes us further and further from

---

tickets on which appears the word " Left." That is to say that the Royalists have almost disappeared. The " Radicals," formerly sitting on the right, now occupy the centre. . . .

indefiniteness; that is to say, it brings us nearer to a truth.

Nevertheless, reply the detractors of the idea of Progress, history reveals no kind of moral progress in humanity, and that is the only kind of progress that matters. Gide is undoubtedly inclined to believe that moral becoming should follow, sooner or later, intellectual becoming. But, above all, it seems to him that we betray the idea of Progress if we regard it only in relation to our own era. The history of mankind is at its beginning. We have only a few records of the grandeur and the decadence of peoples. It is when the idea of Progress is regarded from the infinity of the future that it becomes dazzling. To-day it is still nothing but a nascent idea, poor and weakly. But it, too, will grow and will undoubtedly become our *raison d'être.* . . .

" I have not changed my direction," writes Gide, " I have always walked straight ahead; I continue. . . ." But " now I advance with my steps set towards something. . . ."

BIBLIOGRAPHY AND INDEX

BIBLIOGRAPHY

This bibliography is arranged in two parts.

In the first, relating to France, I have made use of the valuable information already collected by M. Naville, and have specially featured the dates on which Gide's works have been *put upon the market*. Thus the privately printed editions of a work, even when they preceded the ordinary edition by many years, bear only the date of the appearance of the ordinary edition. Similarly, small works collected by the author, sometimes after a very considerable interval, *in a single volume*, bear only the date of the appearance of this volume.

In the second part I have collected, probably for the first time, the principal translations of Gide's works which have appeared abroad.

It is only by way of indication that we have also mentioned critical studies which have appeared in certain foreign countries.

PART I

Works Published in France

1891. *Les Cahiers d'André Walter* (*Œuvre posthume*). Anonymous. Paris: Librairie Académique Didier-Perrin et Cie.

(Review by P. C., Pierre Chrysis, the pseudonym of Pierre Louÿs, appearing only in this edition.) This edition was destroyed by the author's desire, and only a few copies remain of what is properly the original edition.

1891. *Les Cahiers d'André Walter (Œuvre posthume)*. Anonymous. Paris: Librairie de l'Art Indépendant. (Edition of 190 copies.) This *de luxe* edition should have appeared first, but was delayed by the printer.

1892. *Les Poésies d'André Walter (Œuvre posthume)*. Anonymous. Paris: Librairie de l'Art Indépendant.

1896. *Le Voyage d'Urien,* followed by *Paludes.* Paris: Mercure de France.

> *Le Voyage d'Urien* appeared separately in Paris: Librairie de l'Art Indépendant, in 1893.
>
> *Paludes* appeared separately in Paris: Librairie de l'Art Indépendant, in 1895.

1897. *Les Nourritures terrestres.* Paris: Mercure de France.

1899. *Philoctète. Le Traité du Narcisse. La Tentative amoureuse. El Hadj.* Paris: Mercure de France.

> *Le Traité du Narcisse* appeared separately in Paris: Librairie de l'Art Indépendant, in 1894. The cover bore the words: "Traité du" and, below, a design by Pierre Louÿs representing a narcissus. The work was reissued by the same publisher in 1892.
>
> *La Tentative amoureuse* appeared separately in Paris: Librairie de l'Art Indépendant, in 1893.

1899. *Le Prométhée mal enchaîné.* Paris: Mercure de France.

1902. *L'Immoraliste.* Paris: Mercure de France.

1903. *Prétextes. Réflexions sur quelques points de littérature et de morale.* Paris: Mercure de France. The inside title is: Réflexions critiques sur . . .".

> *Réflexions sur quelques points de littérature et de morale* (anonymous) appeared separately in Paris: Mercure de France, in 1897.

The *Lettres à Angèle*, 1898–9, appeared separately in Paris: Mercure de France, in 1900.

De l'Influence en littérature (lecture given at the Libre Esthétique in Brussels, March 29, 1900) appeared separately in Paris: Petite Collection de l'Ermitage, in 1900.

Les Limites de l'Art (lecture) appeared in Paris: Petite Collection de l'Ermitage, in 1901.

1904. *Saül. Le Roi Candaule.* Paris: Mercure de France.

Le Roi Candaule (three-act play) appeared separately in Paris: La Revue Blanche, in 1901.

Saül (five-act play) appeared separately in Paris: Mercure de France, in 1903. This work was written in 1896.

1906. *Amyntas. Mopsus. Feuilles de route. De Biskra à Touggourt. Le Renoncement au Voyage.* Paris: Mercure de France. *Feuilles de Route*, 1895–6, appeared separately without name of place or publisher, undated, in Brussels: Imprimerie N. Vandersypen, in 1899.

1909. *La Porte étroite.* Paris: Mercure de France.

1910. *Oscar Wilde. In Memoriam. Le " De Profundis."* Paris: Mercure de France.

1911. *Nouveaux Prétextes. Réflexions sur quelques points de littérature et de morale.* Paris: Mercure de France.

De l'Importance du public (lecture given at the court of Weimar on August 5, 1903) appeared separately in Paris: Petite Collection de l'Ermitage, in 1903.

1911. *Isabelle.* Paris: the Nouvelle Revue Française.

1912. *Le Retour de l'Enfant Prodigue*, preceded by *Cinq Autres Traités.* Paris: Nouvelle Revue Française. This edition repeats the texts appearing in the 1899 edition, but is completed by:

Le Retour de l'Enfant Prodigue, published separately in Paris: Vers et Prose, in 1907.

Bethsabé, which appeared separately in Paris: Bibliothèque de l'Occident, in 1912.

1914. *Souvenirs de la Cour d'Assises*. Paris: the Nouvelle Revue Française.

1914. *Les Caves du Vatican*. Satire by the author of *Paludes*. Anonymous. Paris: the Nouvelle Revue Française.

1919. *La Symphonie pastorale*. Paris: the Nouvelle Revue Française.

1921. *Morceaux Choisis*. Paris: the Nouvelle Revue Française. In part a new work, containing fragments of unpublished works.

1921. *André Gide (Pages Choisies)*. Paris: Georges Crès et Cie. Bibliothèque de l'Adolescence. No date. (A partly original edition containing several unpublished fragments.)

1922. *Charles-Louis Philippe. Essai biographique*. Paris: Éditions Athéna.

Charles-Louis Philippe (lecture given at the Salon d'Automme, November 5, 1910) appeared previously in Paris: Eugène Figuière et Cie, in 1911.

1923. *Dostoïevski. Articles et Causeries*. Paris: Plon-Nourrit et Cie.

Dostoïevski d'apres sa correspondance appeared separately: Eugène Figuière et Cie, in 1911.

1924. *Incidences*. Paris: the Nouvelle Revue Française.

1924. *Corydon*. Paris: the Nouvelle Revue Française.

Corydon appeared earlier, entitled: *C. R. D. N.* (anonymous), without name of place or publisher (Bruges: Imprimerie Sainte-Catherine), in 1911. In 1920 a fresh enlarged edition was published entitled: *Corydon* (anonymous), without name of place or publisher (Bruges: Imprimerie Sainte-Catherine). The inside title is: " Corydon. Four Socratic Dialogues." The back of the cover is inscribed only: " C. R. D. N. 1920."

1925. *Caractères*. Paris: A l'Enseigne de la Porte Étroite.

1926. *Les Faux-Monnayeurs*. Paris: the Nouvelle Revue Française.

1926. *Si le Grain ne meurt*. Paris: the Nouvelle Revue Française. (Although copies are dated 1924, they were not on sale until October 1926.)

> *Si le Grain ne meurt* appeared previously in Paris without name of publisher (Bruges: Imprimerie Sainte-Catherine) in 1929. (Certain proper names in the text are different from those in the current edition.)

> *Si le Grain ne meurt*, Volume II, appeared in Paris, without name of publisher (Bruges: Imprimerie Sante-Catherine) in 1921. (Certain proper names in the text are different from those in the current edition.)

1926. *Le Journal des Faux-Monnayeurs*. Paris: Éditions Éos.

1926. *Num Quid et Tu?* Paris: Éditions de la Pléiade, J. Schiffrin.

> *Num Quid et Tu?* (anonymous) appeared without name of place or publisher (Bruges: Imprimerie Sainte-Catherine) in 1922.

1927. *Dindiki*. Liége: Éditions de la Lampe d'Aladdin.

1927. *Voyage au Congo. Carnets de route*. Paris: the Nouvelle Revue Française.

1928. *Le Retour du Tchad*, sequel to *Voyage au Congo. Carnets de route*. Paris: the Nouvelle Revue Française.

1929. *L'École des Femmes*. Paris: the Nouvelle Revue Française.

1929. *Essai sur Montaigne*. Paris: Éditions de la Pléiade, J. Schiffrin.

1929. *Un Esprit non prévenu*. Paris: Éditions du Sagittaire.

1929. *Robert*. Supplement to *L'École des Femmes*. Paris: the Nouvelle Revue Française.

1930. *L'Affaire Redureau*, followed by *Faits Divers*. Paris: the Nouvelle Revue Française (Collection *Ne Jugez Pas*).

1930. *La Séquestrée de Poitiers*. Paris: the Nouvelle Revue Française (Collection *Ne Jugez Pas*).

1931. *Œdipe*. Paris: Édition de la Pléïade, J. Schiffrin.

PART II

Translations of the Works of Gide

GERMANY

Le Retour de l'Enfant Prodigue. Berlin: Deutsche Verlags-
Anstalt. Translation by Rainer Maria Rilke.

1909. *Saül*. Berlin: Deutsche Verlags-Anstalt. Translation by
Félix-Paul Greve.

1919. *Le Prométhée mal enchaîné*. Berlin: Deutsche Verlags-
Anstalt. Translation by Franz Blei.

1925. *La Symphonie pastorale*. Berlin: Deutsche Verlags-Anstalt.
Translation by Bernard Guillemin.

1927. *Les Faux-Monnayeurs*. Berlin: Deutsche Verlags-Anstalt.
Translation by Ferdinand Hardekopf.

1928. *Le Journal des Faux-Monnayeurs*. Berlin: Deutsche Verlags-
Anstalt. Translation by Ferdinand Hardekopf.

1929. *Les Nourritures terrestres*. Berlin: Deutsche Verlags-Anstalt.
Translation by Hans Prinzhorn.

1929. *L'Immoraliste*. Berlin: Deutsche Verlags-Anstalt. Translation by Félix-Paul Greve.

1929. *Paludes*. Berlin: Deutsche Verlags-Anstalt. Translation by
Félix-Paul Greve.

1929. *L'École des Femmes. Robert*. Berlin: Deutsche Verlags-
Anstalt. Translation by Käthe Rosenberg.

1929. *Si le Grain ne meurt*. Berlin: Deutsche Verlags-Anstalt.
Translation by Ferdinand Hardekopf.

1930. *Les Caves du Vatican*. Berlin: Deutsche Verlags-Anstalt.
Translation by Ferdinand Hardekopf.

1930. *La Porte étroite*. Berlin: Deutsche Verlags-Anstalt. Translation by Félix-Paul Greve.

1930. *Le Voyage au Congo* and *Le Retour du Tchad*. Berlin: Deutsche Verlags-Anstalt. Translation by Gertrude Müller.

1930. *Isabelle*. Berlin: Deutsche Verlags-Anstalt. Translation by Paul Donath.

1931. *Œdipe*. Berlin: Deutsche Verlags-Anstalt. Translation by Ernst-Robert Curtius.

1931. *Considérations Européennes*. Berlin: Deutsche Verlags-Anstalt. Translation by Ernst-Robert Curtius.

In Preparation

1933. *Corydon*. Berlin: Deutsche Verlags-Anstalt. Translation by Joachim Moras.[1]

Critical Studies

1929. June 20. *Neue Leipziger Zeitung*. Study by Erich Kastner.

November 20. *Deutsche Allgemeine Zeitung* (Berlin). Study by Emil Lucka.

November 20. *Vossische Zeitung* (Berlin). Study by Otto Zarek.

November 22. *Prager Press*. Study by Franz Blei.

November 22. *Rigasche Rundschau*. Study by Frank Thiess.

November 22. *Berliner Tageblatt*. Study by Bernard Guillemin.

November 22. *Generalanzeiger Dortmund*. Study by Erich Kastner.

November 22. *Vorwärts* (Berlin). Study by Frh. Maltzahn.

[1] Some of these works appeared previously with other publishers than the Deutsche Verlags-Anstalt, which undertook, in 1930, the uniform edition of Gide's works.

November 23. *Germania* (Berlin). Study by Otto Forst-Battaglia.

November 23. *Stadt-Anzeiger* (Cologne). Study by Dr. Kurt Voss.

November 24. *Kölnische Zeitung* (Berlin). Study by K.-H. Ruppel.

November 24. *Neue Zürcher Zeitung*. Study by Albert Thibaudet.

November 25. *Braunschweig Landeszeitung*. Study by Dr. Ernst Sander.

November 29. *National Zeitung* (Basel).

December 12. *Das Deutsche Buch* (Leipzig). Study by W.-E. Silskind.

Literarische Welt. Study by Willy Haas.

Mitteilung des Deutschen Buch-Club (Hamburg). Study by Paul Aluens.

Der Bund (Berne). Study by Klaus Mann.

ENGLAND

1905. *Oscar Wilde. In Memoriam*. Oxford: Holywell Press. Translation, Introduction, Notes, and Bibliography by Stuart Mason.

1919. *Prometheus Illbound* (*Le Promethée mal enchaîné*). London: Chatto & Windus. Literal translation by Lilian Rothermere.

1924. *Strait is the Gate* (*La Porte étroite*). London: Jarrolds. Translation by Dorothy Bussy.

1925. *Dostoevsky*. London and Toronto: J. M. Dent & Son. Translation by Dorothy Bussy.

1928. *The Counterfeiters* (*Les Faux-Monnayeurs*). London: Alfred A. Knopf. Translation by Dorothy Bussy.

1928. *Lafcadio's Adventures* (*Les Caves du Vatican*). London: Alfred A. Knopf. Translation by Dorothy Bussy.

1929. *Essay on Montaigne* (*Essai sur Montaigne*). London: Blackmore Press. Translation by Stephen H. Guest and Trevor E. Blewitt.

1930. *The School for Wives* (*L'École des Femmes*). London: Alfred A. Knopf. Translation by Dorothy Bussy.

1930. *The Immoralist* (*L'Immoraliste*). London: Alfred A. Knopf. Translation by Dorothy Bussy.

1930. *Travels in the Congo* (*Voyage au Congo* and *Le Retour du Tchad*) London: Alfred A. Knopf. Translation by Dorothy Bussy.

Critical Studies

1909. September. *Contemporary Review*. " Writings of Gide," by Edmund Gosse.

1920. April 10. *Childhood Living Age*. " Some Memories of a Parisian," by Edmund Gosse.

1924. June 14. *Literary Review*. " Portrait," by Edmund Gosse. *Life and Letters* (London). " The Novels of André Gide," by Francis Bickley.

BULGARIA

1929. *La Symphonie pastorale*. Translation by Vassil Poundeff.
1930. *La Porte étroite*. Translation by Marie Youroukoff.

DENMARK

1931. *L'École des Femmes* and *Robert*. Copenhagen: Jespersen og Pio. Translation by Axel Broe.

SPAIN

La Porte étroite. Published by Calleja.
Corydon. Édition Oriente.

Les Caves du Vatican. Published by Dédalo.
L'École des Femmes. Published by Dédalo.

UNITED STATES

1924. *Strait is the Gate (La Porte étroite).* New York: Alfred A. Knopf. Translation by Dorothy Bussy.

1925. *The Vatican Swindle,* later called: *Lafcadio's Adventures (Les Caves du Vatican).* New York: Alfred A. Knopf. Translation by Dorothy Bussy.

1926. *Dostoevsky.* New York: Alfred A. Knopf. With an Introduction by Arnold Bennett.

1927. *The Counterfeiters (Les Faux-Monnayeurs).* New York: Alfred A. Knopf. Translation by Dorothy Bussy.

1928. *Lafcadio's Adventures (Les Caves du Vatican).* New York: Alfred A. Knopf. Translation by Dorothy Bussy.

1929. *The School for Wives (L'École des Femmes).* New York: Alfred A. Knopf. Translation by Dorothy Bussy.

1929. *Travels in the Congo (Voyage au Congo* and *Le Retour du Tchad).* New York: Alfred A. Knopf. Translation by Dorothy Bussy.

1930. *The Immoralist (L'Immoraliste).* New York: Alfred A. Knopf. Translation by Dorothy Bussy.

1931. *The Counterfeiters (Les Faux-Monnayeurs).* New York: The Modern Library. Translation by Dorothy Bussy. Introduction by Raymond Weaver.

1931. *Two Symphonies (Isabelle* and *La Symphonie Pastorale).* New York: Alfred A. Knopf. Translation by Dorothy Bussy.

Critical Studies

1909. December 25. *Living Age.* Study by Edmund Gosse.
December 25. *Living Age.* " Classic Mythology," by Edmund Gosse.

1923. November 10. *Living Age.* "Lecture of Europe: a French View," by Edmund Gosse.

1925. June 20. *Living Age.* "André Gide Sells Out," by A. Flores.

1927. October. *Bookman.* "André Gide and his First Novel," by A. Flores.

1928. December. *Forum.* "Portrait," by I. Opffer.

1929. *Sewanee Review.* "Dostoievsky and Gide," by Tatiana Vacquier.

1931. January. *The Romanic Review.* "Marcel Schwob and André Gide," by S. A. Rhodes.

"André Gide and his Catholic Critics," by S. A. Rhodes.

April. *Living Age.* "André Gide, Saint or Demon," by Marcel Arland.

1931. December. *Yale Review.* "Memories of a Sentimental Schoolboy," by I. Opffer.

HOLLAND

1928. *Le Retour de l'Enfant Prodigue.* Assen Van Gorcum & Company. Translation by F. G. de Jong.

1929. *Paludes.* Arnhem: review *De Stem,* Van Loghem, Slaterus en Visser. Translation by M. Nijkoff.

1930. *La Symphonie pastorale.* Amsterdam: Amsterdamsche Mij tot voortzetting van de zaken van de Nederlandsche Uitg-Midy. Translation by N. C. Nagel.

1932. *Le Monde de Demain. Vers un Nouvel Ordre* (article by André Gide), in the *Hollandsche Revue.*

HUNGARY

1918. *Les Caves du Vatican.* In the review, *Vasanapi Ujsag,* 1918–19. Translation by G. Hönig.

1926. *L'Immoraliste.* Société Franklin. Translation by Albert Gyergyai.

1929. *La Symphonie pastorale.* In the *Nyugat* review, published later by Éditions Panthéon.

1929. *Isabelle.* In the *Nyugat* review; published later by Éditions Panthéon. Translation by Albert Gyergyai.

1931. *L'École des Femmes.* In the *Nyugat* review. Translation by Albert Gyergyai.

1931. *Jeunesse.* In the *Nyugat* review. Translation by Albert Gyergyai.

In Preparation

Le Retour de l'Enfant Prodigue. Translation by André Németh.

ITALY

1912. *Le Voyage d'Urien.* Published under the title: *Voyage sur l'Océan Pathétique.* Florence: Boldini. Translation by A. Onofri.

1920. *Le Prométhée mal enchaîné.* Florence: Valecchi. Translation by G. Papini.

1925. *La Porte étroite.* Milan: Bottegia di Poesia.

1930. *L'École des Femmes.* Milan: Libreria degli Omenoni. Translation by C. V. Ludovici.

Critical Studies

1929. March 17. *Italia Letteraria.* Essay by Gian Siro Ferrata.

1930. September. *La Coltura.* Essay by Sergio Solmi.

La Vita e il Libro (1st series). Study of *La Porte étroite,* by G. A. Borgese.

La Stampa. Several studies by G. Pettinato.

Pégaso. Several studies by P. Pancrazi.

JAPAN

Les Cahiers d'André Walter. Hiougadô. Translation by Katsumi Hanajima.

L'Immoraliste. Shinchôsha and Kaizôsha. Translation by Atsushi Ishikawa.

La Porte étroite. Shinchôsha and Kaizôsha. Translation by Yoshio Yamanonchi.

La Symphonie pastorale. Shinchôsha and Kaizôsha. Translation by Isamu Inoué.

Paludes. Daïichishobô. Translation by Däigaku Horiguchi.

Le Prométhée mal enchaîné. Shunyôdô. Translation by Yokaï Okubo.

Les Caves du Vatican. Iwanamishoten. Translation by Atsushi Ishikawa.

Dostoïevski. Hiougadô. Translation by Sanemitsu Mushakoji.

1933. *La Symphonie pastorale.* Atsushi. Translation by Kawaguchi.

Critical Studies

1932. September. *Shicho.* " André Gide," study by Tadashi Ijima.
Shibasoten. " Nature and Purity," study by Tetsutaro Kawakami.

NORWAY

1921. *La Porte étroite.* Oslo: Aschehoug. Translation by Lorentz Eckhoff.

1926. *La Symphonie pastorale.* Oslo: Aschehoug. Translation by Lorentz Eckhoff.

POLAND

1901. *Le Prométhée mal enchaîné.* Lwow: H. Altenberg. Translation by Zénon Przesmycki.

1901. *Philoctète*. In the review *Chimera*, No. 9. Translation by Zénon Przesmycki.

1907. *Le Roi Candaule*. Translation by A. Nowaczynski. Performed at Cracow, February 1907.

1910. *Le Retour de l'Enfant Prodigue*. *Nowa Gazeta*. Translation by Waclaw Rogowicz.

1929. *Les Faux-Monnayeurs*. Warsaw: Édition Roj. Translation by Jaroslaw Iwaszkiéwicz and Hélène Iwaszkiévicz.

Critical Studies

1911. *La Nouvelle France littéraire*, by Jean Lorentowicz, the last chapter of which is a study of André Gide, followed by a bibliography of André Gide and the Polish translations of his works.

Several articles in the *Viadomosci Literackie*.

SWEDEN

1920. *La Porte étroite*. Stockholm: Gebers. Translation by Harald Heyman.

1921. *L'Immoraliste*. Stockholm: Gebers. Translation by Harald Heyman.

1932. *Les Faux-Monnayeurs*. Stockholm: Falskmyntarna, Spektrums Förlag.

CZECHOSLOVAKIA

1899. *Philoctète*. Em. de Lesehrad. Translation by Prochàzka.

1904. *Le Prométhée mal enchaîné*. Moderni Revue. Translation by Prochàzka.

1910. *La Porte étroite*. Kamila Neumannova. Translation by Prochàzka.

1912. *Le Traité du Narcisse*. *Philoctète*. *Le Prométhée mal enchaîné*. Kamila Neumannova. Translation by Prochàzka.

1913. *L'Immoraliste*. Kamila Neumannova. Translation by Fleischner.

1914. *Bethsabé*. Moderni Revue. Translation by Groh.

1914. *Le Roi Candaule*. Kamila Neumannova. Translation by Prochàzka.

1918. *Saül*. Stara Rise. Translation by Marek.

1919. *Isabelle*. Kamila Neumannova.

1928. *Voyage au Congo*. Pokrok. Translation by Horsky.

1929. *Le Retour de l'Enfant Prodigue*. Svoboda. Translation by Marek.

1930. *Les Caves du Vatican*. Topic.

1930. *L'École des Femmes*. *Robert*. Aventinum. Translation by J. Mala and O. Radl.

1932. *Les Faux-Monnayeurs*. Druzst. Prace. Translation by Heyduk.

Oscar Wilde. In Memoriam. Srdee.

In Preparation

Si le Grain ne meurt. Janda. Translation by Winter.

JUGOSLAVIA

(*Translations in Serbian-Croatian*)

1925. *L'Immoraliste*. Zagreb: Obzor. Translation by J. Horvath.

1929. *La Porte étroite*. Zagreb: Zabavna Biblioteka. Translation by A. Bonifacié.

1931. *La Symphonie pastorale*. Zagreb: Biblioteka Narodnih Norina. Translation by Lj. Wiesner.

1931. *La Porte étroite*. Lyubljana: Ceposlovna Kujizek. Translation by B. Vodusck.

Bethsabé. Revue Vijenac.

1932. *Le Retour de l'Enfant Prodigue*. Translation by A. B. Simié and A. Bonifacié.

Les Caves du Vatican. Translation by M. Ristio.

Critical Studies

1925. *Jugoslavenska* (Njiva). Study by A. Bonifacié.
1929. *Letopis Matice Srpske.* Study by M. Ristié.
1929. *Savremenik.* "Efforts and Victories of André Gide," by
     I. Srepel.
1930. *Gens d'Occident* (Zagreb). Study by A. Bonifacié.

TURKEY

La Porte étroite. Stamboul: Matbaerlik ve Nesriyat. Translation by Burhan Umit.

INDEX